80s STYLE

DESIGNS
OF THE
DECADE

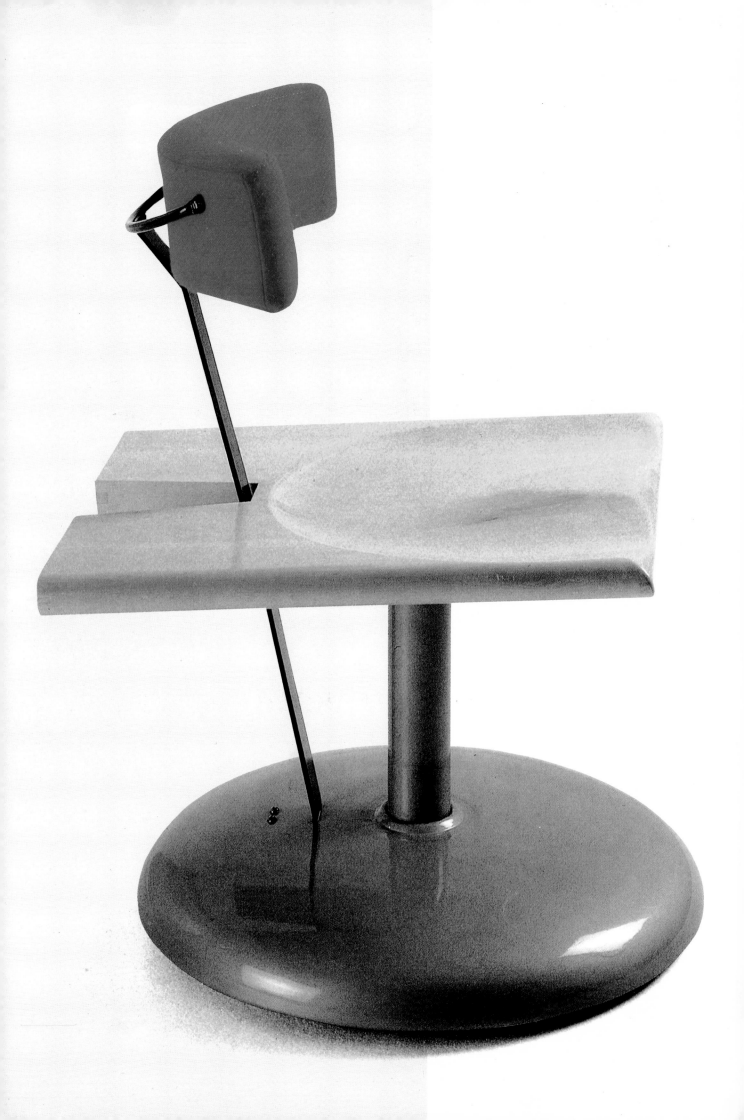

80s STYLE

DESIGNS OF THE DECADE

BY ALBRECHT BANGERT AND

KARL MICHAEL ARMER

•

FOREWORD BY ETTORE SOTTSASS

ABBEVILLE PRESS • PUBLISHERS • NEW YORK

GAETANO PESCE
Chair, *Greenstreet*
Wire, plastic
Prototype
Manufacturer: Vitra, West Germany (1987)

Foreword © 1990 Ettore Sottsass
Text © 1990 Albrecht Bangert
© 1990 John Calmann and King Ltd
and Cross River Press

Library of Congress
Cataloging-in-Publication Data

Bangert, Albrecht, *1944–*
    80s style, designs of the
    decade/by Albrecht Bangert and
    Karl Michael Armer; foreword by
    Ettore Sottsass.
    Includes index.
    ISBN 1-55859-117-6
    1. Design–History–20th
    century-Thames, motives.
    I. Armer.
    Karl Michael, *1950–*
    II. Title.
    III. Title: Eighties style, designs of
    the decade.
    NK1390.B26 1990
    745.4′442–dc20   90–638
                                                 CIP

Translated by Stewart Spencer
(Foreword by Caroline Beamish)

Typeset by Rowland
Phototypesetting Ltd,
Bury St Edmunds, Suffolk
Printed in Hong Kong

First edition

✱ CONTENTS

This letter is not intended to carry the same weight as the epistles written by philosophers and apostles of ancient times; letters provoked by events with catastrophic implications for the tribe, the nation, the planet. This is just an ordinary letter, a letter like a friendly boomerang: once you have received it I hope it will come back to me, possibly to reassure me.

This is a letter about the Eighties, about the symbols, the words and the phrases that we have selected for use in pursuing our lives through the decade

Dear designers,

To tell you the truth, I don't know if this letter is addressed to you, or to 'Design' itself (the Spirit that pursues us all), or to myself, in order to clarify my thoughts. It is

✱ A LETTER TO THE DESIGNERS

perhaps a truism that every letter is addressed to someone, even if that person is unknown (even if that person is oneself). For this I beg your indulgence.

known as the Eighties; about the symbols, words and phrases we have employed to mark out the stage on which, during this time, we have played out our existence; and lastly about the symbols, words and phrases with which we have attempted, and still attempt to cross the time threshold.

There is no doubt that during this decade the creation and consumption of Design has exploded like a Nova. Industrial logic, as it proceeds towards its destination (wherever that may be) has identified a potent force in Design, a five-star argument, in fact, for continuing the distribution throughout the planet of millions of products, for communicating with ever increasing sections of the world's populations. The project is not simply to broadcast the benefits of consumption, but to communicate at a deeper level as well, opening the soul to its own secret wishes, unbridled longings, inexpressible desires.

In my opinion the most urgent need for nearly everybody, as the peoples of the world gradually gain self-confidence and approach a more sophisticated awareness of the possibilities life offers, is the need for an identity, a desire to 'be', to exist, to possess substance, whether real or imaginary. This is as true for whole tribes and populations as it is for small clans, small family groups, for people on their own, for individuals.

Now, as I said before, Design has become a powerful force because it is nothing more nor less than a metaphor for existence, a metaphor for the land and the sea, for rooms, implements, clothes, gestures – and also for the dreams, the aspirations, the knowledge and the ignorance which we debate endlessly with ourselves and with others.

The problem today is that once contact has been made with people's secret souls – once the tribe (or the populace, the clan, the family, the single man or woman) has been made to understand that absolutely anyone is capable of designing, or dreaming, desiring, possessing, then nothing can stop them from dreaming, desiring, designing. A chain reaction is set off: the Nova explodes. As I see it, the chain reaction was set off in the Sixties. Now at the end of the Eighties, the flames, the smoke and vapours of the explosion can be seen more clearly.

Dear friends, I think one could say that we are only now beginning to feel the buffeting of the post-cataclysmic winds. We are about to be cauterized or burnt up in tempestuous flames, we are about to be suffocated or poisoned by the gases escaping from the earth's crust. It is important to be aware of this, and to talk about it.

It is important to know that we may be trapped and crushed by these great industrial mechanisms, whose logic and systems can never be fully mastered, let alone controlled.

Alternatively, we may be trapped and crushed by the mechanisms of seduction proffered by industrial culture, aimed as they are at reaching deep into the hearts and minds of absolutely everyone, without any exceptions.

I believe that our only way of escape is to know exactly where we stand, and not to delude ourselves that we can act 'outside' the great plan that industrial 'culture' has in store. Any attempt to do so, to build up a culture outside or parallel to industrial culture is, at present, more or less doomed to failure; to being absorbed, engulfed in the onrush of primitive power, overwhelmed by the irresistible charm of industrial culture.

I do not believe that any destiny awaits us at present other than that proffered by industrial-technological logic. This is not the destiny of individuals, of individual cases or events. It is global, planetary, a huge historical event. I see nothing on the horizon to indicate any movement towards another culture, certainly nothing forceful enough to suggest that industrial culture is about to be superseded.

I think I can say that with calm certainty, and I think I can also say that the territory, or territories over which we can operate are those where existence and the future of industry meet head-on. In other words, that the debate about Design belongs within these precise limits, within this anxious, dramatic, complicated, urgent landscape.

I believe I can also state that the aim of Design is more than ever to propose metaphors, i.e. to propose ever vaster systems of figurative language which will give new dignity, new clarity, new serenity to existence, cowering as it is before the barbaric invasion of industrial and cultural technology which threatens to overpower it.

Escaping to the South or the North, to the East or West, into private solipsism, acts of aggression, unsatisfactory romantic nostalgia, or obsessional technological rhetoric will leave no mark. It merely serves to oil the sophisticated wheels of industrial logic in motion.

I believe that it is high time that we who term ourselves designers opposed the primitive barbarism of industrial culture, putting in its place something more dignified, something more conscious of the value of existence; we must create a radiant vision of people's desires for serenity, for happiness, for play, for pleasure.

There! This is the letter I have been so bold as to address to other friends who like me call themselves designers. This letter brings good wishes, nothing more, and is written in the hope that, like a boomerang, it will return to me bringing with it hope and good luck.

ETTORE SOTTSASS

Anyone searching for a single phrase with which to sum up the design scene of the 1980s need look no further for a thematic title than the principal work by the German philosopher Immanuel Kant, *The Critique of Pure Reason*.

Certainly, were we to review the multifarious trends that influenced styles and beliefs in

From a psychological point of view, design in the 1980s bears all the signs of juvenile rebellion. All the distinguishing features are there: a rejection of ossified structures, exuberant excess, muscular vitality, extreme swings of mood, a delight in shocking other people, dreams of overnight success, self-infatuation and a barely developed inclination to think of longer-term objectives, still less of some future utopian state. Design is always a mirror of particular lifestyles, and the 1980s were marked by the peculiar intensity with which people lived in the here-and-now and on the

 INTRODUCTION

the 1980s – punk, high-tech, low-tech, post-modernism, minimalism, deconstructivism, and their various historical variants, to name but a few – the common feature they all seem to share is their high degree of irrationality, almost of bizarreness, and the fact that even in their contradictions they were wilfully extreme.

surface of things. Hedonism was more highly rated than morality: enjoyment was the most important principle. In consequence, design did not need to have a particular style as it had to do in previous decades: every style was now acceptable, provided only it was psychologically satisfying. Or, more pointedly, good living was more important than good form. And this seemed to overturn those principles of design, which concerned the moral aim to improve the world: cinema superseded Bauhaus, Vidal Sassoon replaced Dieter Rams, and Braun gave way to colour.

This is not intended to sound as critical as it might. The most important thing about this decade was not so much what happened in design but the fact that it happened at all, since the international style which typified 'good form' and which the Bauhaus had helped to shape had become a moribund language like Latin or Ancient Greek, still useful, no doubt, but somewhat remote from real life. Even worse, it had now become a kind of dictator hounding alien dogmas with inquisitorial zeal. The rational solutions provided by functionalism rested on a standardized type of thinking of the kind produced by computers and therefore undifferentiated: solid, 'optimized' and well thought-out, but boring and without feeling. (Think of the cars that come out of wind-tunnels.)

Reaction to Reason's benevolent tyranny was bound to be all the more violent after so many years of repression, and so indeed it turned out to be, with Memphis and Punk Baroque and *secrétaires* with ornamental columns. Had there been some seismograph that allowed us to measure the *Zeitgeist* as expressed in design objects produced in the last thirty years, it would, by and large, follow the straight and narrow line of Reason during the 1960s and 1970s, and then veered dramatically in the 1980s between the most violent extremes.

Ups and downs, thesis and antithesis, movement and countermovement: such dualism is typical of the 1980s. It is this that made the decade so exciting and, at the same time, so hard to summarize. Design in the 1980s was constantly torn back and forth between two opposing poles. Like every youthful revolt, it reeled between protest and passive conformity, or, to use a vocabulary specific to design, between provocation and decoration. Instability was followed by stabilization, the challenges posed by punk and Memphis gave way to the reassurance of a neo-conservative, post-modernist aesthetic whose decorative unpretentiousness was then again opposed by minimalism's meagre fare. There was thus an infinite number of opposites, each of which left its mark on design in the 1980s at some point or other: high-tech and traditionalism, cultivated elegance and barbarous brutality, artistry and craftsmanship, coolness and passion, logic and emotion, abstraction and representationalism, overexcitement and understatement, and imaginary disasters and an idealistic world.

Only the briefest outline can be given here of this slalom-like manoeuvre which, veering from side to side between the multiplicity of options, took place at breakneck speed. The different trends and fashions followed each other so quickly, that it sometimes seemed as though the answer had come before the question, that reaction preceded action. The fashionable and unfashionable were suddenly indistinguishable. Consumers and designers lost their footing and began to gyrate in every direction. Not that that mattered. Or, rather, it did matter, inasmuch as there was a remarkable side-effect to all this, namely, the disappearance of the avant-garde. There was, after all, no *garde* left to be *avant*. It was simply steamrollered out of the way – and it quickly learned its lesson. Avant-garde art was superseded by spectacle: success is now measured in numbers of copies produced and minutes of media coverage.

There is a tendency to describe the result of all this as pluralism. Its positive side is that during the 1980s much was produced that was beautiful, novel and genuinely remarkable. The decade was colourful, creative and highly productive in terms of design. Some of its finest products will figure on the following pages and (wherever appropriate) will be discussed with fitting enthusiasm. But one of the tasks incumbent on any writer who undertakes this kind of retrospective survey is to look behind the brightly coloured pictures and to think not just in aesthetic categories. A number of dark shadows will then be found to cast themselves across the cheerful design puzzle of the decade that has just ended.

One of them is the superficiality already mentioned. Liberation from the constraints of functionalism and rationalism soon encouraged designers to lose all sense of restraint. Objects were created whose utter imbecility was rescued from public ridicule only by their claims to be treated as art. Other designers discovered in art history a kind of self-service store which allowed them to hide their lack of ideas behind the smokescreen of stylistic quotation. The cuddlesome wish to please on the part of many post-modernist objects and the provocations of many would-be artists inspired a style of design of flamboyant triviality. Not only is this trend continuing, it inevitably calls into question all serious attempts at design.

The breath-taking speed with which changes have taken place has led to a deep disquiet on the part of the general public. As is always the case in such situations, they turn for guidance to those authorities that set the going rate, be they prominent names, the false security of historical design, or those rules of behaviour that they read about in magazines. Lifestyles, not design styles, are what we now set greatest store by, and even these, to quote the Italian designer Andrea Branzi, are 'changed like TV stations'. People have become like 'zappers' in their everyday lives, changing stations by remote control, following not their own ideas but behavioural patterns

and ritualized buying habits imposed on them by others, and bending like straws in the wind of fashion. The result, in a word, is a state of extreme alienation and rootlessness. For all the designs that have been on offer, we have not been enriched in consequence, but only made the poorer.

Extensive media reporting on design matters has intensified modes of cult-like behaviour and turned design objects into fetishes. Independently of its utilitarian value, design has become a codified form of non-verbal communication, allowing us to judge our fellow humans at a glance and place them in their social group. As a result of this, furniture is no longer bought in response to our own individual wishes but because of the impact we want it to have upon others. To a certain extent this has always been so, but the phenomenon is particularly marked in an age when design is a way of signalling our lifestyle to others. In extreme cases we surround ourselves with furniture that is alien in spirit and live in a simulated reality. Each of us is familiar with those theatrically stage-managed domestic interiors in which every piece of furniture and every single accessory is calculated to be exactly right: standardized individuality – a paradoxical way of life.

A further aspect which is not unproblematical is the cult of the star designer, a cult for which the designers themselves are not to blame, but which first began to make itself felt in the course of the 1980s. The result was an overestimation of the designer's own abilities and a compulsion to

produce (for stars must always be in the news). But any designer for whom the only things that matter in life are commercial success and the degree of notoriety that he enjoys will quickly lose his integrity and become a sort of design junkie producing junk design. But we need good designers far more urgently than we need media clowns. The cult of star designers and marketing strategies on the part of the producers threaten our design culture by introducing too many aspects alien to design, diluting the design process and finally reducing it to the art of packaging. It had in any case already led to a deeply unhealthy development for, whereas design in the 1950s, 1960s and 1970s was primarily aimed at democratization (good design for as wide a market as possible), design in the 1980s has clearly followed the path of 'aristocratization' (more expensive objects for a new élite). This is a process that should be reversed as quickly as possible. The quality of a design object should not be dependent on how much money was invested in it.

Aristocratization, however, was the only really dubious development that the 1980s had to offer. All the other escapades were merely the outcome of revolutionary chaos on board the good ship *Design*, a vessel that will no doubt enter calmer waters during the 1990s. The ebullient breaking of form in the 1980s deserves our wholehearted welcome. The shocking irrationality of Memphis and deconstructivism, of fantastically beautiful textiles which are deliberately difficult to look after, of technological products that do not exclude both wit and spontaneity – these are trends which, though in individual cases somewhat curious, in the main have a positive effect by bringing a certain poetry back into lives that have grown increasingly abstract and ever more strictly organized, and by offering us occasions for enjoyment and simple astonishment. For this is now more important than a pure and sterile functionalism which, in its absolute state, is inhuman precisely because it strives to attain the perfection of machines.

But enough of the 1980s. Let us look instead to the future. How will things develop? The 1990s promise a wide variety of trends for which we wait with bated breath.

First, we can expect a unified style of design finally to emerge. Recent decades were altogether one-sided. Design in the 1960s and 1970s was largely a product of the left half of the brain, that hemisphere which is the home of rational, analytical thinking. In just as extreme a way, design in the 1980s was a product of the right half of the brain, the half responsible for imagination and emotion. There are already early indications that the 1990s will see these qualities combined. Reason and emotion, analytical acumen and artistic sensitivity will no longer face one another as enemies, but complement each other in wise and balanced harmony. Perhaps we shall see a collaboration between Ettore Sottsass, Memphis's spiritual guide, and Dieter Rams, the guiding light behind the style associated with the name of Braun. Surprising encounters of this kind are certainly in the air.

Second, the trends of the 1980s will not stop overnight. They will last for another two to three years, perhaps in even more extreme forms. Designers determined to make a spectacle of themselves in the media or at international trade fairs need to be extreme – extremely loud or extremely quiet – at least until such time as something new replaces them. They need to shock and cause offence, or to be so unassumingly tasteful and palely interesting that people sit up and take notice. Minimalism will therefore always be with us, as will good, old-fashioned craftsmanship. At the same time, Punk Baroque will find more and more new supporters, and bad taste will still be cultivated with the help of kitsch and camp art, of parody and a style that derives from children's comics. By no means negligible areas of design will have all the obscure charm of high-budget 'B' films.

Third, the present state of uncertainty that affects the vast majority of those who buy design products will continue as before. To instil a sense of certainty, manufacturers need to switch increasingly from PR measures to large-scale and expensive advertising campaigns to promote limited editions and the classics of yesteryear.

Fourth, the avant-garde of design consumers will consciously distance themselves from design objects. This is a natural process of emancipation. In the 1980s, consumers were sold on cult objects; in the 1990s, by contrast, they will choose to be the master, rather than the slave of design. We shall see interiors in which expensive design furniture is displayed with conscious casualness and even with disrespect: Memphis tables will be hidden beneath a floral tablecloth, Ron Arad's concrete record player will suffer the indignities of country-and-western music, and so on. The best style is not to have any. (Those ultra-progressives who have been saying this for years will of course furnish their homes in strictly middle-class style and relish the scatter cushion's subtle joys.)

Fifth, ecological issues will increase dramatically in importance. Hitherto, design has paid scant attention to ecology, but the situation is now so grave that designers simply cannot avoid having to think of how they use scarce resources, recycling, cheap replacement materials, obsolescence, and so on.

Sixth, the 1990s are bound to see an increase in new ideas emanating not only from those Eastern bloc countries that have grown more liberal in recent years but also from Third-world countries, such as Brazil and Argentina. With their multicultural roots, their vitality and creativity, Sao Paulo and Buenos Aires, especially, have the potential to become a second Milan. Spain, by contrast, shows signs of stagnating in smug complacency after a lightning start that may perhaps prove to have been overrated. Also waiting in the wings, so to speak, are Australia, Canada, and Singapore, although it remains to be seen what their contribution will prove to be like.

Seventh, the most important countries in terms of design in the 1990s will again be Italy and Japan, and possibly also Germany. Italy will provide the new ideas, since so many positive qualities are concentrated here that it is simply bound to create the best designs. Among these qualities are a delight in improvisation and playful innocence, pleasure in experimentation, an anti-authoritarian urge to call things into question and thus to create something new, and a constructive nihilism that tears things down and builds them up once more. If Japan is influential in setting the tone, it is because East and West rub together there like tectonic plates that give rise to earthquakes which keep on changing the world of design.

There are very many designers in Japan who are visionary, rigorously perfectionist and sensitive – Samurais of aesthetics. Germany could become important since it is close in terms of national temperament to the style we expect to see in 1990s design, a style that will be marked by a mixture of rationality and emotionality. German industry will also be increasingly design-orientated (a trend that will certainly be more pronounced there than in France, say, or Great Britain), in addition to which Germany can currently call on some of the world's most important designers to help it on its way. One thinks of Richard Sapper, Dieter Rams, Frogdesign and Ingo Maurer.

Eighth, important impulses will come from microelectronics and from the development of new materials. Three-dimensional objects can be made flat, thanks to the use of microchips. In turn these surfaces must be designed. One area of product design is concerned increasingly with graphic design. Memory alloys, new synthetic materials and microelectronics make it likely that design objects in future will be able to alter their shape and colour. Perhaps the time is not long off when we shall be able not only to dim the brightness of a lamp but to 'turn down' the colour

of a cupboard. Or, by using remote control, to order shelving to assume particular shapes determined in advance. An unbelievable amount can happen in the space of a mere ten years.

Ninth, there is a noticeable tendency nowadays to express ourselves in strong emotions. In consequence we can expect design trends that communicate well-defined images, psychological associations and sentimental value. The major styles and influences will be (a) archaic and primitive influences; (b) ethnological and exotic styles; (c) colonial and pioneering styles; (d) salon style; (e) urban nostalgia; (f) a provocative noh-style; and (g) meditative, almost empty rooms. Parallel to this, designers will attempt to give their objects greater 'depth' and confer on them an aura that transcends their sheer objectivity. One way of achieving this aim will be to combine previously irreconcilable opposites such as natural and synthetic materials, craftsmanship and computer technology, luxuriousness and minimalism and, above all, high-tech and mysticism. A new technologically inspired romanticism will come into being which is not science fiction but science fantasy, a fascinating style that will aim to communicate warmth and poetry by using the very latest technology.

Tenth, the social status of design and, above all, of interior design will continue to increase. There is, however, a great danger to be avoided here, namely, a withdrawal into the beautiful, air-conditioned world indoors. The outside world will be seen as something hostile, as something irreparably lost. A hole in the ozone layer? Acid rain? Climatic disaster? Why should we care? It's warm and comfortable here inside. What such visionaries as Gaetano Pesce and Shiro Kuramata predicted years ago – Pesce in 1972 with his *Habitat for Two People in an Age of Great*

Contaminations and Kuramata in 1979 with his projected *House to be Built in a Defunct Urban Environment* – is finally coming true: designers must not create a space in which survivors can live out their lives of luxury like twentieth-century troglodytes. The world of shopping malls, arcades and those shrines where we worship the gods of entertainment has finally permeated the private sphere. This flight into the interior is particularly pronounced in Japan, in the spectacular, ingenious interiors of Tokyo and Osaka, and in the USA, where mega-mansions with their cosy cocoons and couch potatoes signal in no uncertain terms our turning away from the outside world. If beauty and pleasure in life can be experienced only indoors and under artificial lighting, this is bound to bode ill for the outside world and for Nature. Perhaps we ought, from time to time, to contemplate the colours of a maple leaf in autumn, the movements of an albatross in flight or the plumage of a toucan in order to see that *this* kind of 'design' is infinitely better than almost anything produced by the hand of humankind. In the brilliance of its forms, its colours and ideas, every zoo and botanical garden far surpasses the best that the world of design can show.

This is something that all of us – designers and design aficionados – ought to recall in all humility at least once in the course of every day. What use are even the most beautiful vases if there are no longer flowers to put in them?

KARL MICHAEL ARMER

ALBRECHT BANGERT

In no area of design did the boom of the 1980s assume such extreme proportions as it did in the field of furniture. Furniture emerged from the background to dominate the scene, with individual items presented as priceless works of art. Ettore Sottsass's *Carlton* shelving, Toshiyuki Kita's *Wink* armchair,

1 ✱ FURNITURE

Philippe Starck's *Pratfall* chair and Hans Hollein's *Marilyn* sofa became the icons of 1980s lifestyle, one which sought to escape everyday banality through these venerated objects and to found a new 'aristocracy', visible to the outside world by means of status symbols.

It must be acknowledged, therefore, that furniture design in the 1980s was largely an élitist affair. Anyone familiar with the prices paid for pieces by famous designers (the regular purchase prices, be it added, not those paid for collectors' items) would know that £8000 for a sofa or bookcase can scarcely be considered a democratic price. Good design gives the producer a monopoly, and gives it him on a plate: the specific item of furniture in this particular form cannot be bought anywhere else. But this designer monopoly is often overexploited to stimulate demand, especially by means of limited editions. Cheaper pieces of furniture, on the other hand, are turned out in bland, third-rate imitations of what were originally brilliant ideas on the part of their designers. There are very few mass-produced pieces of furniture by prominent designers, and even these often give a pale and sickly impression, as though the designer were keeping back his really good ideas for his better-paying customers. This is not a positive development. Good design should not be so prohibitively expensive that it remains the preserve of the monied classes. We do not need a system of apartheid in the world of design. Good design should be available to all at not unreasonable prices. That is why – to borrow an image from publishing – we need not only original publications in hard covers but also inexpensive paperbacks containing the very same text. There is still a lot to do here, and the 1980s have led us the wrong way. Avant-garde design or the name of a famous designer are not sufficiently compelling reasons to add a series of noughts to an otherwise reasonable price. This is not how things ought to be. We need a lot of naive Don Quixotes to change this situation.

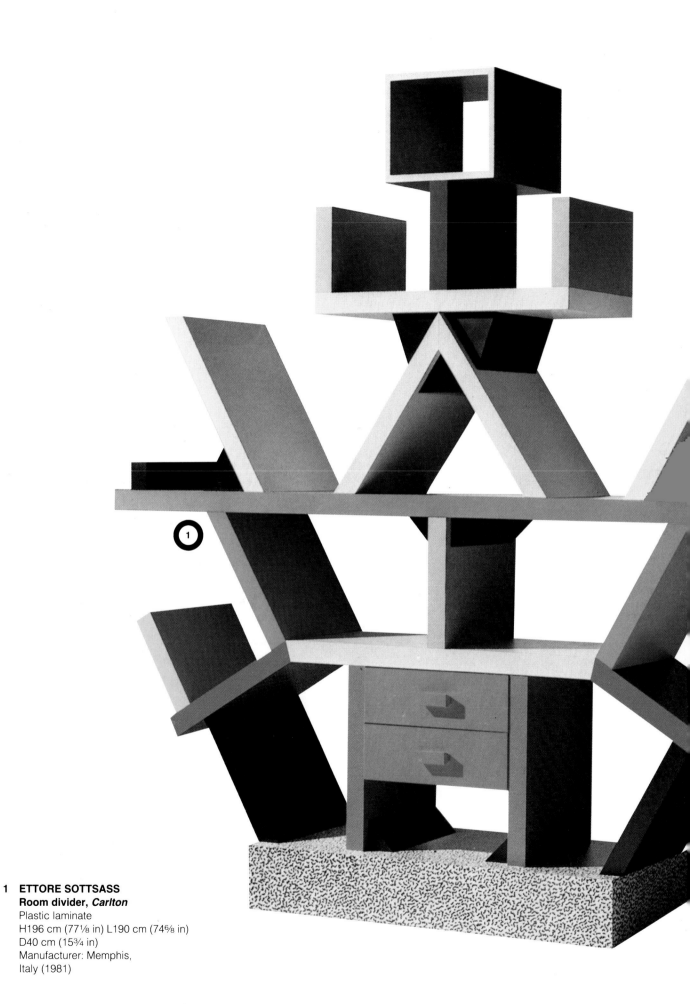

1 **ETTORE SOTTSASS**
Room divider, *Carlton*
Plastic laminate
H196 cm (77⅛ in) L190 cm (74⅝ in)
D40 cm (15¾ in)
Manufacturer: Memphis,
Italy (1981)

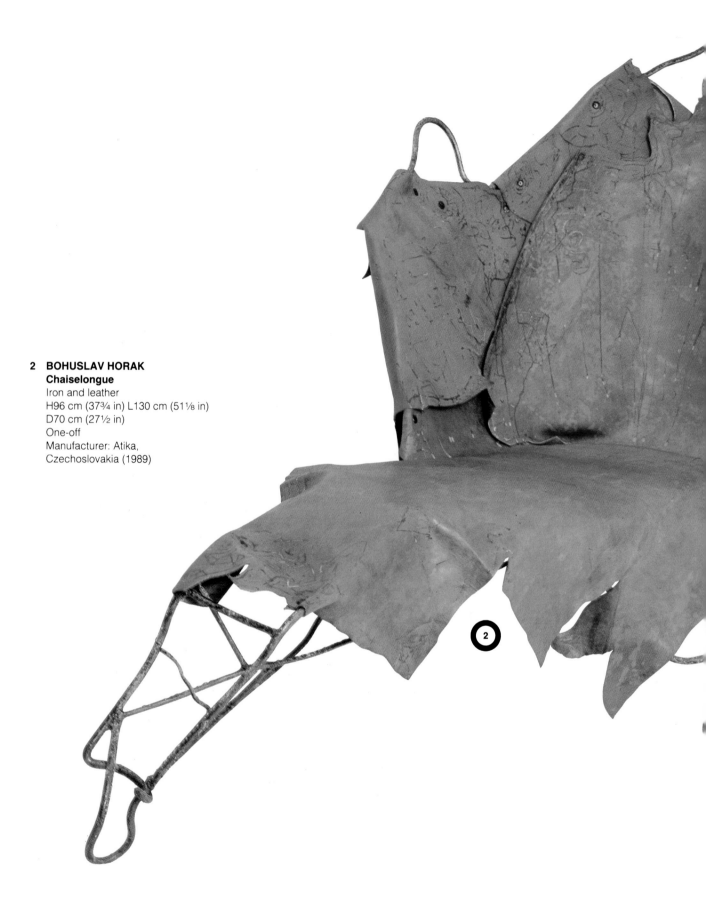

2 **BOHUSLAV HORAK**
Chaiselongue
Iron and leather
H96 cm (37¾ in) L130 cm (51⅛ in)
D70 cm (27½ in)
One-off
Manufacturer: Atika,
Czechoslovakia (1989)

2

This ought to be one of the challenges for design in the 1990s, which is currently enervated and lacking any sense of direction – small wonder after such a hectic decade. At the beginning of the 1980s design and function still had a great deal in common. (You still remember what function was?) It then increasingly became an opportunity for decoration – in the case of Memphis, with a liberating *naïveté* and ironic wink, and a calculated commercialism from post-modern furniture *couturiers*. In the face of the increasingly free interplay of colours and forms, it was no doubt unavoidable that at least one area of design should develop into a decorative (and highly stylized) branch of fine art. Individual items of furniture were no longer satisfied with their traditional role as a table or chair but presented themselves as pieces of sculpture, unique artefacts and collectors' pieces in limited editions, or, even worse, as political statements. But who wants to sit on a political statement? And so, dear designers, if you want to make a political statement, express it in words, write it down, but do not dress it up as a chair. Or as a work of art.

Among those designers who chose not to create works of art, many strove in the direction of Art's more popular little brother, the Cult Object. Their aim was not to finish up in museums and galleries but on the pages of *Paris Match*, *The Sunday Times*, or *Stern*. Images, lifestyle codes and cultural-philosophical statements became more and more important in design, so that it took only a small step to snuff out the final spark of rationality, leaving neither functionality, nor decoration, nor art playing the leading role, but only the labyrinthine landscapes of the psyche. Design became dissociated from the actual object and became a branch of psychotherapy. It was no longer chairs and tables that were designed, but egos, fantasy worlds of the imagination.

Thrones and gilded luxury beds, barbaric fetishes and totems are not so much items of furniture as outward descriptions of inner states, materialized daydreams and embodied illusions – and, more often than not, emotional support and ego boosters for the clinically insecure. Thus the development ended: from a functional to a decorative object, than to an object of art or cult ritual, furniture finally became a form of psychological software.

By the end of the 1980s, everything was possible in the field of design, but it was a situation in which the new suddenly became the old. The well-established design stars successfully attempted an avant-garde somersault, propelling themselves backwards, from the front line of provocation to the lush meadows of conservative values such as 'craftsmanship' and 'functionality'. Among the works produced in the name of progressive retrogression were carefully crafted and traditional pieces of furniture which were discreet to the point of invisibility – pieces by Ron Arad, Philippe Starck, Oscar Tusquets Blanca or Jasper Morrison. After so hectic a decade it is finally time for a breather. All quiet on the furniture front.

The mastermind. He has always struck lucky and hit the bull's-eye. In 1958 he designed the first large-scale Italian computer to look like a container deposited on our planet from outer space. The control buttons on this black box were like those of some seductive toy. Even today, thirty years later, Ettore Sottsass's Elea 9003, with its brilliantly designed user-surface, is still considered a stroke of genius by other computer designers. Sottsass scored another direct hit in 1968 with his Valentine typewriter, entirely in red, an object which

came to embody Pop Art and the design of that whole period. Working unconsciously, but with an infallible feel for the spirit of the age and a fair degree of astuteness, Sottsass became the leading figure in radical Italian design in the 1970s and thus an early influence on the New Design of the 1980s. The extreme ideas that Sottsass had already thought up and sketched out decades earlier were implemented during the 1980s with apparently playful ease, in collaboration with a group of young and talented designers who together founded Memphis. With them he overturned traditional

design principles and transformed a discipline which, until then, had been geared in the main to production and functionality, into a visually communicative spectacle. Like Sottsass himself, design became a media event, a visual sensation, and even a subject for light entertainment.

Following the sensations created by Memphis, the maestro has now set out in search of new adventures, applying the experiences gained in the world of design to architecture, and thereby fulfilling his life's ambition by building Sottsass houses.

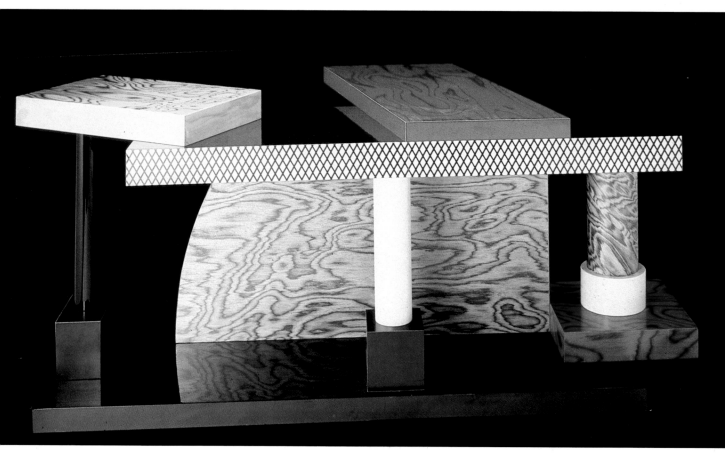

3 ETTORE SOTTSASS
Console, *Tartar*
Reconstituted veneer and plastic laminate
H78 cm (31 in) W195 cm (77 in)
D85 cm (33½ in)
Manufacturer: Memphis, Italy (1985/6)

5 ETTORE SOTTSASS
Dining table, *4 Gopuram*
Pear wood, lacquered wood
Limited batch production
H74 cm (29 in) W124 cm (48¾ in)
L228 cm (89⅝ in)
Manufacturer: Design Gallery,
Italy (1988/9)

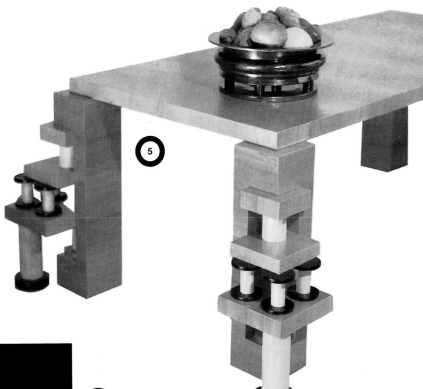

6 ETTORE SOTTSASS
Cabinet, *Mobile Giallo*
Wood, briar, gilded wooden knobs
H146 cm (57½ in) W46 cm (18 in)
L132 cm (51⅞ in)
Manufacturer: Design Gallery,
Italy (1988/9)

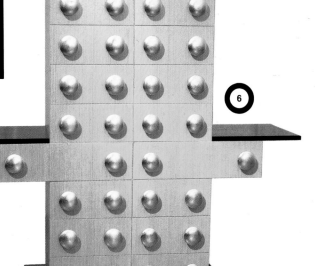

4 ETTORE SOTTSASS
Sideboard, *Freemont*
Reconstituted veneer, plastic laminate,
aluminium and gilded wood
H183 cm (72 in) W190 cm (75 in)
D60 cm (24 in)
Manufacturer: Memphis, Italy (1985/6)

7 MICHELE DE LUCCHI
Table, *Cairo*
Metal, lacquered wood
H72 cm (28½ in) D55 cm (21¾ in)
Manufacturer: Memphis, Italy (1986/7)

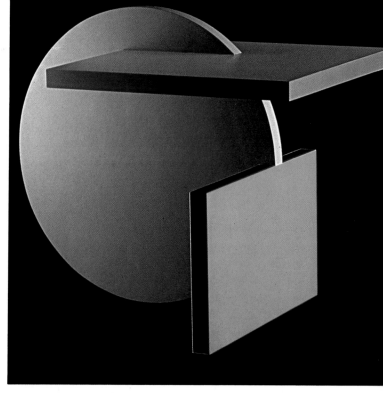

The best '-ism' is optimism. *The works by Michele de Lucchi illustrated here are not only representative of Memphis's early history, they also typify (at least in part) the whole of Italian design, which Ettore Sottsass once described as being 'more colourful, joyful, optimistic and with a sense of humour'. In its early days, Memphis was like a teenager, not giving a damn for the '-isms' of its forefathers but trusting with carefree abandon in its own vitality and spontaneity. This uncontrolled and playful force continues to affect us today, even though it now involves a certain melancholy nostalgia. Those, indeed, were the days.*

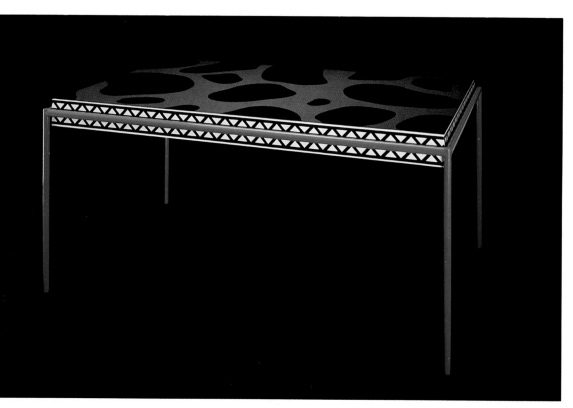

9 MICHELE DE LUCCHI
Table, *Burgundy*
Plastic laminate and painted metal
H72 cm (28½ in)
W155 cm (61 in)
D105 cm (41½ in)
Manufacturer: Memphis, Italy (1985/6)

8 MICHELE DE LUCCHI
Side table, *Continental*
Plastic laminate and timber
H60 cm (23 in) W60 cm (23 in)
L90 cm (34 in)
Manufacturer: Memphis, Italy (1984/5)

10

10 MICHELE DE LUCCHI
Chair, *First*
Metal and wood
H90 cm (35⅜ in) W59 cm
(23¼ in) D50 cm (19⅝ in)
Manufacturer: Memphis, Italy (1983)

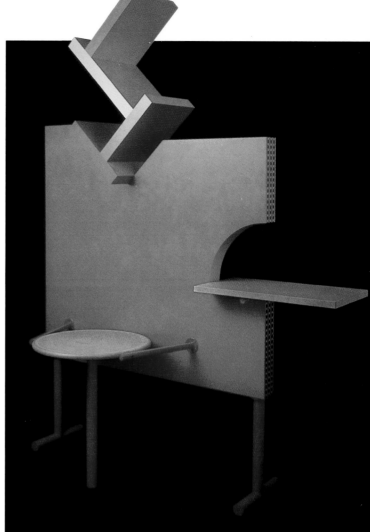

12 MICHELE DE LUCCHI
Room divider, *Scarlet*
Plastic laminate and metal
H243 cm (96 in) W180 cm (71 in)
D85 cm (33½ in)
Manufacturer: Memphis, Italy (1985/6)

Stylistic mutations. *Items of
furniture and household objects are
losing their status of timeless
validity. Instead of being sensible
and boring, coffee tables, chairs
and cupboards are now in a state of
permanent change, voluntarily
submitting themselves to the
influences, for example, of
Caribbean and African art and to
artistic trends such as Cubism and
De Stijl. It works, as long as it lets us
have a good laugh and is powerful
as a composition. Interior design
has become a kind of software, as
interchangeable as packaging,
printed with 'Op Art', 'Africa' and
'Suburbia', if not at random, then
consciously undiscriminating. One
of the basic ideas behind*

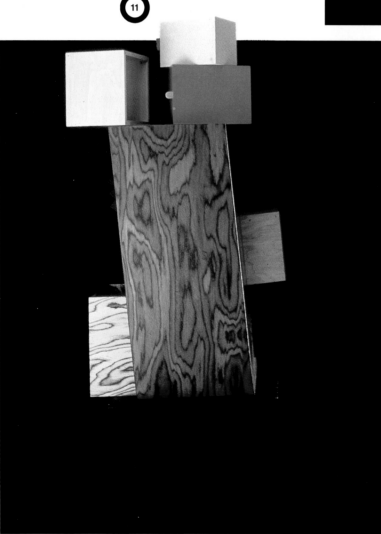

*Memphis's manifesto is to subject
items of furniture to the same kind of
principle as obtains in the fashion
industry, where collections change
from year to year. Graphic design
and three-dimensionality, form and
colour are mixed together like a
series of rapid takes in an abstract
video film.*

11 MARCO ZANINI
Cabinet, *Amazon*
Reconstituted veneer and
lacquered wood
H205 cm (71 in) W80 cm (31½ in)
D51 cm (20 in)
Manufacturer: Memphis,
Italy (1985/6)

14 NATHALIE DU PASQUIER
Chair, *Pilar*
Wood and plastic laminate. The back
and seat have fabric-covered cushions.
H98 cm (38½ in) W54 cm (21¼ in)
D53 cm (20¾ in)
Manufacturer: Nathalie du Pasquier;
made by Pier-Luigi Ghianda, Italy (1985/6)

13 NATHALIE DU PASQUIER
Sideboard, *Emerald*
In wood and plastic laminate
with a curved mirror
H190 cm (75 in) W100 cm
(39½ in) D40 cm (16 in)
Manufacturer: Memphis,
Italy (1985/6)

15 NATHALIE DU PASQUIER
Chair, *Mercedes*
Lacquered wood with fabric-
covered seat cushion
H98 cm (38½ in) W55 cm
(21½ in) D50 cm (19½ in)
Manufacturer: Nathalie du
Pasquier/Pier-Luigi Ghianda,
Italy (1985/6)

16 LEWIS & CLARK
Chair, *Temple*
Designed for the 'Surface and Ornament
Competition'. Designed as a fantasy, the
chair won first prize. 'For a deity who sits
enthroned while tiny imaginary
worshippers perform exotic rituals'
H150 cm (59 in) D120 cm (47 in)
L120 cm (47 in)
Manufacturer: Formica Corporation,
USA (1984/5)

More is more. *'Less is more' – this
maxim by the Bauhaus guru Mies
van der Rohe remained
unchallenged for decades and
became the unwritten law that
governed what we call 'good form',
But, in the 1980s, first architecture,
then design began, as it were, to
put on make-up and to call the
resultant style 'post-modernist'.
Luxury was no longer proscribed
but was back in vogue, demanding
a new Art Deco. Why be simple
when you can be opulent?
Everything was embellished and
brightened up, while buildings were
hung, like Christmas trees, with
decorations quoting every kind of
style. The more the merrier. Often
enough the effect was merely*

17 **MASSIMO MOROZZI**
Table, Tangram
In seven parts
Wood in different colours
Manufacturer: Cassina, Italy (1983)

*curious, though undeniably
ostentatious – and that indeed was
the aim. The two pieces of furniture
reproduced here are typical of the
post-modernist spirit:
architectonically trimmed, they play
with classical quotations, displaying
a discreet gigantomania, offering
scope for conversation and serving
the aim of self-stylization. The
temple throne by Jim Lewis and
Clark Ellefson tells everyone who
might want to know that its owner
considers himself worthy of being
worshipped like a god, while
Massimo Morozzi's Tangram table
allows space to display artistic
sensibilities. The living room
becomes a gallery for the individual
psyche.*

18 CHARLES A. JENCKS
Sun Table and Chairs
MDF painted and glazed.
Table H77 cm (30 in). Small 132 cm (52 in).
Expanded 183 cm (72 in)
Chair H97 cm (38 in). W61 cm (24 in).
L44 cm (17 in)
Manufactured specially for the designer,
available from Max Protech Gallery, New
York

(18)

19 ROBERT VENTURI
Chairs and tables, *Venturi Collection*
Venturi Chairs available in three styles –
Queen Anne, Chippendale or Empire.
Square table top also available in solid
granite. Base and veneer finishes as
above. Laminate finishes in surf white,
floral pattern, black, yellow or burgundy.
H62 cm (28½ in). L122 cm, 138 cm or
152 cm (48 in, 54 in or 60 in)
Manufacturer: Knoll International, USA

(19)

(20)

'I wanna be loved by you'. Huskily murmured into a microphone by Marilyn Monroe in one of her songs, these words could equally well sum up the whole of post-modern design, for here is a stylistic trend whose raison d'être consists in being attractive, image-enhancing and not too demanding, rather like a minor film star with whom one likes to be seen at a party. All of these aspects are hinted at in Hans Hollein's Marilyn sofa, a sex-charged piece of living-room furniture that screams the word HEDONISM in capital letters and which, therefore, has often been used in advertising luxury products as the symbol of a specific lifestyle. Together with a number of other items of furniture reproduced on the following pages, Marilyn shows the craving for admiration that typifies post-modern design, even in the choice of materials. A predilection for 'blonde' materials such as gold and bright bird's-eye maple is particularly striking, suggesting a preference for blondes. During the 1960s, before he made a name for himself with luxury designs for the rich and famous, Hans Hollein was one of the most revolutionary and visionary young architects of his generation. And the same was true of Robert Venturi. Venturi, however, remains a rough diamond. His table and chair collection for Knoll is a Disneyland version of the history of furniture with an emphasis on parodistic charm, subtly subversive wit and that 'messy vitality' he himself so admires.

20 HANS HOLLEIN
Sofa, *Mitzi*
Wood frame, plywood back and side
Padding in polyurethane of different
hardnesses, covered in fabric
H97 cm (38 in) D87 cm (34 in)
L210 cm (82 in)
Manufacturer: Poltronova,
Italy (1984/5)

21 HANS HOLLEIN
Sofa, *Marilyn*
Wood frame, padding in polyurethane of
different hardnesses
H93 cm (36 in) D75 cm (29 in)
L238 cm (93 in)
Manufacturer: Poltronova,
Italy (1984/5)

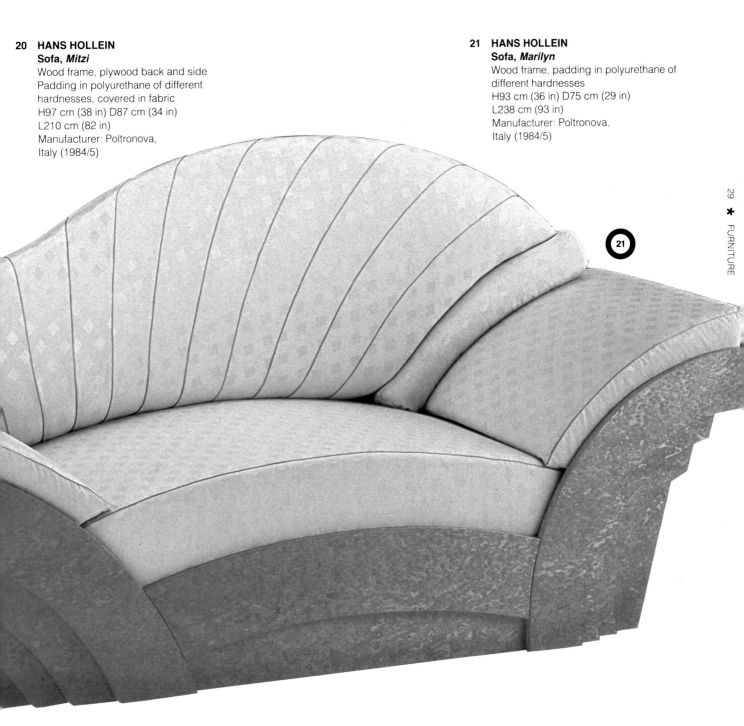

21

Escapades of escapism. There is clearly a lack of romance in modern people's lives. Something inside City dealers, production managers, stockbrokers and art directors cries out for escape into some other world. To escape into a wide-screen version of some golden age, long since past, when power, luxury and romance prevailed, is a pipedream perfectly embodied by a certain type of post-modern show design. Stylistic flourishes from the history of art, and marketable names such as Sun Chair, Serenissimo *and*

Stanhope, *evoke reminiscences of Egypt, Venice, Art Deco, Regency style, Empire style and an aristocratically hedonistic love of life. Furniture like this makes all women feel like Cleopatra and men feel like sun-gods. This is the 'world according to Hollywood', a world which always leaves the purchasers free to play the roles of their dreams. Of course, such pleasures are not cheap, but you may at least save on psychiatrist's bills.*

22 LELLA & MASSIMO VIGNELLI & DAVID LAW
Table, *Serenissimo*
The legs are four large-diameter metal columns treated to evoke Venetian stuccowork. They are interconnected by a natural-finish metal framework. The top is treated plate glass, giving a semi-opalescent effect.
H70-72 cm (27½-28½ in) L160 cm (63 in) W145 cm (57 in)
Manufacturer: Acerbis International, Italy (1985/6)

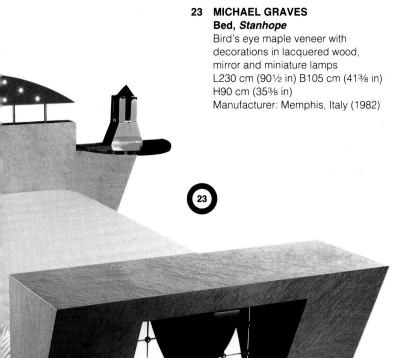

23 MICHAEL GRAVES
Bed, *Stanhope*
Bird's eye maple veneer with
decorations in lacquered wood,
mirror and miniature lamps
L230 cm (90½ in) B105 cm (41⅜ in)
H90 cm (35⅜ in)
Manufacturer: Memphis, Italy (1982)

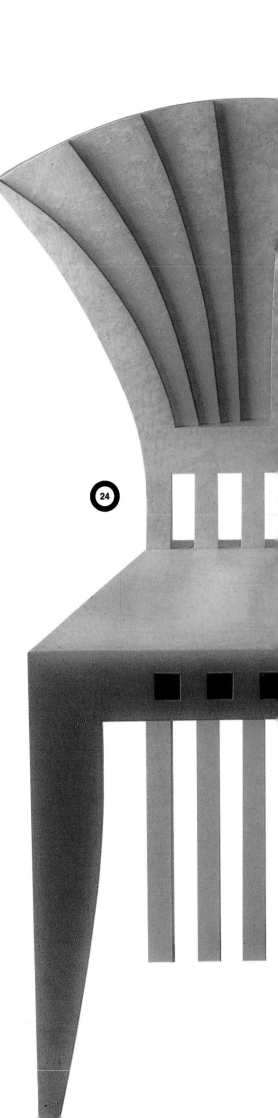

24 CHARLES JENCKS
Chair, *Sun Chair*
Wood
H97 cm (38¼ in) W61 cm (24 in)
L44 cm (17⅜ in)
Manufacturer: Sawaya & Moroni,
Italy (1985)

25 NORBERT BERGHOF, MICHAEL A LANDES, WOLFGANG RANG
Writing desk, *F1 Frankfurter Schrank*
Bird's eye maple, ebony, burl, solid maple, ivory, horn, brass, goldleaf, marble, granite
H230 cm (90½ in) W75 cm (29½ in)
D40 cm (15¾ in)
Manufacturer: Draenert Studio, Germany (1985/6)

A new model: modern Biedermeier. 'Biedermeier' in Germany recalls a sleepy dreamy age when people had time to write each other love letters and when they travelled by stagecoach. Rooms were well-lit and modest, furniture suitably solid and built of light-coloured wood with geometrical patterns inlaid and stained in black.

The fact that the post-modernism of the 1980s has gone back to these very same ideals and that the revolutionaries such as the Italian architect Adolfo Natalini of Superstudio once at the forefront of stylistic change now render homage to the Biedermeier secrétaire is surprising perhaps, but wholly understandable with the change in values during that decade. Following the revolutionary iconoclasm of 1968, Goethe's living room has now been found to exercise an irresistible fascination – a question, perhaps, of life imitating the Elective Affinities of art: solid, carefully fashioned furniture is once again being built and sold to a ready market. The secrétaire with golden towers by Berghof, Landes and Rang, Natalini's writing desk with monumental columns that swivel and close, and Hollein's elegant black, gold and maple sideboard deserve to figure just as prominently in a catalogue of eighties' style as do the jarring, graphic patterns produced by Memphis. The world is not turned upside down by pieces such as these, but invests in them instead.

26 ADOLFO NATALINI & GUGLIELMO RENZI
Cabinet, *Volumina*
Wood
A study cabinet designed for reading,
writing, collecting and storing. Two tall
columns of cypress or walnut or cherry-
wood contain and support a lift-top desk.
The interiors are in wengee or Japanese
maple. All the wood has been seasoned
for up to forty years. Limited batch production
H179 cm (70½ in) W123 cm (48½ in)
D (open) 79 cm (31 in); (closed) 40 cm (15¾ in)
Manufacturer: Sawaya & Moroni, Italy (1987/8)

26

27

**27 NORBERT BERGHOF, MICHAEL
LANDES & WOLFGANG RANG**
Armchair, *Frankfurter Stuhl FIII*
Maple, brass, gold, marquetry
Produced in a limited batch of 100
H83 cm (32⅝ in) W63 cm (24⅞ in)
D54 cm (21¼ in)
Manufacturer: Draenert Studio,
West Germany (1986/7)

28

28 HANS HOLLEIN
Side table, *Schwarzenberg*
Aniline-dyed briar, wood and gilded wood
H82 cm (32⅜ in) L160 cm (63 in)
D47 cm (18½ in)
Manufacturer: Memphis, Italy (1981)

29

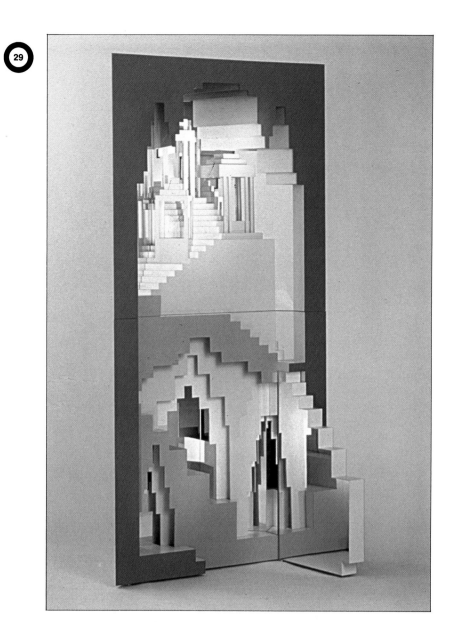

30

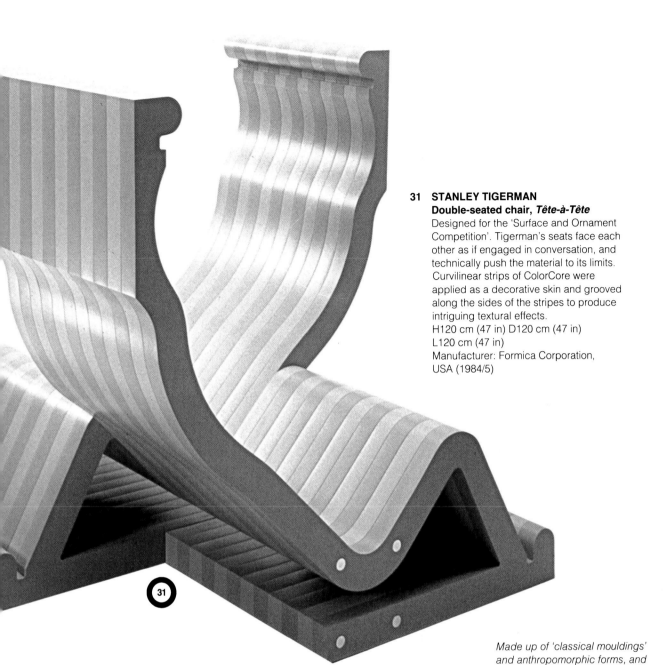

31 STANLEY TIGERMAN
Double-seated chair, *Tête-à-Tête*
Designed for the 'Surface and Ornament
Competition'. Tigerman's seats face each
other as if engaged in conversation, and
technically push the material to its limits.
Curvilinear strips of ColorCore were
applied as a decorative skin and grooved
along the sides of the stripes to produce
intriguing textural effects.
H120 cm (47 in) D120 cm (47 in)
L120 cm (47 in)
Manufacturer: Formica Corporation,
USA (1984/5)

Academic paper tigers. *'The
design was intended for an
intimately related couple who could
read the same page of the Sunday
New York Times simultaneously on
opposite sides of the page.' Thus
the Chicago-born architect and
pupil of Mies van der Rohe, Stanley
Tigerman, describing his
lollipop-coloured chaise. On a
design like this, you don't just read
the paper, you can also engage in
conversation on architectural topics.*

*Made up of 'classical mouldings'
and anthropomorphic forms, and
well suited to witty rhetoric, this
piece – called Tête à Tête by
Tigerman – was exhibited in 1983
as his contribution to the 'Formica
ColorCore Surface & Ornament
Exhibition'.*

*The same event was further
distinguished by a corner cupboard
with a temple town of neo-classical
micro-architecture designed by
Charles Moore, Tigerman's
post-modern colleague. The
ColorCore competition clearly
shows the various ways in which
plastic laminate is used in New
Design on both sides of the Atlantic,
while at the same time underlining
the fundamental difference between
American ways of thinking and
Italian practices à la Memphis.*

29, 30 CHARLES MOORE
Corner Cupboard
ColorCore. Designed for the 'Surface and
Ornament Competition'. Moore used
the material to express his preoccupation
with Classical decorative motifs.
H approx 183 cm (72 in)
Manufacturer: Formica Corporation,
USA (1984/5)

32 DEREK FROST
Stereo cabinet
A stereo cabinet with three lift-up lids containing a counter, two turntables and mixing controls. Three sliding doors conceal a television on a swing arm, amplifiers, and storage for CDs and cassettes. The lower level has three storage drawers. Finished in blue matt cellulose with white-gold oil gilding. The silver doors are by Yumi Katayama.
One-off
H98 cm (38½ in) W127 cm (50 in)
D55 cm (21½ in)
Manufacturer: Derek Frost Associates, UK (1987/8)

32

33 JOHN HUTTON/DONGHIA DESIGN STUDIO
Club chair, *Luciano*
Hardwood frame, finished wood legs,
fabric upholstery
H92 cm (36 in) W92 cm (36 in)
D92 cm (36 in)
Manufacturer: Donghia Furniture and
Textiles, USA (1988/9)

(33)

34 JOHN HUTTON
Sofa, *San Marco*
Hardwood frame, hand-tied springs,
fabric upholstery
H96.5 cm (38 in) W244 cm (96 in)
D102 cm (40 in)
Manufacturer: Donghia Furniture and
Textiles, USA (1988/9)

Good ol' fifties. *Ah, the fifties,
when the world was still OK! What
memories those years evoke:
petticoats and pomade, rock 'n' roll,
the Cold War and sexual
repressiveness. But perhaps the
decade of our imagination was a
land of cockayne transfigured by
the filters and soft-focus lenses of
our memory. One thing, however, is
true: the chairs of the period still
had crumple zones like those
unforgotten screen goddesses
Marilyn Monroe, Gina Lollobrigida,
Sophia Loren and Anita Ekberg.
John Hutton's upholstered furniture
recalls these voluptuous forms,
while Derek Frost's self-indulgent
radiogram is a time machine
disguised as a piece of furniture.*

(34)

Pet with teddy-bear ears. *If there is one piece of furniture that deserves the description of 'classic of the '80s' and 'one of the decade's leading designs', it is the Wink armchair by the Japanese industrial designer Toshiyuki Kita. Adjustable joints inside the frame allow the chair to be placed in supine or sitting positions, just like a human body, while its 'ears' can also be made to waggle. In creating this brilliant design (realized in conjunction with the Italian firm of Cassina), Kita not only earned a place for himself in the holy of holies of New York's Museum of Modern Art, he also pulled off a coup in the world of product design. Its more elegant middle-class relative, the Veranda system, was also developed by Cassina. It too can be adjusted by means of interior joints but, like Arflex's couch, it is sadly lacking the amiable originality of Kita's comical wing chair. The same*

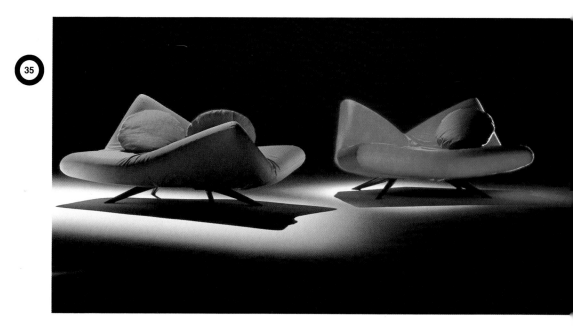

35 **FABRIZIO BALLARDINI &
FULVIO FORBICINI**
Sofa, *Ribalta*
Metal frame, cast iron base,
polyurethane foam upholstery
Each angle can be modified to six
different positions.
H80 cm (31½ in) W118 cm (46½ in)
L162 cm (63¾ in) Height to seat 41 cm (16⅛ in)
Manufacturer: Arflex, Italy (1988/9)

*is true of Wink as it is of all new
inventions in furniture building: the
first solutions (always assuming the
idea is fresh and inspiring) are
generally the best and most radical.
A chair like Wink – like the chairs by
Thonet or Freischwinger – can only
be varied but never improved.*

37–39 VICO MAGISTRETTI
Two-seat sofa, *Veranda*
Frame of folding steel units, polyurethane
foam and polyester padding
H75/110 cm (29½/43⅜ in)
W180 cm (70⅞ in) D155 cm (61 in)
Manufacturer: Cassina, Italy (1983)

36 TOSHIYUKI KITA
Armchair, *Wink*
Black ABS, adjustable metal frame,
polyurethane and dacron padding
H38/95 cm (15/34⅜ in) L90/200 cm
(35⅜/79¾ in)
W78 cm (30⅝ in)
Manufacturer: Cassina,
Italy (1981)

40 JAVIER MARISCAL
Wheeled chair, *Biscuter*
Metal, fibreglass, upholstery
H31 cm (12¼ in) W56.5 cm (22¼ in)
D77 cm (30¼ in)
Manufacturer: Akaba, Spain (1988/9)

40

41

41 PEPE CORTES &
JAVIER MARISCAL
Chair, *Trampolin*
Steel, wood
H67 cm (26⅜ in) W (total) 55 cm (21⅝ in)
D55 cm (21⅝ in)
Manufacturer: Akaba, Spain (1986/7)

42 PAOLO DEGANELLO
Armchair, *Torso*
Steel frame and elastic webbing, padded
with polyurethane foam and polyester.
Feet with black ABS points. Fabric or
leather upholstery; the seat and back can
be of different materials. A sofa and a bed
are available in the same style.
H82 cm (32 in) D88 cm (34 in)
Manufacturer: Cassina, Italy (1984/5)

43, 44 BORGE LINDAU & BO LINDEKRANTZ
Chair, *Planka*
In enamelled plywood with leather, sheet-metal or fabric seat. The swivelling base plate is enamelled steel and the seat frame and neck frames are chrome-plated
H110 cm (43 in) W42 cm (16½ in)
D68 cm (27 in)
Manufacturer: Lammhults, Sweden (1985/6)

46 JOCHEN HOFFMANN
Sofa, *Trio*
Versatile sofa which can be used as a two-seater with two leg rests, a three-seater with one leg rest or a four-seater. The head rests are also adjustable. The beech frame is supported by lacquered-finished metal. The upholstery comes in a variety of different fabrics.
Manufacturer: Firma Franz Fertig, West Germany (1985/6)

**45 PETER MALY
Armchair,
Zyklus**
In chromed steel
tubing, with the
upper part in
coloured
lacquer. The
cover material
and the leather
are available in
various
combinations
and colours.
H72 cm (28¼ in)
W75 cm (29½ in)
L85 cm (33½ in)
Manufacturer:
COR-Sitzkomfort,
West Germany
(1985/6)

45

46

47 DANILO SILVESTRIN
Desk, *Hommage à Mondrian*
Lacquered wood.
H80 cm (32 in) W90 cm (35 in) L190 cm (74 in)
Manufacturer: Rosenthal Einrichtung, West Germany (1984/5)

48 BURKHARD VOGTHERR
Chair, *T-Line*
Metal, polyurethane moulded foam,
integrated fabric in various colours
H100 cm (39 in) W75/76 cm (29½ in)
D68/75 cm (26/29 in)
Manufacturer: Arflex, Italy (1984/5)

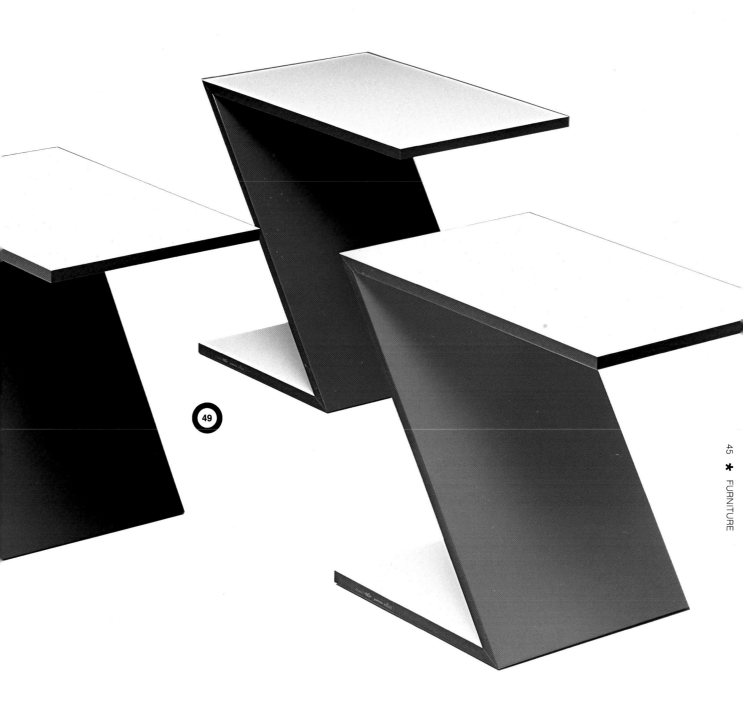

49 **DANILO SILVESTRIN**
Table, *Hommage à Rietveld*
Lacquered wood. The formal
reduction to three surfaces is
emphasized by colour.
H60 cm (23 in) W46 cm (18 in)
L69 cm (27 in)
Manufacturer: Rosenthal Einrichtung,
West Germany (1984/5)

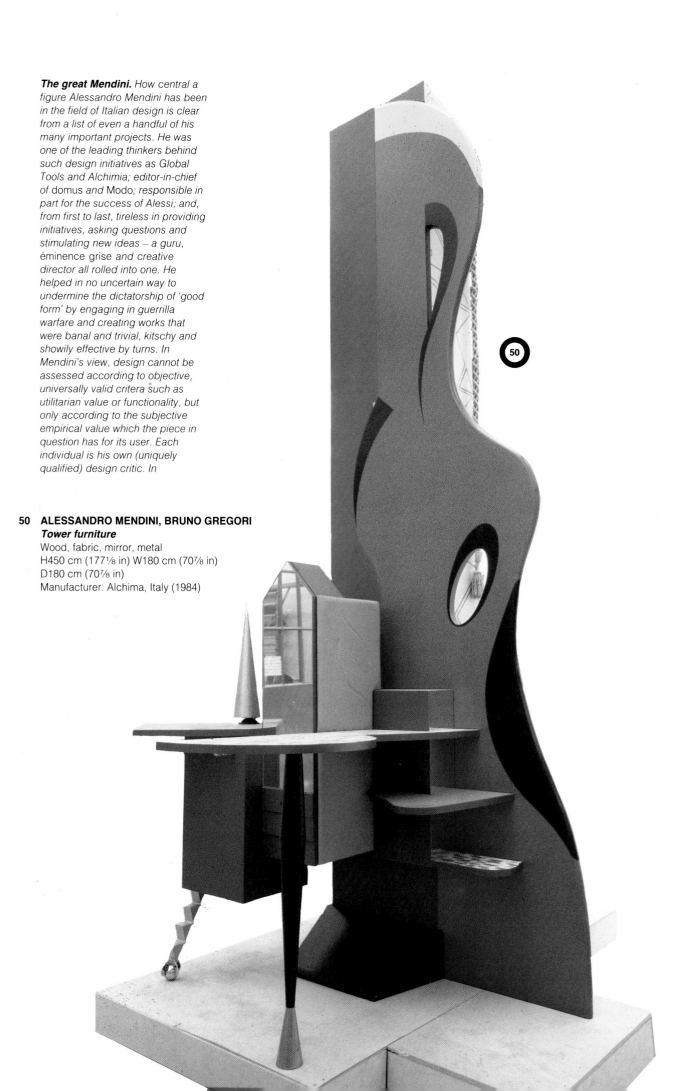

The great Mendini. *How central a
figure Alessandro Mendini has been
in the field of Italian design is clear
from a list of even a handful of his
many important projects. He was
one of the leading thinkers behind
such design initiatives as Global
Tools and Alchimia; editor-in-chief
of* domus *and* Modo; *responsible in
part for the success of Alessi; and,
from first to last, tireless in providing
initiatives, asking questions and
stimulating new ideas – a guru,
éminence grise and creative
director all rolled into one. He
helped in no uncertain way to
undermine the dictatorship of 'good
form' by engaging in guerrilla
warfare and creating works that
were banal and trivial, kitschy and
showily effective by turns. In
Mendini's view, design cannot be
assessed according to objective,
universally valid critera such as
utilitarian value or functionality, but
only according to the subjective
empirical value which the piece in
question has for its user. Each
individual is his own (uniquely
qualified) design critic. In*

50 ALESSANDRO MENDINI, BRUNO GREGORI
Tower furniture
Wood, fabric, mirror, metal
H450 cm (177⅛ in) W180 cm (70⅞ in)
D180 cm (70⅞ in)
Manufacturer: Alchima, Italy (1984)

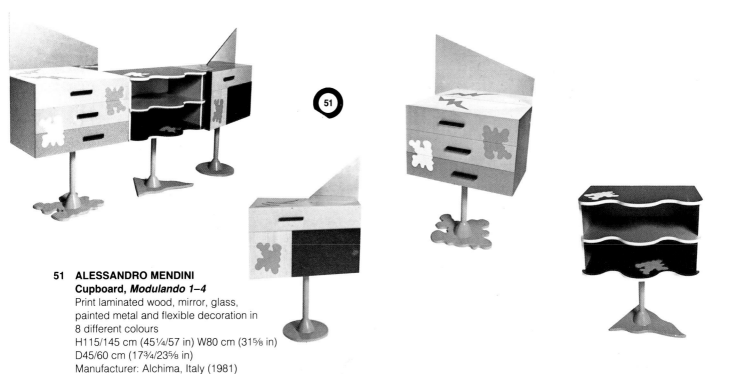

51

51 ALESSANDRO MENDINI
Cupboard, *Modulando 1–4*
Print laminated wood, mirror, glass,
painted metal and flexible decoration in
8 different colours
H115/145 cm (45¼/57 in) W80 cm (31⅝ in)
D45/60 cm (17¾/23⅝ in)
Manufacturer: Alchima, Italy (1981)

advancing this view, Mendini no
doubt earns his place among the
spiritual fathers of that pluralism in
design that is so often quoted
today. Next to his importance as an
original thinker, his design work
leaves a more mixed impression.
Novel and witty it undoubtedly is;
but it lacks the ultimate in originality.
The way he works is not by creating
something completely new in every
detail but by going back to
something that already exists,
quoting it, changing it and
arranging it anew. Mendini is the
founder and undisputed master of
parodistic redesign and of what
might be called the 'style-cocktail'.
Worthy, commonplace furniture
suffers strange permutations under
the assault of Mendini's imagination
and is transformed into iridescent
birds of paradise. No doubt more
surprises are in store for us in
Mendini's Genetic Laboratory for
Visual Surprises.

52

52 ALESSANDRO MENDINI
Sofa and armchair, *Maracatu*
Wood, upholstery
H88 cm (34⅝ in) W166 cm (65⅜ in)
and 94 cm (37 in) D80 cm (31½ in)
Manufacturer: Vitra International,
Switzerland (1988/9)

(54)

(55)

(53)

53 MASAKI MORITA
Table, *Stream*
Table in steel with a polyurethane coating
and matt paint finish
One-off
H70 cm (27½ in) W300 cm (118 in)
D60 cm (23⅝ in)
Manufacturer: Kikuchihara, Japan (1986/7)

54 MAURIZIO PEREGALLI
Armchair, *Poltrocino Cromo*
Chair of 1.5 cm (⅝ in) square steel tube,
chromed, with black self-finished
polyurethane seat. Part of the *Zeus
Collection*
H68 cm (26¾ in) L53 cm (20⅞ in)
D42 cm (16½ in)
Manufacturer: Noto, Italy (1986/7)

55 PASCAL MOURGUE
Table
Three-legged café table on castors. The
legs are of black-lacquered metal. One
version has a double shelf, the other a
mirrored and sanded tray with hollow centre
H72 cm (28⅜ in) Di75 cm (29½ in)
Manufacturer: Artelano, France (1986/7)

56

56 MARIO BOTTA
Armchair, *Sesta*
Perforated and stretched-steel painted
frame with seat and cushions in leather or fabric
H95 cm (37½ in) W100 cm (39½ in)
D100 cm (39½ in)
Manufacturer: Alias, Italy (1985/6)

Sofa, *Sesta*
Two-seater sofa with perforated
stretched-steel frame. Seat and cushions
in leather or fabric
H95 cm (37½ in) L155 cm (61 in)
Manufacturer: Alias, Italy (1985/6)

57   FOSTER ASSOCIATES
Office system, *Nomos*
Die-cast aluminium, steel tube
A system of workstations and tables
Manufacturer: Tecno, Italy (1986/7)

57

Furniture engineering. *Unlike post-modern architects, high-tech architects have shown a marked reserve in the field of design. We have seen nothing by Richard Rogers, while Renzo Piano and Jean Nouvel have produced no more than the occasional table or chest of drawers. By contrast, Norman Foster has designed or, rather, constructed an unconventional office system with the same degree of concentration that he brought to the Hong Kong and Shanghai Bank. It is, to borrow a term from the Russian Constructivists, the work of an 'artist-engineer'. The modular construction system of tubular steel, aluminium and plastic allows the observer to see the principles on which the design is constructed. Were Gustave Eiffel alive today, his design would not have been very different. The most fascinating detail of the Nomos system is the magnificent way in which wire is used both structurally and functionally: all the power- and connecting cables are held together in flexible cords using plastic clips like nerve fibres in the spinal column. What name should we give this anatomical incursion into the world of engineering? High-tech or Bio-tech? There are interesting parallels here with the 'Organic Design' associated with the Turin of the 1940s and 1950s, when Carlo Mollino and others crossed modern technology with fragments of saurian ribs and backbones in designing a new style of furniture.*

58   **NORMAN FOSTER**
Office system, *Nomos* (detail)
Wire management
Manufacturer: Tecno, Italy

Tame tigers. *How many young hotheads have been warmly welcomed by industry and embraced with such enthusiasm that the revolutionary breath has been squeezed out from their lungs. It gives one pause for thought that two such important designers as Philippe Starck and Alessandro Mendini, whose limited editions are often striking for the boldness of their ideas, both withdraw their claws when working on* mass-produced objects. Both *Starck's* Dr Glob *and Mendini's* San Leonardo armchair *are discreet to the point of anonymity. Mendini's chair would hardly catch one's eye in the pages of a mail-order catalogue, while Philippe Starck's chairs are a compilation of older designs from a veritable ancestral portrait gallery, evoking associations from Eileen Gray and Bauhaus to the ultralight furniture designed by Fritz August Breuhaus for the passenger zeppelins of the 1930s, and from Carlo Mollino and Gio Ponti to Vico Magistretti's stacking chairs, to name only some of the influences on his work. The piece in question is like a screen projection: too many images superimposed produce a non-image. And tame tigers lose their teeth more quickly.*

(59)

59 PHILIPPE STARCK
Stacking chair, *Dr Glob*
Polypropylene, steel tubing
H46 cm (18 in) W47.5 cm (18¾ in)
D48 cm (18⅞ in)
Manufacturer: Kartell, Italy (1988/9)

62 ALESSANDRO MENDINI
Armchair, *San Leonardo*
Collection
Leather club armchair, designed
in traditional form
H100 cm (39½ in) W102 cm (40 in)
D85 cm (33½ in)
Manufacturer: Matteo Grassi,
Italy (1985/6)

60

60 **PHILIPPE STARCK**
Chair, *Von Vogelsang*
Steel tubing frame with bent perforated
metal seat. All varnished in light metal
grey.
H71.5 cm (28 in) W54 cm (21 in)
D51 cm (20 in)
Manufacturer: Aleph, Italy (1985/6)

61

62

61 **PHILIPPE STARCK**
Table/seat, *Mickville*
Three-legged folding structure in steel
tubing with turned sheet-steel top,
varnished in metal azure and semi-
opaque black
Total H80.5 cm (32 in) H of surface
48 cm (19 in) D38 cm (15 in)
Manufacturer: Aleph, Italy (1985/6)

63

63 PHILIPPE STARCK
Chair, *Pratfall*
Varnished black steel tubing frame with
bent plywood back lacquered in semi-
opaque black. Seat is covered in black
leather.
H86 cm (34 in) W61.5 cm (24 in)
D78 cm (31 in)
Manufacturer: Aleph, Italy (1985/6)

64 PHILIPPE STARCK
Table, *Titos Apostos*
Three-legged, folding table of steel
tubing, with turned sheet-steel plates and
top, varnished in metal, gold and silver
H71 cm (28 in) D85 cm (33½ in)
Manufacturer: Aleph, Italy (1985/6)

64

The ubiquitous Monsieur Starck.
UBIK is the name of one of Philippe Starck's most famous chairs. It is also the name of a mysterious being in Philip K. Dick's eponymous science-fiction novel. In this nightmare-like odyssey through simulated realities in a dying man's brain, the ubiquitous UBIK keeps on appearing. (His name derives from the Latin ubique, 'everywhere'.) Philippe Starck is a fan of Dick's and would like to be like UBIK – omnipresent, involved in a thousand different projects, working faster than the speed of light and jetting all round the world at faster than the speed of sound. And whenever you open design magazines, there is the man himself: UBIK! The Café Costes UBIK, the Concorde UBIK, the three-legged stool UBIK, the designer stubble UBIK, the Andy Warhol of design UBIK. But no matter, any friend of Philip K. Dick is a friend of ours. For Dick not only wrote Blade Runner, he even had a far better title for it: Do Androids Dream of Electric Sheep?

65 PHILIPPE STARCK
Armchair, J. (Serie Lang)
Steel, aluminium, polyurethane foam
Three-legged armchair with black leather upholstery and a single metal leg at the back. The frame is of cast aluminium and the body of tubular steel.
H86 cm (33⅞ in) W66 cm (26 in)
D60 cm (23⅝ in)
Manufacturer: Driade, Italy (1986/7)

66 SHIRO KURAMATA
Bar stool, *BK 86000*
Chromed tubular steel, laminated wood
Limited batch production
H90 cm (35½ in) W36 cm (14⅛ in)
D15 cm (6 in) Di of seat 33 cm (13 in)
Manufacturer: Pastoe, Netherlands (1988/9)

67 SHIRO KURAMATA
Armchair, *Sing Sing Sing*
Chair of tubular steel with back and seat of
metal slats, moulded plastic base: in silver,
buffed chrome or nickel
H89 cm (35 in) W54 cm (21¼ in) D59 cm
(23¼ in)
Manufacturer: XO, France (1986/7)

(66)

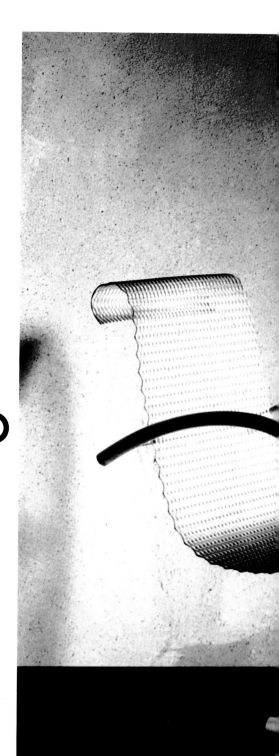

(67)

Maximum minimalism. *There is no
doubt that Shiro Kuramata is one of
the very few very great designers of
the late twentieth century. His
spectacular design concepts for the
Lucchino Bar and Caffe Oxy in
Tokyo and his Issey Miyake
boutiques throughout the world
have influenced whole armies of
interior designers, while his almost
impossibly high standards have
also left them deeply frustrated. In
furniture design as well, he is the
undisputed master of the creative
void. His objects often seem to
hover in a state of suspension on
the very brink of disintegration. A
sense of immateriality, of something
invisible but none the less
suspected, gives his furniture a
certain trance-like aura, surrounding
it with a dome of timelessness and
silence beneath which seconds
could last an eternity. But however*

*meditative they may appear,
however much they resemble holy
relics, they are firmly anchored in
the here-and-now, in a present on
which they, too, have left their mark.
The impression made by
Kuramata's minimalist designs is
neither mean nor pitiful, but
sensuous, allusive and filled with
rich associations. Chests of drawers
resemble spaceships, cupboards
dance, armchairs hover in the air,
tables glow with light. The most
extreme example of Kuramata's
state-of-the-art high-tech
romanticism is his Blues in the
Night, a table with several dozen
red diode tubes that glow inside its
transparent acrylic surface. There is
no better working environment than
this for the well-dressed hacker on
his night-time voyage of discovery
and adventure through other
people's data files.*

68

68 SHIRO KURAMATA
Chair, *How High the Moon*
Expanded metal, steel tube
H69.5 cm (27⅜ in) W95.5 cm (37½ in)
D82.5 cm (32½ in)
Manufacturer: Kurosaki, Japan (1986/7)

69

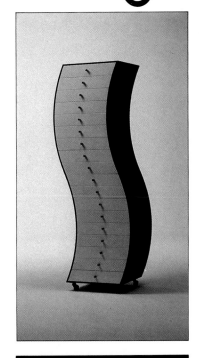

69 SHIRO KURAMATA
Chest, *Side 1, Side 2*
Chest of drawers in black ash with
lacquered wood available in two different
shapes and in a castor-mounted version
Limited batch production
H170 cm (67 in) W63 cm or 45 cm
(24⅞ in or 17¾ in) D50 cm or 60 cm
(19⅝ in or 23⅝ in)
Manufacturer: Cappellini International
Interiors, Italy (1986/7)

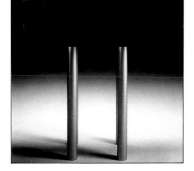

70

70 SHIRO KURAMATA
Chest, *Solaris*
Chest of drawers in cherrywood or ash
The drawers can be opened from both sides.
H155 cm (61 in) W140 cm (55⅛ in)
D80 cm (31½ in)
Manufacturer: Cappellini International
Interiors, Italy (1986/7)

71 SERGI DEVESA BAJET
Coffee table, *Chincheta*
Sheet aluminium painted in epoxy
H31 cm (12¼ in) Di 100 cm (39½ in)
Manufacturer: Disform, Spain (1988/9)

(71)

73 ANNA CASTELLI-FERRIERI
Armchair, *4814*
Technopolymers blend, steel
A new injection moulding process
creates a random spotted material.
H73 cm (28¾ in) W65 cm (25½ in)
D97 cm (38¼ in)
Manufacturer: Kartell, Italy (1988/9)

72 PERRY A. KING AND SANTIAGO MIRANDA
Book shelf system, *Bloom*
Steel
D33 cm (13 in) L100 cm (39½ in) or
150 cm (59 in). Uprights: H200 cm
(78¾) to 303 cm (119⅝ in)
Manufacturer: Tisettanta, Italy (1988/9)

Back to nature. Nostalgic incursions into the past also left their mark on the sort of design that we saw at the end of the decade. No longer was there any sign, as far as furniture was concerned, of that industrial design from which the new genre initially developed before establishing itself as an independent art form.

Jaime Tresserra Clapés is a former goldsmith who is one of the new generation of designers in Barcelona. His secrétaire – richly worked and winged like some exotic insect – resembles an outsize casket of jewels.

The London-based design artist Matthew Hilton uses fin-shaped objects cast in aluminium as legs to support a glass-topped coffee table, while antelope legs of silver attached to a wooden cone support a circular tabletop. Such quotations from nature, cast in metal like holy relics, constitute the magic aura of his designs. A new art nouveau is not far off.

75 MATTHEW HILTON
Table, *Flipper*
Glass, cast aluminium
H38 cm (15 in) W95 cm (37½ in)
L95 cm (37½ in)
Manufacturer: SCP, UK (1988/9)

74 MATTHEW HILTON
Antelope Table
MDF, aluminium, wood, stainless steel
A small, three-legged table with two legs of aluminium and one of oak. The top is of MDF and stainless-steel inlay.
Limited batch production
H70 cm (27½ in) Di 85 cm (33½ in)
Manufacturer: Matthew Hilton, UK (1987/8)

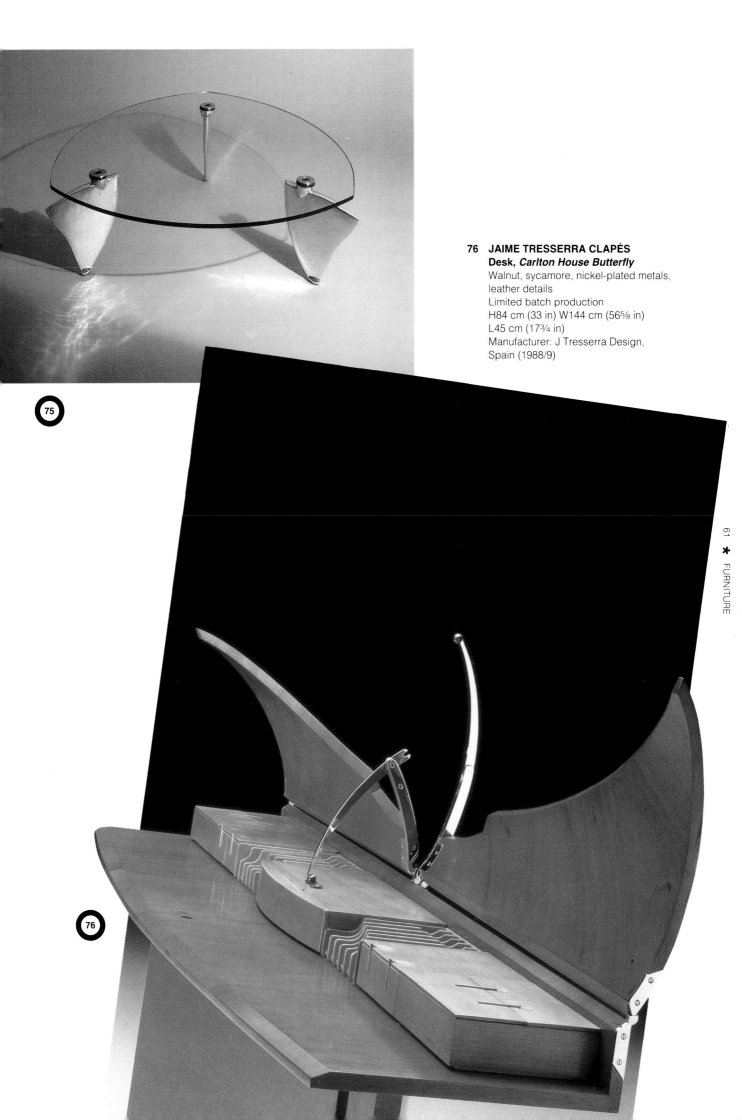

76 JAIME TRESSERRA CLAPÉS
Desk, *Carlton House Butterfly*
Walnut, sycamore, nickel-plated metals,
leather details
Limited batch production
H84 cm (33 in) W144 cm (56⅝ in)
L45 cm (17¾ in)
Manufacturer: J Tresserra Design,
Spain (1988/9)

75

76

77 ZAHA HADID
Wavy Back Sofa
Lacquered wood, felt, wool
Prototype of a sofa in lacquered wood,
upholstered in wool
H120 cm (47¼ in) W70 cm and (max)
200 cm (27½ in and 78⅜ in)
L380 cm (149½ in)
Manufacturer: Zaha Hadid
with Michael
Wolfson, UK (1987/8)

Post-modern streamline. *The
stylistic spectrum of the late 1980s
was enriched in spectacular fashion
not only by the science-fiction
illustrations, suggesting the idea of
speed, of Massimo Iosa Ghini, a
former draughtsman on children's
comics but now a prominent
designer, but also by the
crumbling new buildings of the
London-based painter-architect
Zaha Hadid and by the filigree
furniture constructions by the art
engineer Santiago Calatrava.*

*The Italian designer Iosa Ghini
seems to have his foot pressed
firmly down on the accelerator
pedal, to judge by the wings and
streamlined shapes that he uses to
give his objects a sense of optical
speed. An engineer, Calatrava
constructs elaborate wing assembly
parts, folding them together to
produce items of furniture which in
turn become beautifully shaped
examples of structural engineering.
In the case of the architect Zaha
Hadid, the dynamically
constructivist world of the Russian
revolutionary artists – a world not
realized in its day – lives on in
London as a deconstructivist
reinterpretation.*

78 SANTIAGO CALATRAVA
Reclining chair, *Espada DS-150*
Leather, wood, chromed steel
H42 cm (16½ in) W65 cm (25½ in)
L200 cm (78¾ in)
Manufacturer: de Sede, Switzerland (1986/7)

79 MASSIMO IOSA-GHINI
Armchair
Wood, leather, chrome
H75 cm (29½ in) W55 cm (21½ in)
D75 cm (29½ in)
Manufacturer: Memphis, Italy (1986/7)

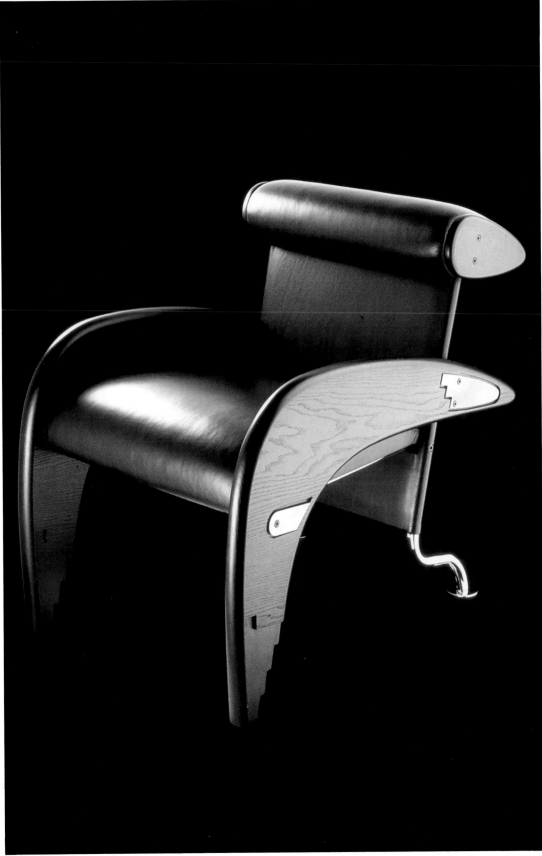

(79)

80 BOŘEK ŠÍPEK
Chaise longue, *Sni*
Steel, polyurethane foam, wood
A chaise longue in the *Prosim* range of
living-room furniture with a steel frame
padded with cold-worked polyurethane
foam. The visible frame is of polished
matt cherry-wood and the seat and arm
covers are of black leather.
H100 cm (39½ in) W165 cm (65⅜ in)
D84 cm (33 in)
Manufacturer: Driade, Italy (1987/8)

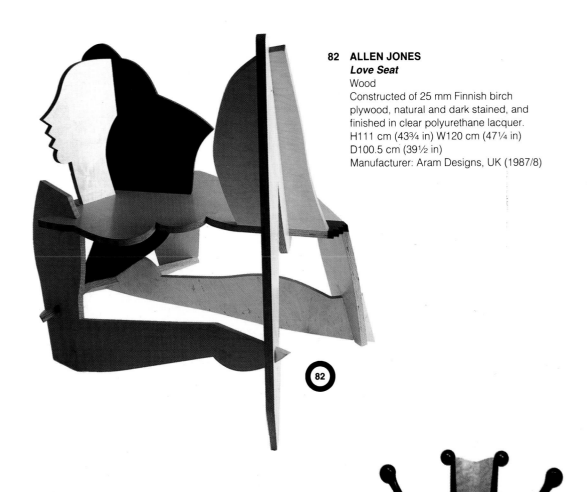

82 ALLEN JONES
Love Seat
Wood
Constructed of 25 mm Finnish birch
plywood, natural and dark stained, and
finished in clear polyurethane lacquer.
H111 cm (43¾ in) W120 cm (47¼ in)
D100.5 cm (39½ in)
Manufacturer: Aram Designs, UK (1987/8)

83 BOŘEK ŠÍPEK
Chair, *Ernst und Geduld*
Ebony, padouk, maple
Limited batch production
H70 cm (27½ in) W60 cm (23½ in)
D45 cm (17¾ in)
Manufacturer: Neotu, France (1988/9)

81 CHRISTOPHER ROBERTSON
Chair
Oak, steel, laminate
One-off
H70 cm (27½ in) W80 cm (31½ in)
L120 cm (47¼ in)
Manufacturer: RCA Furniture Workshops,
UK (1986/7)

84 GAETANO PESCE
Armchairs, *Dalila Uno, Due, Tre*
Hard polyurethane, epoxy finish
H75/89 cm (29½/35 in) W49/71 cm
(13⅝/27⅞ in) D55/64 cm (21⅝/25¼ in)
Manufacturer: Cassina, Italy (1981)

85 GAETANO PESCE
Chair, *Feltri*
Felt
Prototype of a chair made from thick
wool felt. The lower part is impregnated
with polyester resin to provide support
and resistance. The seat is fixed to the
supporting frame by hemp strings that
also trim the soft edges of the chair, and
the whole is completed by a mattress of
quilted fabric and down padding.
H140 cm (55⅛ in) W74 cm (29 in)
D64 cm (25⅛ in)
Manufacturer: Cassina, Italy (1987/8)

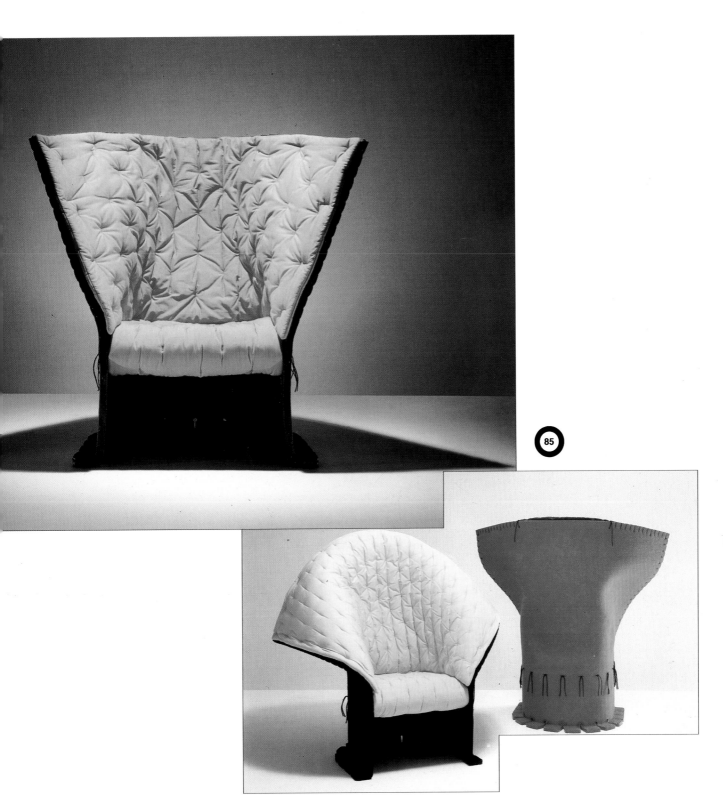

85

Felt for the Third World. *Like
Sottsass and Kuramata, Gaetano
Pesce – a New Yorker by adoption
– is one of the major figures of
avant-garde design. As long ago as
the 1960s, all three of them began
to lay the foundations for a new
formal language of the 1980s.*

*Pesce in particular began at an
early age to question traditional
views of uniform industrial design
and to demand a greater sense of
individuality. Even the utilitarian
object, he argued, must be a mirror*
of the imperfect human individual. It
is this belief which persuaded him,
in his Delilah chairs, to give
expression to the symptoms of old
age, to muscles, sinews and bones,
and to sprinkle sand in the polyester
to produce the effect of a pitted
skin. In the case of the Delilah chair,
the individualized mass-produced
article remained an ideal that
lacked the technological means to
realize it. Seven years later Peace
devised a new technology for
working in felt which brought him
one step closer his avowed ideal of
producing an individualistic and
highly expressive body architecture.
His Feltri furniture is draped round
people like some protective mantle.
It can be manufactured in larger or
smaller quantities and as cheaply or
as exclusively as required. Pesce
considers felt to be an ideal material
which, because it is recycled,
stands a chance of being accepted
in Third-World countries. For the
present, however, his felt furniture
remains restricted to design
galleries and the most exclusive
furnishing stores.

86 SETSUO KITAOKA
Screen, *Byobu*
Folding screen in colorcore
Each panel 24 cm (9½ in) by 24 cm
(9½ in) by 14 cm (5½ in)
Prototype (1985/6)

87 KAZUKO FUJIE
Screen, *Coquille*
In plywood with a Japanese linden
veneer and natural grain finish
H180 cm (71 in) W400 cm (157 in)
D150 cm (59 in)
One-off (1985/6)

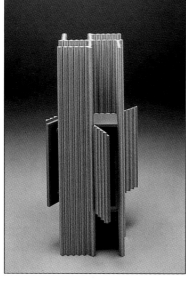

A cardboard lounge chair. Little
Beaver *is the name of Frank Gehry's
easy chair and footstool. It is as big
as a lounge chair but the frame is
not made from the expensive
jacaranda. It is not upholstered in
down, nor are its feet made of
aluminium. It is made entirely of
ordinary corrugated cardboard, cut
in strips and pasted ogether.*

*To the éminence grise of the
Little Beaver's creator (Gehry has*
been awarded the Pritzger Prize for
Architecture, the architectural
equivalent of the Nobel Prize), the
mischievous joke implied by the
chair depends for its effectiveness
on our expectations of what
constitutes the prototypical lounge
chair, expectations that are further
undermined by the somewhat
surprising choice of material. Our
feeling of uncertainty is further
fuelled by the Little Beaver's edges,
which look as though some rodent
has been gnawing them. A
calculatedly unfamiliar treatment of
the material turns an ordinary object
into something extraordinary.
Experiments in the field of tension
between material and form are also
a part of Japanese tradition and
have found expressive use as a
stylistic device in works by the
architects Kazuko Fujie and Setsuo
Kitaoka.

88 FRANK O GEHRY
Chair and stool, *Little Beaver*
Cardboard
A chair and stool that use a 'poor'
material to create a rich object.
Limited batch production
Chair H87 cm (34¼ in) W81 cm
(31¾ in) D86 cm (33⅞ in)
Stool H41 cm (16⅛ in) W44.5 cm
(17½ in) D56 cm (22 in)
Manufacturer: Vitra International,
Switzerland (1987/8)

88

69 ★ FURNITURE

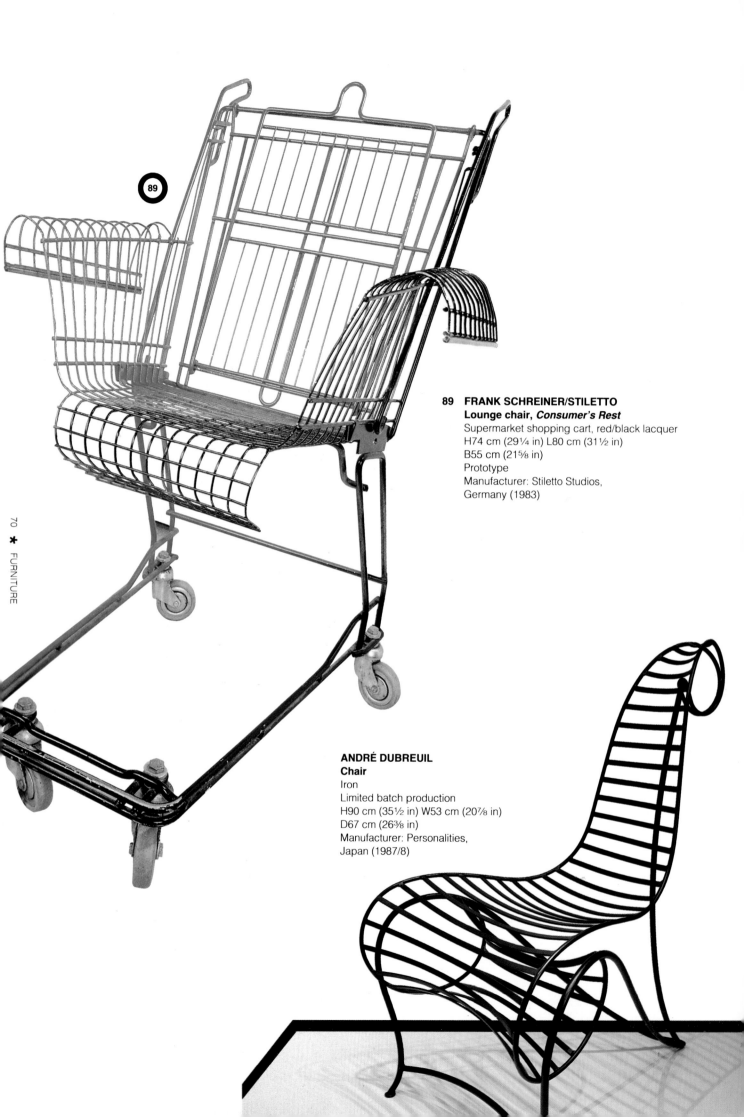

89 FRANK SCHREINER/STILETTO
Lounge chair, _Consumer's Rest_
Supermarket shopping cart, red/black lacquer
H74 cm (29¼ in) L80 cm (31½ in)
B55 cm (21⅝ in)
Prototype
Manufacturer: Stiletto Studios,
Germany (1983)

ANDRÉ DUBREUIL
Chair
Iron
Limited batch production
H90 cm (35½ in) W53 cm (20⅞ in)
D67 cm (26⅜ in)
Manufacturer: Personalities,
Japan (1987/8)

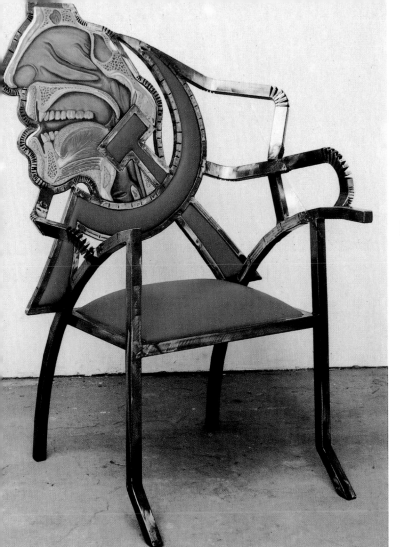

90 SIEGFRIED MICHAIL SYNIUGA
Chair, *Hotel Ukraina*
Leather, steel, printed
H110 cm (43¼ in) W58 cm (22⅞ in)
D58 cm (22⅞ in)
Manufacturer: Siegfried M. Syniuga (1985)

91 TOM DIXON
Chair
Cast iron, found objects
One-off
Manufacturer: Tom Dixon, UK (1986/7)

Raiders of bad taste. *Increasingly, both 'action' artists and conceptual artists have taken to producing provocative junk designs in limited editions of up to 100 copies, offering them to jaded art collectors who already have everything. They cannibalize fragments from everyday rubbish dumps, cobbling together readymades of studiously sophisticated bad taste. The provocation must, of course, evaporate, for the more hideous the objects, the more exquisite the pleasure of their high-brow clientèle who can only respond to visual stimuli in excess. Here are a few examples for all those readers who are addicted to films such as* Attack of the Killer Tomatoes *and John Water's Odorama movies, or to Gloria Spencer, the 'World's Largest Gospel Singer' (all 45 stones of her).*

Raiders of bad taste II.
Pornography can be made out of everything, so why not also out of design? The items of furniture on these two pages would not look out of place at a Sado-Masochists' Club in a better residential area. The sexual allusions, the suggestions of fetishistic rituals are laid on with a trowel. A rubber throne for women with the whip hand? Well, why not. Welcome to the wonderful world of designer sex.

92

92 ANONYMOUS
Chair, *Schlauchsessel*
Metal, rubber tyres
H120 cm (47¼ in) W70 cm (27½ in)
L150 cm (59 in)
One-off

93 AXEL STUMPF
Table, *Kumpel 1*
Pickaxes and glass
H50 cm (19⅝ in) W60 cm (23⅝ in)
Manufacturer: Axel Stumpf,
Germany (1986)

(93)

(94)

94 SUSANNE NEUBOHN
Stool, *Floh*
Plastic, lacquered steel, rubber
Limited batch production
H46 cm (18 in) W50 cm (19⅝ in)
D40 cm (15¾ in)
Manufacturer: Berliner Zimmer,
West Germany (1988/9)

(95)

95 SUE GOLDEN
Mirror
One-off
H46 cm (18 in) W25.4 cm (10 in)
Manufacturer: Sue Golden, UK (1986/7)

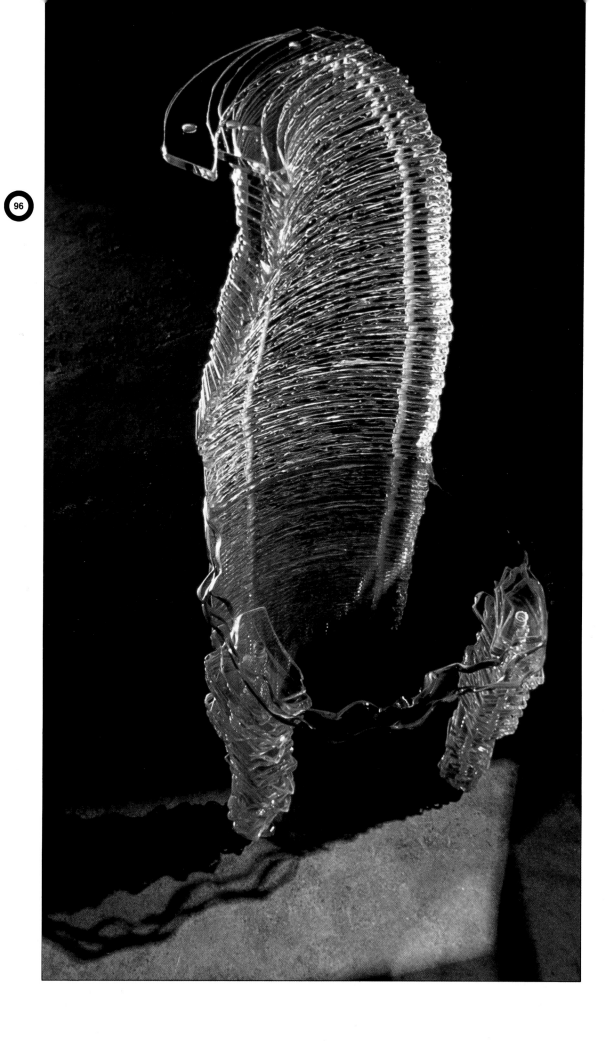

96 DANNY LANE
Stacked chair
Float glass, steel
One-off
H100 cm (39⅜ in) W50 cm (19⅝ in)
D60 cm (23⅝ in)
Maker: Glassworks, UK (1986/7)

99 DANNY LANE
Table, *Shell*
Hand-finished curved glass
The base is composed of five L-shaped
legs arranged in a fan, united at one
end by a pivot pin.
H40 cm (15¾ in) W125 cm (49¼ in)
L125 cm (49¼ in)
Manufacturer: Fiam, Italy (1988/9)

97 DANNY LANE
Table
Glass, steel
One-off
H37 cm (14½ in) W60 cm (23⅝ in)
L120 cm (47¼ in)
Maker: Glassworks, UK (1986/7)

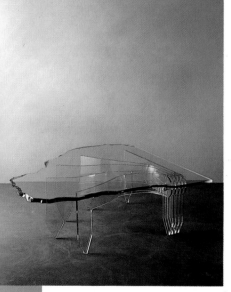

98 DANNY LANE
Table, *Atlas*
Curved glass surface and sheet glass legs
H40 cm (15¾ in) W70 cm (27½ in)
L140 cm (55⅛ in)
Manufacturer: Fiam, Italy (1988/9)

Artificial ruins. *When the
London-based painter Danny Lane
takes his hammer to armour-plated
glass, the results of this act of brutal
aggression are bizarrely shaped
building bricks that can be used to
construct a world of poetic objects.
Sophisticated methods such as this
meant that during the 1980s
utilitarian objects were increasingly
sucked into the maelstrom of art
and élitist limited editions. At his
Metropolitan Glassworks in
Hackney, once the capital's
working-class quarter, Danny Lane
not only smashes glass in order to
piece it together again, he also
combines a social vision with the
practical exercise of his art:
together with his craftsmen and
glasscutters he runs a workers'
cooperative in a Victorian building.*

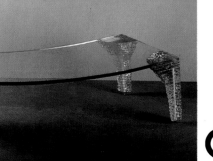

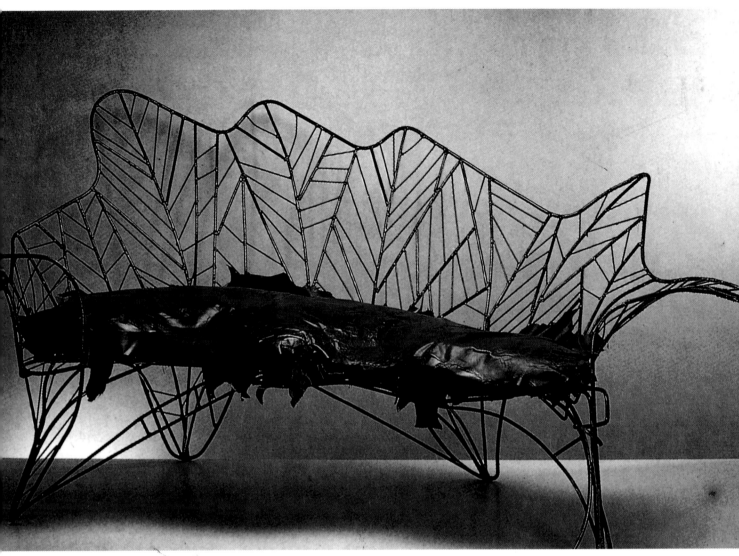

(100)

Prague Spring. *Since 1987 Prague has had its own Memphis group. It is called* Atika *and consists of Vit Cimbura, Bohuslav Horák, Jiri Javurek, Jiri Pelcl and Jaroslav Susta Jr. Together they describe*

101 DANIEL MACK Bentwood Armchair
Wood
A chair made of sugar maple and hickory with a tape seat
H114 cm (45 in)
W61 cm (24 in)
D51 cm (20 in)
Manufacturer: Daniel Mack Rustic Furniture, USA (1987/8)

(101)

themselves as 'angry young designers'. Atika sees itself as part of the same tradition as Archizoom, Alchimia and Memphis and professes support for post-modernism, for which it seeks new and experimental forms of expression. The way the group defines its aims attests to a sense of self-awareness, and signals the mood of upheaval and change that now exists in Eastern bloc states in the wake of Gorbachev's perestroika. Bohuslav Horák's furniture objects provide the most impressive example of Atika's guiding principles: a starkly sculptural component, an emphasis on non-industrial production methods, traditional materials such as wood and leather, and a living regard for nature. Ecological awareness is also in evidence on the other side of the Atlantic, where Daniel Mack designed a chair in conjunction with Mother Nature which harks back to the traditional Adirondack style in which wealthy New Yorkers used to furnish their holiday homes in the years around 1870. It looks like the perfect office chair for 'Robin Hood'.

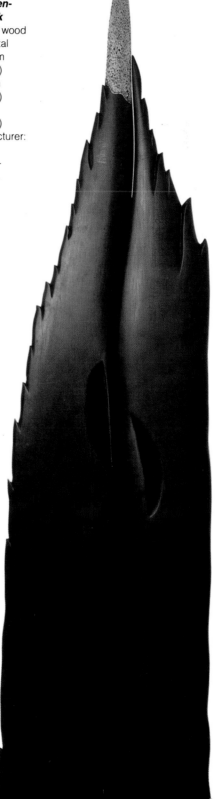

100 BOHUSLAV HORAK
A Rotten Luck Easy Chair
Welded iron wire and leather
H120 cm (47¼ in) L180 cm (70⅞ in)
D37 cm (14½ in)
Manufacturer: Atika, Czechoslovakia (1988)

102 BOHUSLAV HORAK Cupboard, *Flammen- schrank*
Stained wood and metal
H200 cm (78¾ in)
W60 cm (23⅝ in)
D40 cm (15¾ in)
Manufacturer: Atika, Czecho- slovakia (1988)

Pentagon's steel skeleton. *Design in the 1980s is no longer industry's exclusive preserve. Often founded as self-help organizations, studios and workshops such as Ron Arad's One-Off in London, Zeus in Milan and the Pentagon Design Gallery in Cologne have achieved an astonishing degree of popularity.*

Since 1985 the five members of Pentagon have produced furniture in limited editions, interior designs and exhibition interiors made for the most part in untreated steel with a rusty patina to it. Though perfect in design and execution, their cut and polished surfaces give the impression of calculated imperfection. Even in their ideas, these metallurgists from Cologne follow a universal trend, extending furniture design to the point where it becomes a part of the art of interior decorating. They followed up their 'braced shelving' with a model which stands in space like some medieval monastic cell. Adjustable metal shelves can be used for storing books, while a bench and lectern serve as a work station.

103 WOLFGANG LAUGERSHEIMER/PENTAGON
Shelving, *Verspanntes Regal*
Steel, rubber
H240 cm (94½ in) D31 cm (12¼ in) W31 cm (12¼ in)
Manufacturer: Pentagon, Germany (1985)

**104 REINHARD MULLER & MEYER-VOGGENREITER
PENTAGON**
Shelving, *Bibliothek*
Steel, leather, lighting
H240 cm (94½ in) W135 cm (53⅛ in)
L170 cm (66⅞ in)
Manufacturer: Pentagon, Germany (198)

**BEAT FRANK, ANDREAS LEHMANN
ATELIER VORSRUNG
Furniture sculpture, *Sitzkreuz***
Steel and wood
H100 cm (39⅜ in) L300 cm (118⅛ in)
W250 cm (98⅜ in)
Manufacturer: Atelier Vorsprung, Switzerland, in
association with Atelier 6 and E Rothlisberger (1989)

Crossbreeds. *One example of the cross-seat illustrated here is in a hotel foyer in the south of France, another is at a school for actors, while the third is sent on tour to exhibitions around the world. From its base in Berne, Atelier Vorsprung has specialized in sculptures such as this. Discriminating studies, they occupy a sort of no-man's-land between furniture and conceptual art. In terms of their praxis these representatives of avant-garde design in Switzerland may be seen as followers of the Russian Suprematist Kasimir Malevich, whose demand for* non-representational art implied a warning against overexcessive concern for practical considerations when designing objects for everyday use. This champion of a new abstraction of art and utilitarian object regarded the shape of a chair, or table, or bed, as the result of plastic impressions and not of purely functional considerations. Sixty years later Malevich's theories have once again begun to exercise a number of designers. What remained an unrealized idea, a rough outline on paper, for their Russian precursors has now become an important stimulus in an age obsessed with design.

106 HERBERT WEINAND
Desk, *Karajan 1*
Lacquered chipboard, veneer with silk-
screen print, Nirosta, plastic castors,
fluorescent tubes 40W, built-in radio
H180 cm (70⅝ in) W95 cm (37½ in)
L75 cm (29½ in) and 125 cm (49¼ in)
Typewriter table, *Karajan II*
Lacquered chipboard, veneer with silk-
screen print, Nirosta, plastic castors
H120 cm (47¼ in) W65 cm (25½ in)
L65 cm (25½ in)
Both prototypes
Manufacturer: Designwerkstatt, West
Germany (1988/9)

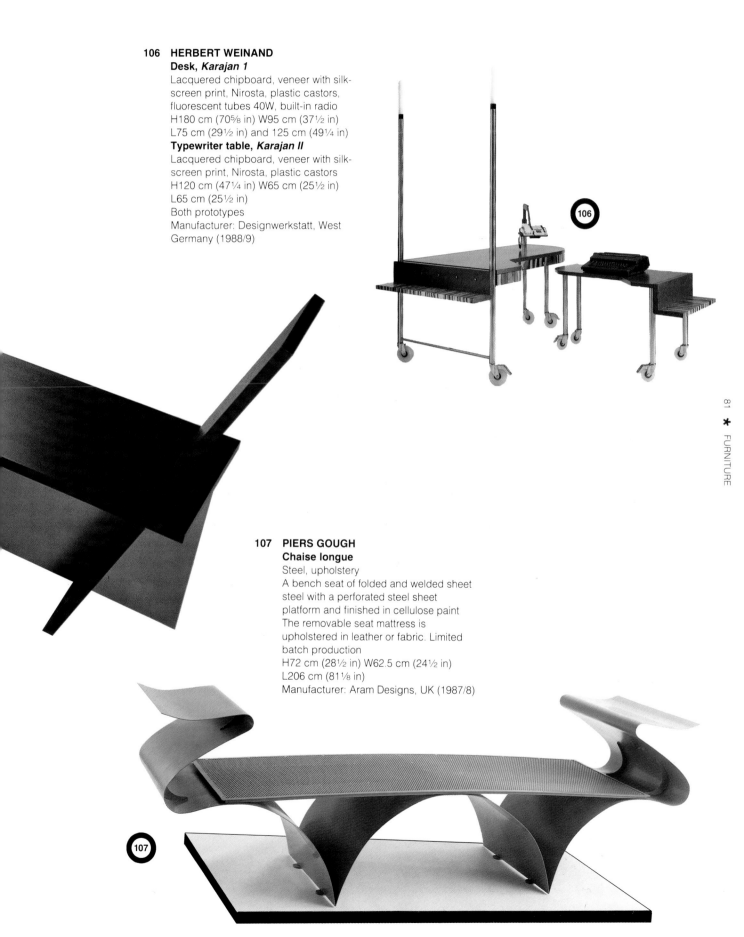

107 PIERS GOUGH
Chaise longue
Steel, upholstery
A bench seat of folded and welded sheet
steel with a perforated steel sheet
platform and finished in cellulose paint
The removable seat mattress is
upholstered in leather or fabric. Limited
batch production
H72 cm (28½ in) W62.5 cm (24½ in)
L206 cm (81⅛ in)
Manufacturer: Aram Designs, UK (1987/8)

Male chauvinist hardware. *There are simply too few opportunities today to show tough and aggressive masculinity. How happy some men today would be to be earthy proletarian types with a packet of Lucky Strikes stuck in the arms of their sweat-stained T-shirts. Instead of which they are prisoners in pin-striped business suits. Well, furniture design offers socially acceptable alternatives to reveal the wild beast lurking inside them. Jean Nouvel, the architect of the grandiose Institut du Monde Arabe, has designed a chest of drawers in the shape of a toolbox, so that its owner can show the world that he doesn't mind getting his hands dirty. In much the same way, Stefan Zwicky's uncomfortable parody of Le Corbusier's Grand Confort armchair exudes angular masculine charm in its rather concrete way. But the most heartwarming gadget for real men is the miniature tank by Paolo Pallucco and Mireille Rivier. In order to underline its no doubt ironical message of cultural criticism, we recommend that its owner combine it with a gallows with droplight attachment.*

109 PAOLO PALLUCCO & MIREILLE RIVIER
Table, *Tankette*
Steel, spring, aluminium smelting
A movable table with a frame of steel channel section and springs. The peripheral wheels are in aluminium smelting. Epoxy powder finish
H34.8 cm (13¾ in) W77.5 cm (30½ in) L125.5 cm (49½ in)
Manufacturer: Pallucco, Italy (1987/8)

108 **JEAN NOUVEL**
Chest, *BAO*
Aluminium
Prototype of an aluminium chest of
drawers that looks like a giant toolbox
H60 cm (23½ in) W120 cm (47¼ in)
D65 cm (25½ in)
Manufacturer: Jean Nouvel, France (1987/8)

110 **STEFAN ZWICKY**
Furniture sculpture, *Grand Confort,*
Sans Confort-Domage à Corbu
Concrete and iron
H67 cm (26⅜ in) W76 cm (29⅞ in)
D70 cm (27½ in)
Manufacturer: Stefan Zwicky (1980)

110

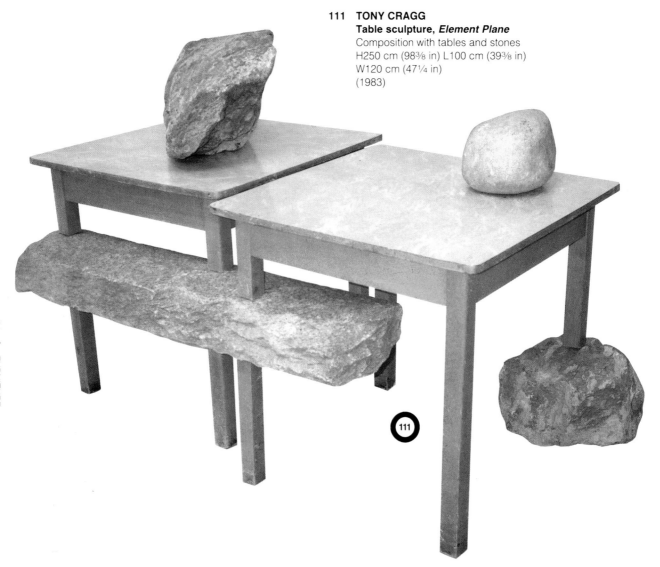

111 TONY CRAGG
Table sculpture, _Element Plane_
Composition with tables and stones
H250 cm (98⅜ in) L100 cm (39⅜ in)
W120 cm (47¼ in)
(1983)

Border traffic between art and design. *The work of the British-born, Wuppertal-based artist Tony Cragg is characterized by the way he transforms and recycles both materials and the structures of his images. What he makes with his transformations are not pieces of furniture but objets d'art. Cragg represented England at the Venice Biennale in 1988, the year in which the young Spanish sculptress Susana Solano was chosen to represent Spain with her sombre iron structures emblematic of suffering. She has now drawn on her experiences and put her principles into practice in designing a storage unit as a first edition for*

Meta Memphis. Threaded bars, machine screws and metal sheeting are used to create an austere cabinet to accommodate books.

Once furniture design had begun in the 1980s to break free from its functional constraints and to turn increasingly to the visual arts, a two-way traffic developed: not only did designers set off on the road to art, artists, too, as the Meta Memphis collection shows, set off on the road to design.

None the less, the imposing bench which the Italian conceptual

artist Pier Paolo Calzolari assembled for Meta Memphis from such strange materials as felt, marble, wood and kiln-fired bricks must be classified as a product of art rather than as a piece of furniture. Calzolari uses the form of the furniture as a metaphor for his artistic message. It is not his intention to help out his fellow designers with his ideas.

112 SUSANA SOLANO
Iron bookcase
Sheet iron and screw rods
H164 cm (64½ in) D70 cm (27½ in)
W70 cm (27½ in)
Manufacturer: Meta Memphis, Italy (1989)

113 PIER PAOLO CALZOLARI
Bench, *Pau*
Felt, firebricks, bentwood, tubing
H80 cm (31½ in) L360 cm (141¾ in)
W113 cm (44½ in)
Manufacturer: Meta Memphis, Italy (1989)

Fast-mood furniture. Bellefast – a cryptic play on words meaning something like 'instant beauty' but also evoking associations of Belfast as a synonym of a world destroyed by aggression and hatred – was intended as their design programme. It was in 1981 that Andreas Brandolini and Joachim B. Stanitzek founded a design studio in Berlin. Their furniture tells crazy tales of tables with horns, four-footed sausages that function as coffee tables, and planks that turn into chairs. In their search for a lost folk culture and sense of cultural identity these Berlin design poets invented 'fast-mood furniture', while the Berlin-based artist Hildegard Erhard, searching in turn for a sense of identity no less relevant in our own time, created a simulated armchair which she called Cement, Cement. The realities of the building industry are used to create design-speak.

It is not so much their pictorial language as their jokey constructions that are the forte of Ginbande, a design studio based in Frankfurt. Items of furniture which fold up out of the ground, new-fangled folding stools, and a table, with seating attached, which rolls out from the wall seek not so much to astonish the observer but to delight the user. Their own delight in innovation has brought these members of the Frankfurt Movement into contact with Vitra Edition, an organization no less fond of experimentation than they are.

114 HILDEGARD ERHARD
Armchair, *Zement, Zement*
Cement sacks and Europallet
H75 cm (29½ in) L110 cm (43⅓ in)
D95 cm (37⅜ in)
Manufacturer: Hildegard Erhard,
West Germany (1987)

115 **BELLEFAST: ANDREAS BRANDOLINI,**
JOACHIM STANITZEK
Table, *Bonanza*
Wood, aluminium, steel, glass
Limited batch production
H51 cm (20 in) W70 cm (27½ in)
L140 cm (55⅛ in)
Manufacturer: Berliner Zimmer,
West Germany (1988/9)

116 **UWE FISHER, KLAUS ACHIM HEINE**
GINBANDE
Table and bench, *Tabula Rasa*
L50/500 cm (19⅝/196⅞ in) W100 cm (39⅜ in)
H80 cm (31½ in)
Manufacturer: Vitra, Germany (1988)

118 WOLF D PRIX, HELMUT SWICZINKY COOP HIMMELBLAU
Armchair, *Vodöl*
Iron, steel tubing, fabric
L250 cm (98⅜ in) H85 cm (33½ in)
W85 cm (33½ in)
Manufacturer: Vitra, Germany (1989)

117 MARY LITTLE
Armchair
Arms and seat in wood on a steel tube
frame. The back is rubber and the feet
turned nylon with a polyester finish
H75 cm (29½ in) W90 cm (35½ in)
D70 cm (27½ in)
Manufacturer: Mary Little, UK (1985/6)

(118)

Farewell to the Bauhaus. *The Bauhaus philosophy has been regurgitated by so many second- and third-class imitators that a sense of aversion, if not of nausea, has necessarily ensued. It has become ever so slightly fashionable to make fun of the right-angled sobriety of the functionalists of the 1920s. But its detractors prove to have feet of clay when they come rigged out in the pretentious vapidity of the Vodöl armchair (the name represents the Viennese pronunciation of the usual word Fauteuil) by Wolf F. Frix and Helmut Swiczinsky, better known as Coop Himmelblau. For all their impressive words ('Architecture must burn, must bleed'), what they have on* *offer here is little more than a tired joke, a satire on Le Corbusier's Gran Confort, one of those pieces of furniture that have no place in the living room but which cry out for media attention as heroes for a day. But even then they ought to offer more than a design on the level of a student prank. By contrast, Mary Little's armchair is understated in the extreme. Curious though it looks at first sight – a mixture of Catalan and Scandinavian styles with a soupçon of late punk – it proves on closer inspection to be cleverly thought-through and functional in a highly original way. It is a genuine armchair, designed to be sat in, while Vodöl is no more than a failed cult object, an aesthetic aberration in the world of interior design.*

121 RON ARAD
Rocking chair, *Big Easy Volume 1*
Mild steel, stainless steel
A hollow structure partly filled with sand
which can be shifted to alter the centre
of gravity; distorted reflections are
emphasized by the chair's movement.
Limited batch production
H75 cm (29½ in) W84 cm (33 in)
D118 cm (46½ in)
Manufacturer: One-off, UK (1988/9)

119 RON ARAD
Chair, *Tinker*
Mild steel, stainless steel, panel beaten
Limited batch production
H95 cm (37½ in) W50 cm (19⅝ in)
D80 cm (31½ in)
Manufacturer: One-off, UK (1988/9)

Apocalypse wow! *For some time now a special literary subspecies – the disaster novel – has flourished in Great Britain. Countless writers from H. G. Wells, John Wyndham and J. G. Ballard to Anthony Burgess, Russell Hoban and Angela Carter have regaled their readers with detailed and inventive accounts of attacks by alien invaders, of nuclear contamination, devastation, flooding and various other forms of disaster. Some of this delight in disaster – but also pleasure in the idea of rebuilding a new world on the ruins of the old one – must have infected the London design scene, for it is striking that four of its most*

prominent representatives – Ron Arad, Nigel Coates, Thomas Dixon and Danny Lane – show a marked propensity for furniture suggestive of the end of time. Their objects create the impression of being somehow wounded, held together by makeshift solutions, ready-made wrecks. Above all, the armchairs designed by Ron Arad (born in Tel Aviv in 1951) look as though they were made for the rulers of some post-atomic nomadic tribe. The reminiscences of escapist fiction and Mad Max films should not,

however, be overstressed. Arad is more than merely the Thonet of steel sheeting. Like Tom Dixon, he is – for want of a better term – a furniture sculptor with a powerful imagination. But such is his unpredictability there may well be more surprises in store not only in his mass-produced furniture but also in the field of architecture, which is where his professional training lies.

122 RON ARAD
Armchair, *Well-tempered chair*
Folded, cut sheet steel
H98 cm (38½ in) W78 cm (30¾ in)
D90 cm (35⅜ in)
Manufacturer: Vitra, West
Germany (1986/7)

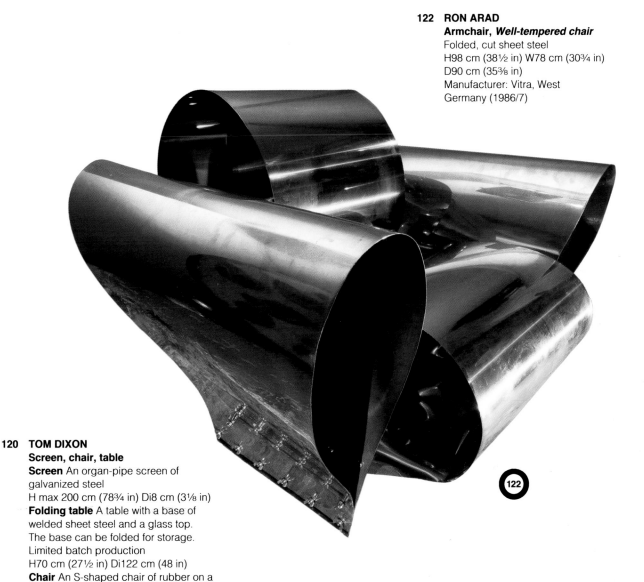

120 TOM DIXON
Screen, chair, table
Screen An organ-pipe screen of galvanized steel
H max 200 cm (78¾ in) Di8 cm (3⅛ in)
Folding table A table with a base of welded sheet steel and a glass top. The base can be folded for storage. Limited batch production
H70 cm (27½ in) Di122 cm (48 in)
Chair An S-shaped chair of rubber on a steel frame and sitting on a cast aluminium base. Limited batch production
H95 cm (37½ in) W40 cm (15¾ in)
D50 cm (19⅝ in)
Manufacturer: Tom Dixon, UK (1987/8)

The 1980s was a theatrical decade. And every theatre producer knows how important lighting is for the success of any production, which explains why it was so central a design factor during this decade. For offices are now much more than just offices, and living rooms are not simply for living in – they are carefully calculated stage sets,

2 ✷ LIGHTING

displays of good taste with which we show how cultured we are or signal a particular lifestyle. Since reception rooms are often buried in the windowless interiors of sprawling building complexes, like burial chambers in the Egyptian pyramids, and since guests are generally received in the evening, after dark, the cry of 'Let there be light' has gained the

force of a categorical imperative. Light alone is capable of showing off an expensive interior design to its very best advantage and even of making it more dramatic in its appeal. Although light is not a material substance, it is an essential part of architectural design and, as such, adds highlights in the truest sense of the word.

The demand for solutions to the problem of lighting was and is enormous, but it is one that the 1980s managed to meet imaginatively: for, in no other area (with the single exception of product design) has there been such a wealth of new techniques, such a profusion of new ideas, concepts and approaches as there has in the area of lighting. The most important development was, no doubt, the halogen revolution which gathered pace in the 1970s, before emerging with full force in the 1980s. High-voltage halogen lamps, and even halogen metal-vapour lamps, flooded rooms with such a brilliant white light that even indoors beautiful people could go on wearing their 'cool' Ray Bans. This was the age of dimmers. A decisive breakthrough occurred in the mid-1980s which was to be very far-reaching: new and tiny low-voltage lamps have made it possible to design avant-garde types of lighting of a kind unknown hitherto. Ingo Maurer made brilliant use of the new opportunities with his *YaYaHo* system, which, bobbing on

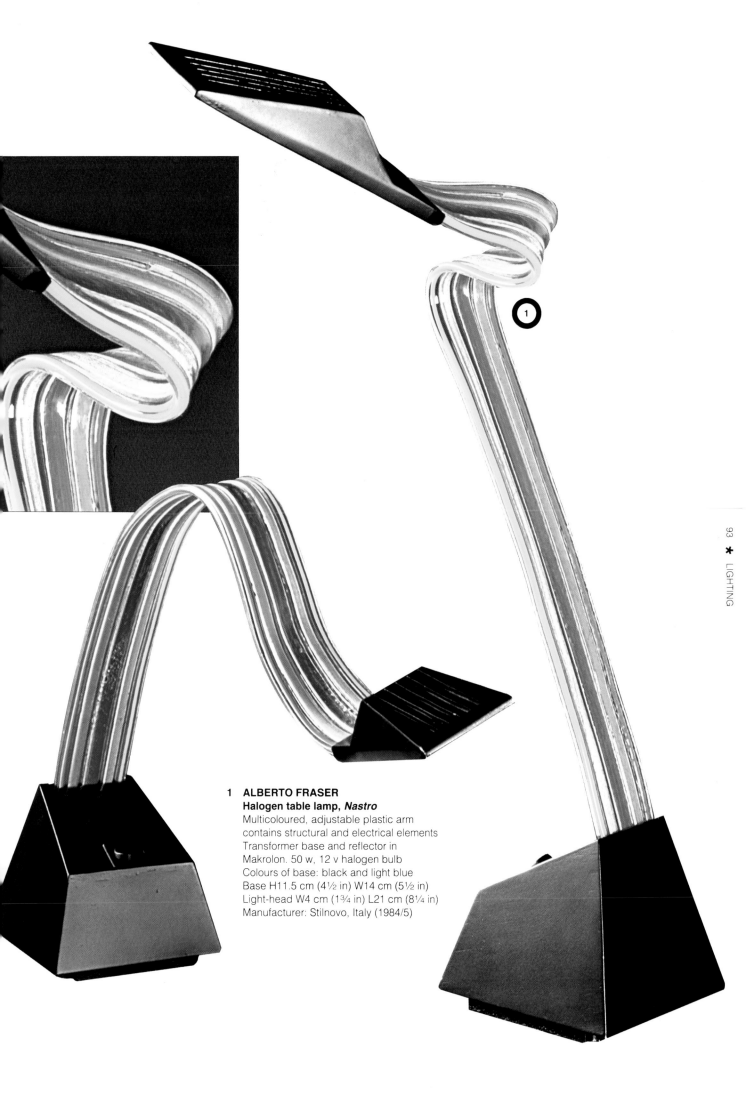

1 ALBERTO FRASER
Halogen table lamp, *Nastro*
Multicoloured, adjustable plastic arm
contains structural and electrical elements
Transformer base and reflector in
Makrolon. 50 w, 12 v halogen bulb
Colours of base: black and light blue
Base H11.5 cm (4½ in) W14 cm (5½ in)
Light-head W4 cm (1¾ in) L21 cm (8¼ in)
Manufacturer: Stilnovo, Italy (1984/5)

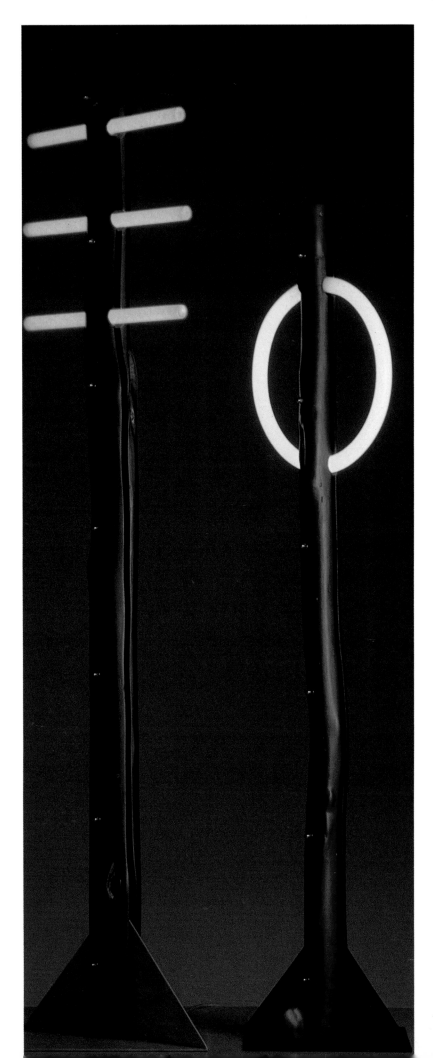

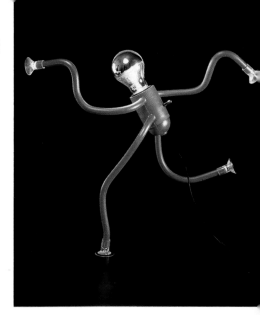

3

**3 CARLO BELLINI &
MARCO FERRERI**
Lamp, *Eddy*
Reinforced thermoplastic
The four flexible limbs are both decorative
and functional. Suction pads can be
attached to each arm.
H57 cm (22⅝ in); arm 26 cm (10¼ in)
L10 cm (4 in) Di 5 cm (2 in)
Manufacturer: Luxo Italiana, Italy (1986/7)

2 HEIKO BARTELS, HARALD HULLMANN/KUNSTFLUG
Floor lamps, *Baumleuchte I and II*
Lacquered wood, metal, neon tubing
H160/180 cm (63/70⅞ in)
Manufacturer: Kunstflug, Germany (1981)

2

high-tensile cables, paved the way for a mobile, poetic style of lighting.

It is strange that, while some lamps have grown smaller and smaller, other forms of lighting have got bigger and bigger. There seems to be a great demand for monumental sculptures with impressive names like Shogun and Agamemnon. There have always been two kinds of lighting: on the one hand, the humble servants that try to make themselves inconspicuous, and, on the other, the majestic, dominating types that cry out

'Look at me, here I am!' It was the latter group which was clearly in the ascendent during the 1980s. With lamps this makes a good deal of sense, since, unlike all the other objects in these pages, lamps are Janus-faced by nature. Whereas chairs or cups are what they are, lamps change their identity depending on whether they are switched on or off. This explains why many designers seem to tend to the view that a light is a light only when switched on: switched off, it becomes a piece of sculpture. During the 1980s this view gave rise not only to a series of highly impressive totemic objects (by Mario Botta, Roberto Marcatti, Ettore Sottsass and the Kunstflug group, to name but a few) but also to a far greater number of deeply pretentious inanities where no expense was spared to produce exactly the same amount of light as a pocket torch can offer.

But such expense is typical. Increasingly often, pure light is being replaced by processed light, in other words, by light that produces graphic effects and subtle interplay by means of grilles and filters, diffusers, reflectors, masks and coloured glass. Not only is the fixture itself designed, so too is its *alter ego*, its shadow on the wall. A number of designers have even gone one stage further and created fictional environments. Taking 'light' and 'city' to be synonyms, James Evanson and Matteo Thun have constructed entire skylines out of illuminated skyscrapers. *Bright Lights, Big City* has become an atmospheric backdrop for the studied theatricality of the individual's private lifestyle.

This is only one example among many of the way in which lights are no longer thought of as abstract sources of light, but as furnishings full of emotional and personal significance. What one sees in consequence are curious hybrids produced by the interaction of technology and imagination, of robots and magicians – lights like *Scaragoo* by the Finnish designer Stefan Lindfors, which is not switched on in some prosaically traditional manner but which lights up when it is touched. This is a technology of 'abracadabra' and a harbinger of the future when 'harmony in heterogeneity' will be the norm. It should come as no surprise, then, to see here a remote-controlled, rice-paper lamp that opens and closes electronically.

4 MARIO BELLINI
Spotlight, *Eclipse 2*

Aluminium

The *Eclipse 2* spotlight uses metal halide and high-pressure discharge lamps to project circles and to illuminate objects and surfaces sharply at an angle ranging from 8 to 72 degrees.

W27.8 cm (10⅞ in) L body 29.5 cm (11⅝ in) L max 41.5 cm (16⅜in) D to top track arm 20.8 cm (8⅛ in)
Manufacturer: Erco, West Germany (1987/8)

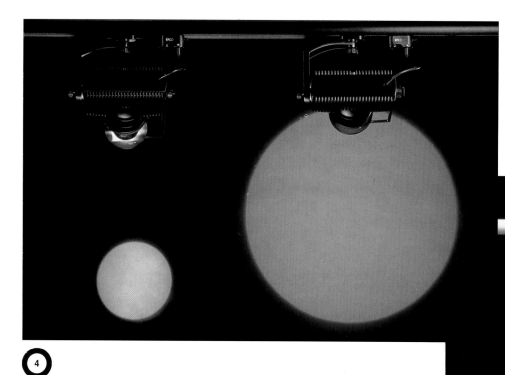

④

The light of reason. *Since the commission to light Norman Foster's spectacular Hong Kong Shanghai Bank the Lüdenscheid firm of Erco has established itself as one of the leading international authorities on lighting systems. Erco sees itself not as a lighting manufacturer but as an architectural designer working in the medium of light. Its stage spots for interior home design are pure hard-core high-tech. To exhaust all the design opportunities offered by filters, attachment lenses, gobos, mirrors and so forth requires something approaching the expertise of a professional lighting designer – or else a very great deal of imagination and a love of experimentation. Although Erco lights are designed by the most varied of design luminaries, they nevertheless share a certain touch, if difficult to define. Perhaps we could call it creative reason or, in a word, 'Erconomy'.*

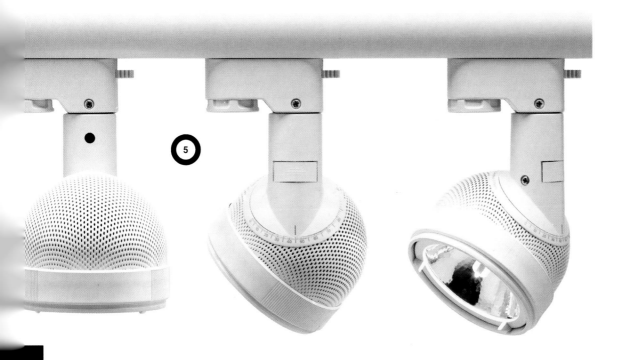

(5)

5 EMILIO AMBASZ & GIANCARLO PIRETTI
Low-voltage spotlight, *Oseris*
Perforated steel plate, black or white
powder coated, and thermoresistant
thermoplast. The spotlights can be
mounted on a three-circuit track, with a
mechanical adapter and a separate
transformer, or on a special low-voltage
track fed by a separate external
transformer. Light can be varied by using
glass colour filters, flood lenses and
sculpture lenses. Special fixing rings,
multigroove baffles and honeycomb anti-
dazzle screens concentrate the light.
H15.6 cm (6 in) W93 cm (36 in) D9.4 cm (3½ in)
Manufacturer: Erco Lighting, West
Germany (1984/5)

(6)

6 BRUNO GECCHELIN
Shuttle Spotlight
The *Shuttle* range of spotlights
consists of a basic oval-shaped
element in two sizes on which
cylindrical casings are fitted
according to the type of lamp used.
Twenty-two different lamps are available
Manufacturer: Guzzini, Italy (1987/8)

Switched-on Porsche. *Design has become an aristocratic business. Names are important not only as an entrée, but also as a guarantee of reputation. 'Porsche', of course, is a magic word that unlocks many doors. Even people who have never heard of Castiglioni, Starck or Sottsass are familiar with this name. It is a name, however, that has ennobled not only fast cars but also sunglasses, watches, pipes, razors and, in this case, lights too. The image is the message, and Ferdinand Alexander Porsche has been marketing this image since 1972 in his own independent design company, while remaining loyal to the style of his brilliant classic, the Porsche 911. With their masculine, matt-black techno-look, all his products embody an aesthetically sublimated, high-tech machismo. In the case of the lamps shown here, however, the potency signal is somewhat low. Is it the fault of the post-modern cones, or the feminine, lipstick red?*

7 FERDINAND ALEXANDER PORSCHE
Floor lamp, *Lettura PL*
Floor version of the *Sintheto* system, with
a high-gloss chromed metal stem and a
base painted matt red, smoky or light grey
Takes two 11W halogen bulbs
H110 cm (43 in) D70 cm (27½ in)
Manufacturer: Luci, Italy (1985/6)

8 FERDINAND ALEXANDER PORSCHE
Pendant lamp, *Soffitto*
Floor version of the *Sintheto* system, with a
high-gloss chromed metal stem,
a base painted red,
smoky or light grey,
red or yellow reflector,
and a pearl grey diffuse
100W halogen lamp,
fitted with a dimmer
H186 cm (73¼ in)
Manufacturer: Luci, Italy (1985/6)

7

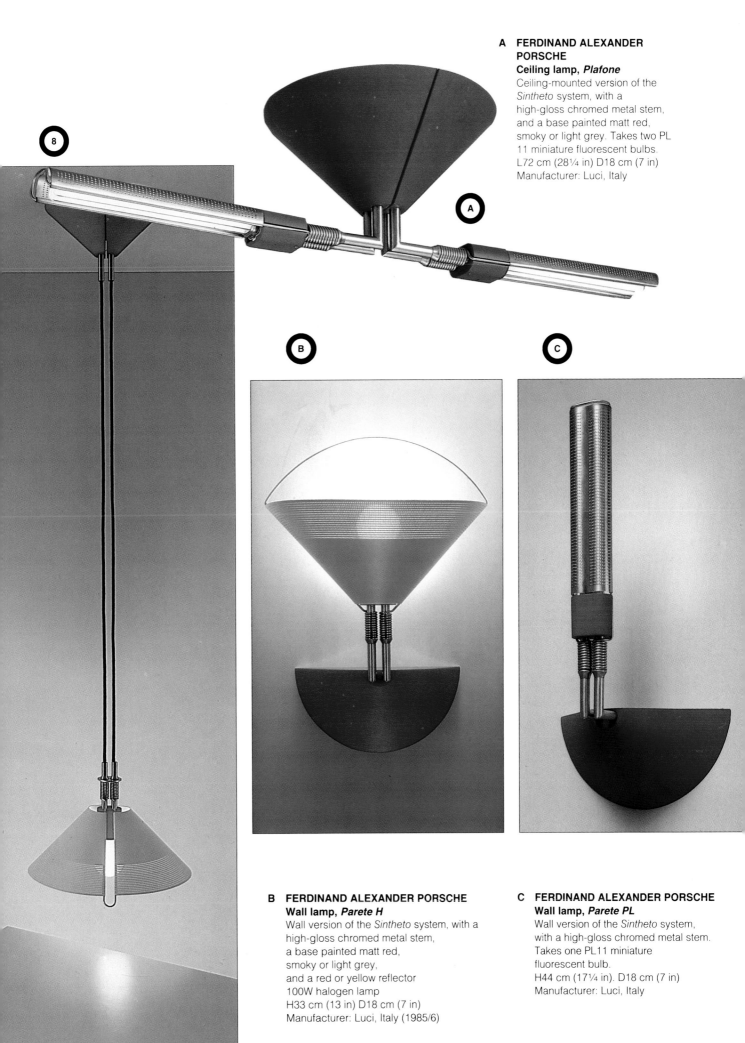

A FERDINAND ALEXANDER PORSCHE
Ceiling lamp, *Plafone*
Ceiling-mounted version of the
Sintheto system, with a
high-gloss chromed metal stem,
and a base painted matt red,
smoky or light grey. Takes two PL
11 miniature fluorescent bulbs.
L72 cm (28¼ in) D18 cm (7 in)
Manufacturer: Luci, Italy

B FERDINAND ALEXANDER PORSCHE
Wall lamp, *Parete H*
Wall version of the *Sintheto* system, with a
high-gloss chromed metal stem,
a base painted matt red,
smoky or light grey,
and a red or yellow reflector
100W halogen lamp
H33 cm (13 in) D18 cm (7 in)
Manufacturer: Luci, Italy (1985/6)

C FERDINAND ALEXANDER PORSCHE
Wall lamp, *Parete PL*
Wall version of the *Sintheto* system,
with a high-gloss chromed metal stem.
Takes one PL11 miniature
fluorescent bulb.
H44 cm (17¼ in). D18 cm (7 in)
Manufacturer: Luci, Italy

High-tech-magic. *In designing YaYaHo and its successors, Ingo Maurer created the most innovative, influential and frequently copied lighting system of the 1980s. It is a system which has shown the way for design in the coming decade by pulling out all the stops in terms of modern technology and thereby producing the complete opposite – magic: high-wire performers; acrobats of light, that glide and float and hover, casting off their clumsy bodies. A round of applause for Ingo Maurer's Flying Circus!*

9 **INGO MAURER**
Pendant lights, *YaYaHo*
In glass, porcelain, ceramic, metal and plastic. This low-voltage cable system has two mounting parts and four different lighting elements. All the elements are movable, either vertically or horizontally. Two-pin halogen 20W and 50W lamps and 50W reflectors Cables: L60 metres (197 feet) Lighting elements: maximum D from string 50 cm (19½ in) Manufacturer: Design M Ingo Maurer, West Germany (1985/6)

10 **INGO MAURER**
Lamp, *Fukushu*
Takes a halogen 12V/50W light source, with transformer/ dimmer. The bases are matt nickel-plated. Iron rods with flexible ends in red and blue. Adjustable height. Multi-mirror reflector swivels through 360 degrees. H62 cm (24⅜ in) W36 cm (14⅛ in) Manufacturer: Design M, Ingo Maurer, West Germany (1986/7)

11 **INGO MAURER & TEAM**
Lighting system, *Bakaru*
Multi-mirror precise reflector, adjustable through 360 degrees. Takes a 20W lamp Manufacturer: Design M, West Germany (1986/7)

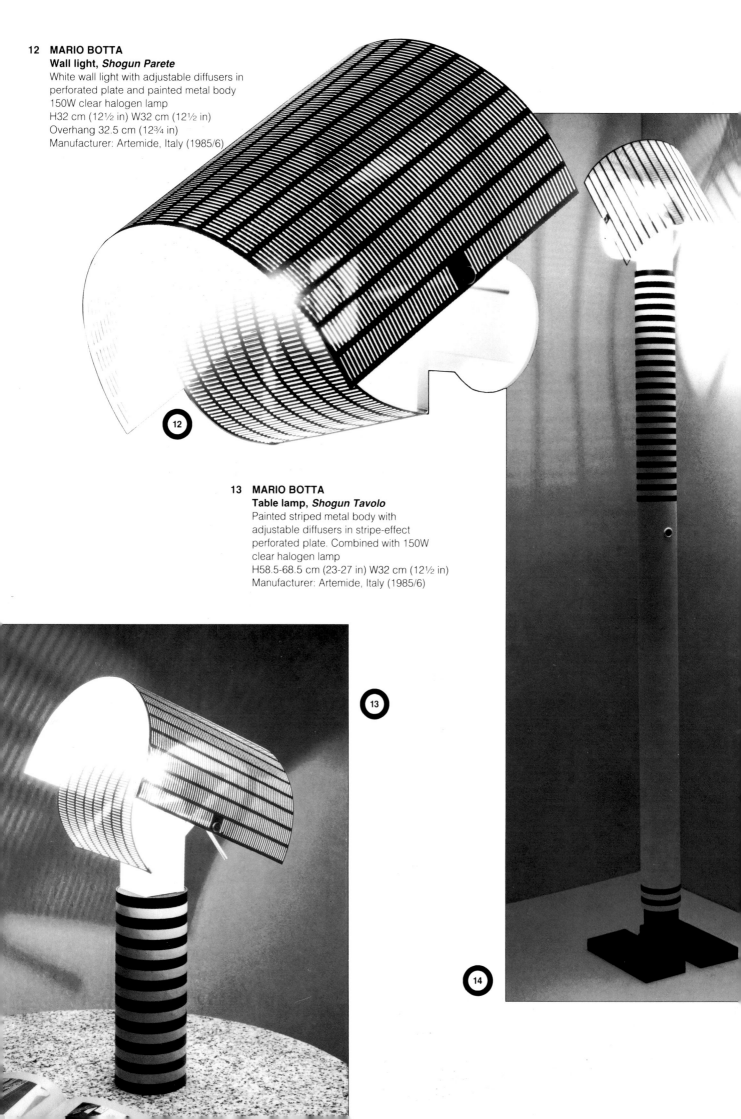

12 MARIO BOTTA
Wall light, *Shogun Parete*
White wall light with adjustable diffusers in
perforated plate and painted metal body
150W clear halogen lamp
H32 cm (12½ in) W32 cm (12½ in)
Overhang 32.5 cm (12¾ in)
Manufacturer: Artemide, Italy (1985/6)

13 MARIO BOTTA
Table lamp, *Shogun Tavolo*
Painted striped metal body with
adjustable diffusers in stripe-effect
perforated plate. Combined with 150W
clear halogen lamp
H58.5-68.5 cm (23-27 in) W32 cm (12½ in)
Manufacturer: Artemide, Italy (1985/6)

14 MARIO BOTTA
Floor lamp, *Shogun Terra*
Painted striped metal body with
adjustable diffusers in stripe-effect
perforated plate. 150W clear halogen lamp
H213 cm (84 in) W32 cm (12½ in)
Manufacturer: Artemide, Italy (1985/6)

15 EMILIO AMBASZ
Adjustable halogen lamp, *Agamennone*
Body in extruded, painted aluminium. The
base is in black-coated metal
H200 cm (78 in) D46 cm (18 in)
Manufacturer: Artemide, Italy (1984/5)

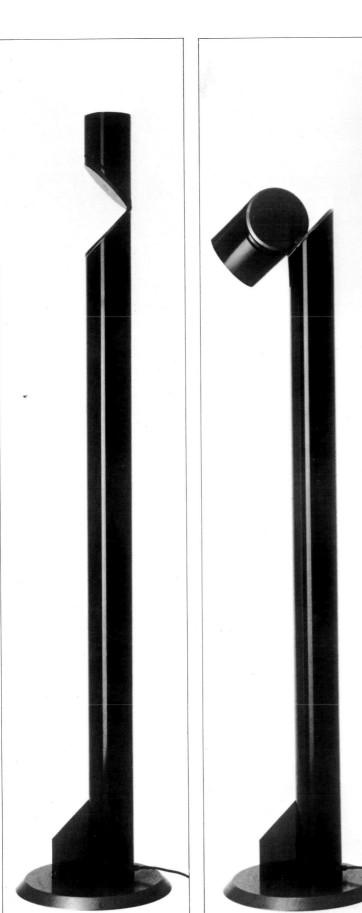
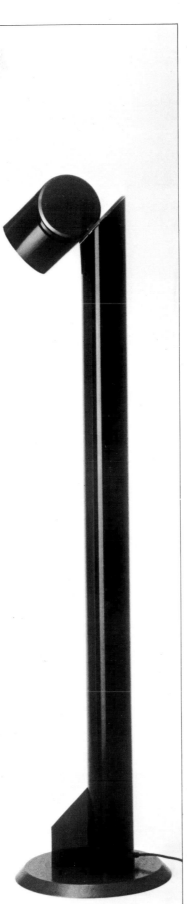
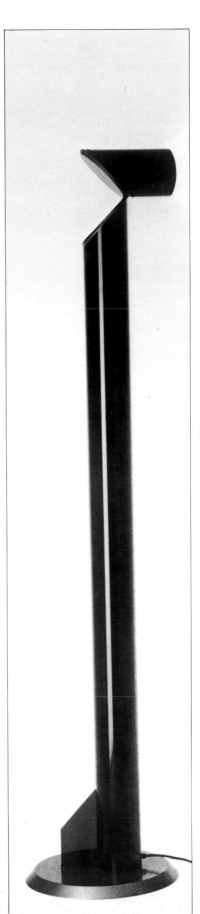

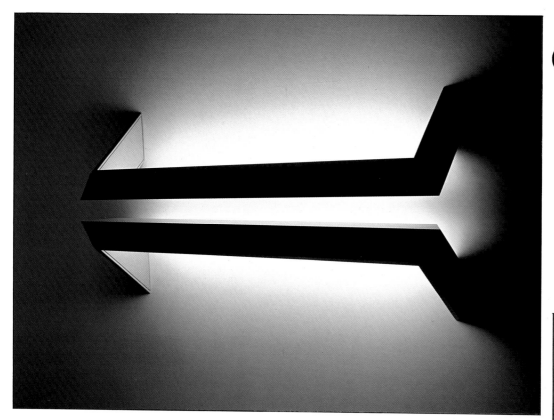

16 MASAYUKI KUROKAWA
Lighting fixture, *Angolo Slit T Bar*
Painted steel
W11.6 cm (4½ in) L from 77-91 cm
(30-35 in)
Manufacturer: Yamagiwa Corporation,
Japan (1984/5)

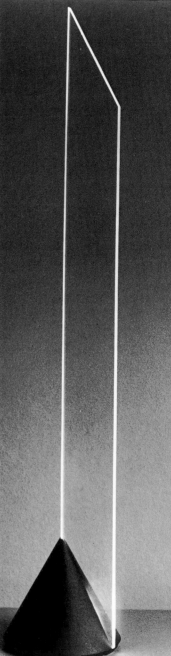

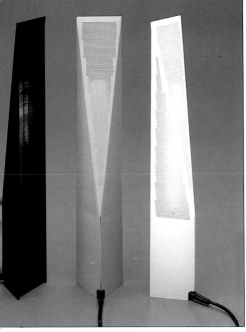

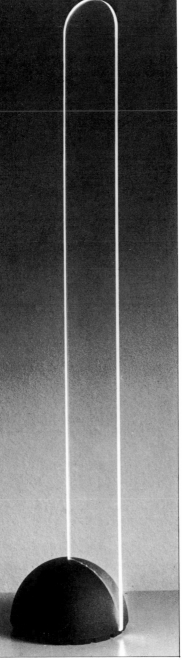

18 MART A A VAN SCHINDEL
Desk lamp, *Bishop*
Aluminium
Available in white, black, blue or yellow
Takes an 11W fluorescent tube 500/800 Lux
Limited batch production
H43 cm (17 in) W7 cm (2¾ in) L7 cm (2¾ in)
Manufacturer: Martech, The
Netherlands (1986/7)

20 PIOTR SIERAKOWSKI
Floor light, *Nautilus*
Aluminium, nextel
Black column and base with insert, in grey
with grey switch or red with red switch
Takes a maximum 500W halogen lamp
with full-range dimmer
H182.9 cm (72 in)
Base: W43 cm (17 in) D36.5 cm (14⅜ in)
Column: W20.3 cm (8 in) D7.6 cm (3 in)
Manufacturer: Koch & Lowy, USA (1986/7)

17, 19 FRANCO ALBERTO BERG
Light sculptures, *Argon, Radon, Xenon*
Base in grey cast iron; panels
in hardened acrylic
D24 cm (9 in) H124 cm (48 in)
Manufacturer: Berg Licht & Objekt,
West Germany (1984/5)

East meets West. *Try an experiment: three of the five lamps on these pages are from Italy, while the other two are from Japan. Guess where each of them comes from. (If you already know the answer, ask a friend to do the test instead.) You will perhaps be surprised to discover that the lamps which look as though they are made in Japan actually come from Italy, while the ones that look made in Italy hail in fact from Japan. This shows that a form of global language has developed in design which, far from being bland and the result of compromise, brings together the best of both worlds. As we shall see in a later section, this has had a particularly beneficial influence in the world of modern tableware.*

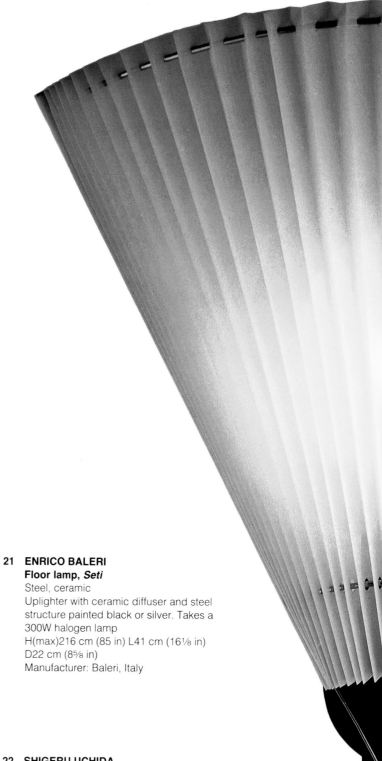

21 ENRICO BALERI
Floor lamp, *Seti*
Steel, ceramic
Uplighter with ceramic diffuser and steel structure painted black or silver. Takes a 300W halogen lamp
H(max)216 cm (85 in) L41 cm (16⅛ in) D22 cm (8⅝ in)
Manufacturer: Baleri, Italy

22 SHIGERU UCHIDA
& STUDIO 80
Floor lamp
Steel, melamine, aluminium
The shade, of perforated aluminium and baked melamine in silver metallic, can be tilted to compose patterns on walls and ceilings. The height is adjustable. Takes a 75W mini-halogen lamp
H143 cm-195 cm (56¼ in-76¾ in) W50 cm (19⅝ in) D50 cm (19⅝ in)
Manufacturer: Chairs (Matsushita Electric), Japan (1986/7)

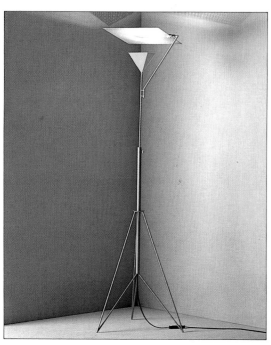

24 ROBERTO MARCATTI
Floor lamp, *Arcade*
Lamp with two adjustable floodlights. Takes
two small 50W halogen lamps. In black and
metallized grey finishes, epoxy-painted
Part of the *Zeus Collection*
H65 cm or 135 cm (25½ in or 53⅛ in)
D15 cm (6 in)
Manufacturer: Noto, Italy (1986/7)

23 AFRA & TOBIA SCARPA
Wall lamp, *Butterfly Parete*
Lamp giving diffused light with a 150W
halogen bulb. Housed in the metal
structure, the bulb is shaded by two glazed
pieces of glass and a fixed fan-shaped
diffuser made of a pleated fireproof fabric.
The stem and wall mount are made of
painted metal.
H57 cm (22⅜ in) W50 cm (19⅝ in)
D25 cm (9⅞ in)
Manufacturer: Flos Italy (1986/7)

25 SHIRO KURAMATA
Floor lamp
Steel, electric wire
H170 cm (67 in) D6 cm, 32 cm or 40 cm
(2⅜ in, 12½ in or 15¾ in)
Manufacturer: Ishimaru, Japan (1986/7)

Variations on a theme by Sapper.
In 1970, Richard Sapper designed Tizio for Artemide. It immediately became a cult object and the archetypal modern desk lamp. Its cool aesthetic set the standard by which all its successors were measured. As these pages show, not even the young design stars of the 1980s have been able to improve on Tizio: all they have done is provide a series of commentaries on it. Marie-Christine Dorner's Dragon (which, in spite of its name, looks more like a tap) and Oscar Tusquets Blanca's charming Bib Luz, slinking out of its book-like transformer like a spy, bear a faint family resemblance to Tizio, while De Lucchi & Fassina, by contrast, pay homage to the grandfather of every functional desk lamp, George Carwardine's Anglepoise of 1934.

26 **JOSEP LLUSCA**
Table lamp, *Anade 4169*
Aluminium, iron
Metallic lamp with adjustable arm, halogen lamp with transformer and two-way switch
H60 cm (23⅝ in) L65 cm (25½ in)
Di20 cm (8 in)
Manufacturer: Metalarte, Spain (1986/7)

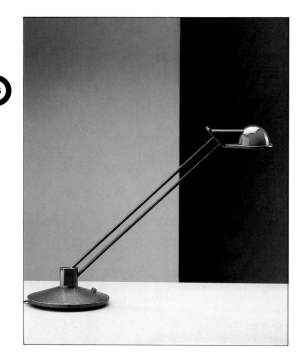

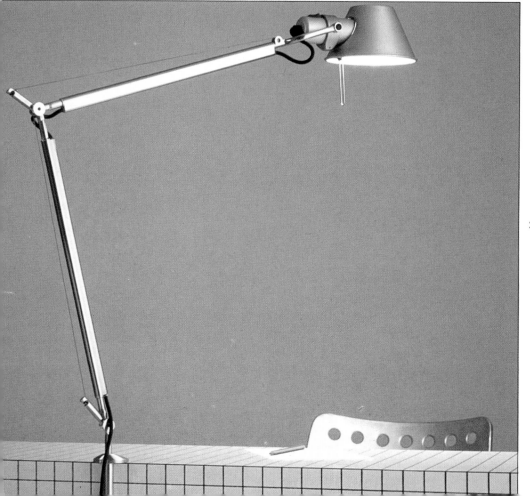

27 **MICHELE DE LUCCHI &
GIANCARLO FASSINA**
Desk lamp, *Tolomeo*
Aluminium
Clamp base with adjustable arm made of polished grey aluminium
L (max) 135 cm (53⅛ in) D15 cm (6 in)
Extendable arm L120 cm (47¼ in)
Manufacturer: Artemide, Italy (1986/7)

28 OSCAR TUSQUETS BLANCA
Library lamp, *Bib Luz*
Aluminium, chrome
A matt silver aluminium box houses the transformer, dual-voltage switch and on/off switch. The rod swivels and the chrome lamp holder swings through 90 degrees. Takes a 50W/12V halogen lamp. Wall-mounted and table versions are also available.
H28 cm or 62 cm(11 in or 24⅜ in) L50 cm or 88 cm (19⅝ in or 34⅝ in) Manufacturer: BD Ediciones de Diseño, Spain (1986/7)

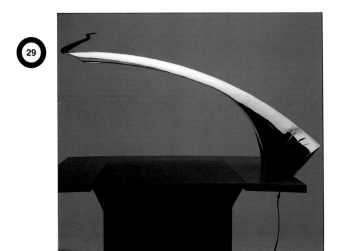

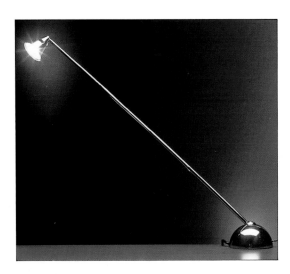

29 MARIE-CHRISTINE DORNER
Table lamp, *Dragon*
Polished aluminium, wood
Balancing on the edge of a table or desk, *Dragon* has a transformer concealed in its sides and the switch is its crest. Takes a halogen lamp.
H45 cm (17¾ in); (on table) 39 cm (15⅜ in) L90 cm (35⅜ in) D8 cm (3⅛ in) Manufacturer: Idée, Japan (1986/7)

30 CHRISTIAN THEILL
Table lamp, *Antenna*
Chromed iron, aluminium, brass, wood
Adjustable light taking a 50W/24V halogen lamp
L33 cm to 91 cm (12⅞ in to 35⅞ in)
Di12 cm (4¾ in)
Manufacturer: Targetti Sankey, Italy (1986/7)

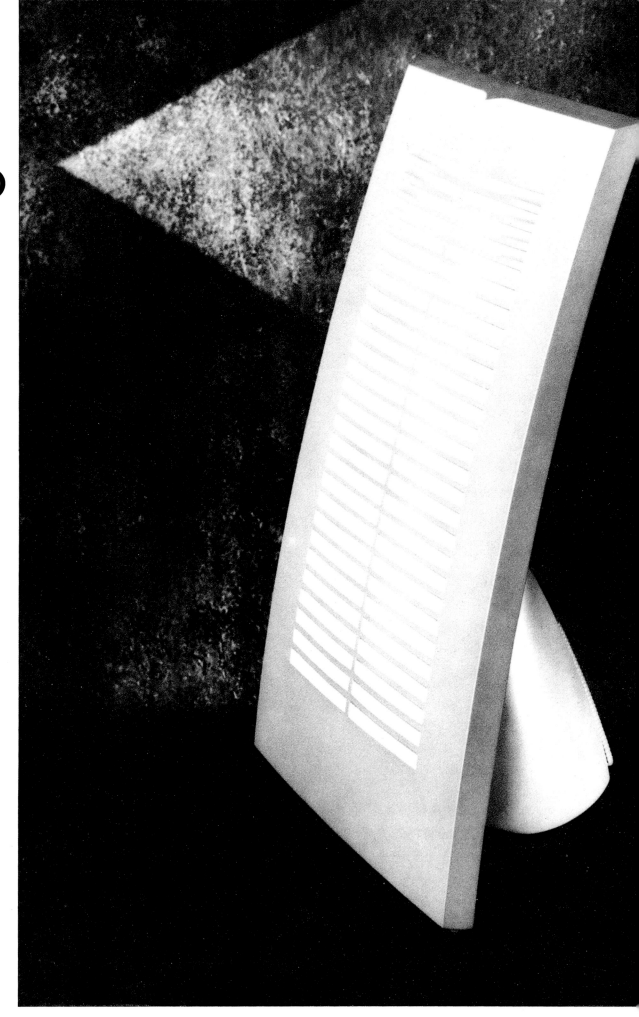

 32

Light comedy. *Why should a lamp have to look like a lamp? Thanks to the development of compact and innovative light sources, there is no longer any need for it to do so. And since our post-modern style of home décor demands theatrical solutions to the problems of interior design, designers now indulge with a clownish delight in disguising their creations. Lamps come looking like sacks and bags, hats and balloons, lighthouses, cranes and off-shore oil rigs. Will the party never end? Of course it will. The wilder they come, the faster they die. Whether a lamp becomes a classic in this commedia del luce or whether it remains yet another sad-faced clown is a tightrope walk with a highly uncertain outcome.*

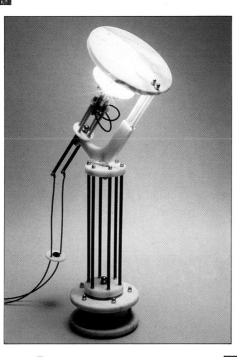

32 PHILIPPE STARCK
Table lamp, *La lune sans le chapeau*
Steel coated in grey epoxy, paper
H68 cm (26¾ in) W24 cm (9⅜ in)
D24 cm (9⅜ in)
Manufacturer: Les Trois Suisses,
France (1986/7)

33 PETER BREMERS
Table lamp
Corian marble
H40 cm (15¾ in) D18 cm (7 in)
Manufacturer: Neotu, France (1986/7)

 33

34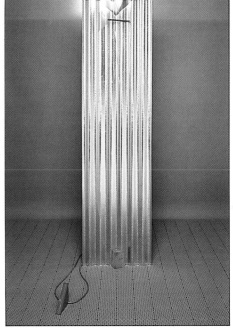

31 PHILIPPE STARCK
Table lamp, *Ray Menta*
Cast aluminium body
The lamp takes a PL miniature fluorescent bulb.
H30.5 cm (12 in)
Manufacturer: XO, France (1986/7)

34 THOMAS EISL
Uplighter
Corrugated aluminium
One-off
H183 cm (72 in) W48 cm (18⅞ in)
D22 cm (8⅝ in)
Maker: Thomas Eisl, UK (1986/7)

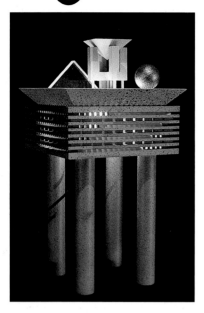

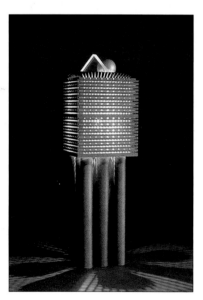

35 JAMES EVANSON
Table light, *Lightstruck*
From the *Lighthouse Collection*. In
lacquered wood with removable lucite
accessories in neon colours
H38 cm (15 in) W23 cm (9 in) L23 cm (9 in)
Manufacturer: Art et Industrie, USA (1985/6)

36 JAMES EVANSON
Floor lamp, *Hi-beam*
From the *Lighthouse Collection*
In lacquered wood with removable
lucite accessories in neon colours
H53 cm (21 in) W18 cm (7 in) L18 cm (7 in)
Manufacturer: Art et Industrie, USA (1985/6)

37 JAMES EVANSON
Lamps, *Lighthouse Collection*
In lacquered wood with removable lucite
accessories in neon colours
Manufacturer: Art et Industrie, USA (1985/6)

The new pets. Modern life can be fairly lonely. And there is a type of modern design which intensifies this sense of loneliness by surrounding us with 'cool' and self-contented objects that demand respect but do not offer friendship. Too much Breuer, too much Braun can get you down. And sometimes, in the unrelenting functionality of your 'domestic factory' of a home, you feel an atavistic desire for company. It is then that Martine Bedin's brightly coloured hedgehog lamp comes snuffling up and Michele de Lucchi's striped giraffe raises its long neck to draw us back to the world of our childhood when we were rather less rational than we are now.

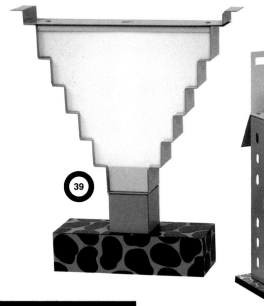

39

38

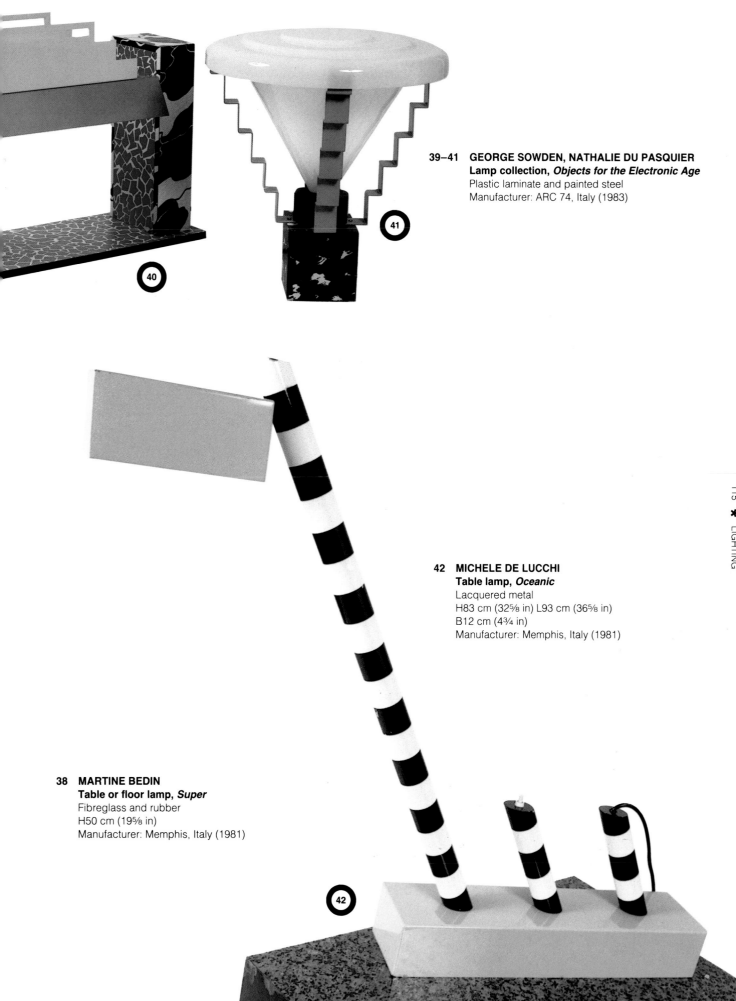

39–41 GEORGE SOWDEN, NATHALIE DU PASQUIER
Lamp collection, *Objects for the Electronic Age*
Plastic laminate and painted steel
Manufacturer: ARC 74, Italy (1983)

42 MICHELE DE LUCCHI
Table lamp, *Oceanic*
Lacquered metal
H83 cm (32⅝ in) L93 cm (36⅝ in)
B12 cm (4¾ in)
Manufacturer: Memphis, Italy (1981)

38 MARTINE BEDIN
Table or floor lamp, *Super*
Fibreglass and rubber
H50 cm (19⅝ in)
Manufacturer: Memphis, Italy (1981)

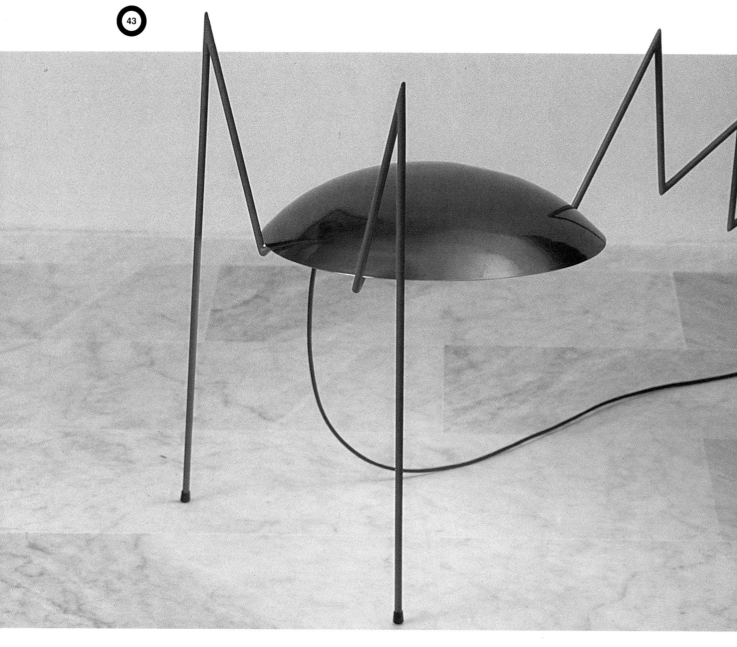

43

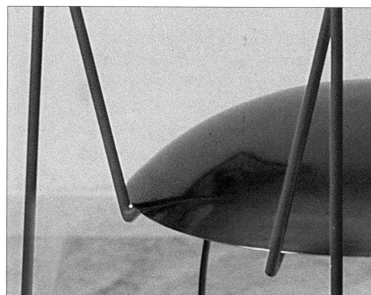

44

43, 44 JAVIER MARISCAL & PEPE CORTES
Floor lamp, *Araña*
In polished epoxy-coated steel, with
tungsten lamp
H27 cm (10½ in) L60 cm (23½ in)
W20 cm (8 in)
Manufacturer: BD, Spain (1985/6)

45 JAVIER MARISCAL
Table lamp, *Valencia*
In sanded steel, with matt nickelled
structure and painted red and blue
elements. The bright chrome steel frame is
supported on a black marble base. 25W lamp
H70 cm (27½ in) W20 cm (8 in)
Manufacturer: BD, Spain (1985/6)

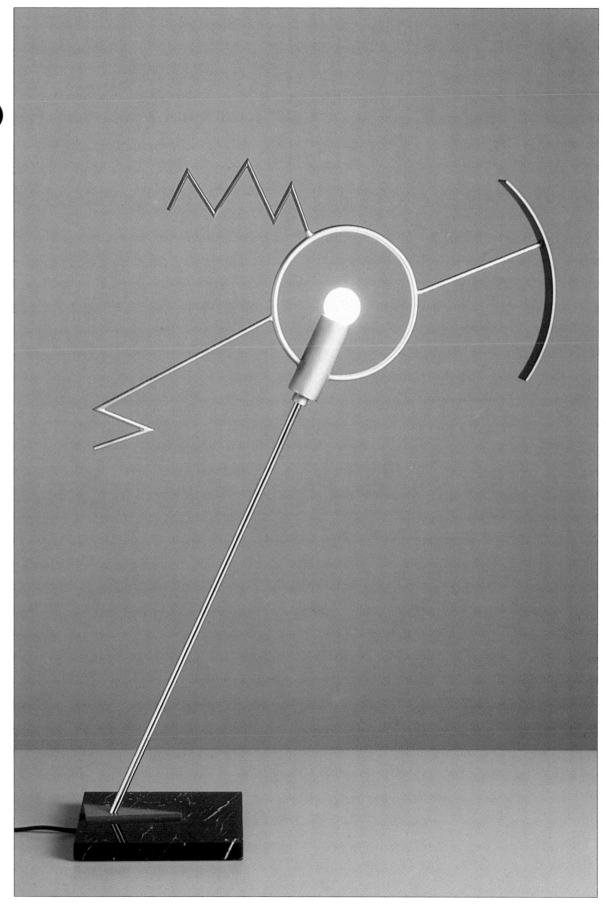

46

46 THOMAS EISL
Shelf unit with light
Galvanized steel, sterling board,
aluminium
A one-off shelf unit suitable for a
corner or free-standing, with two
light bars and corrugated sheets as
conductors. Takes eleven 5W 12V lamps.
H210 cm (82⅝ in) W83 cm (32½ in)
D60 cm (23½ in)
Manufacturer: Thomas Eisl, UK (1987/8)

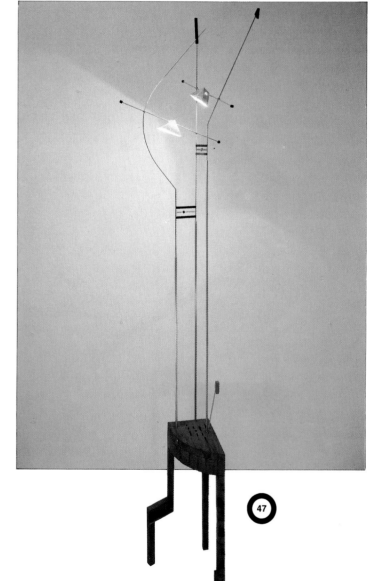

47

47 THOMAS EISL
Floor lamp
Wood, aluminium
A floor-standing light in aluminium,
yew and ebony with two adjustable
reflectors. Takes two 50W 12V
halogen lamps. One-off
H215 cm (84½ in)
Manufacturer: Thomas Eisl, UK (1987/8)

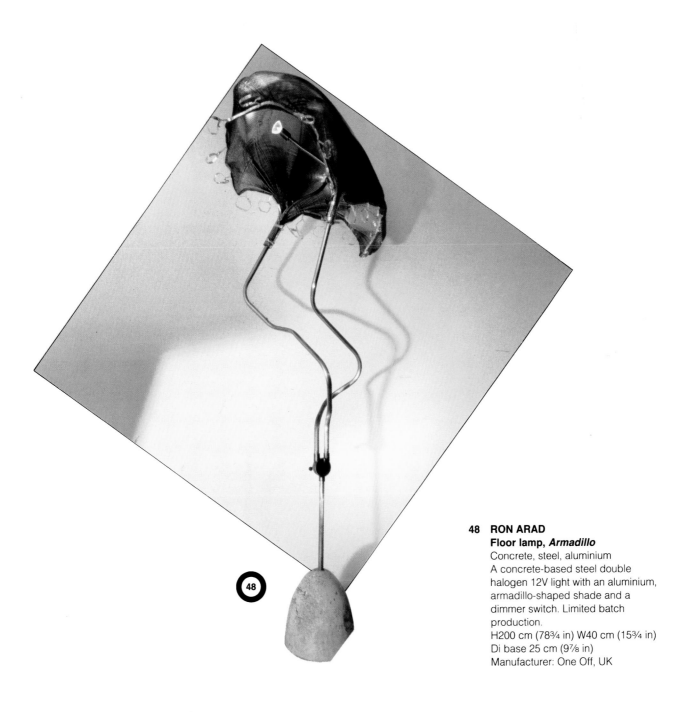

48 RON ARAD
Floor lamp, *Armadillo*
Concrete, steel, aluminium
A concrete-based steel double
halogen 12V light with an aluminium,
armadillo-shaped shade and a
dimmer switch. Limited batch
production.
H200 cm (78¾ in) W40 cm (15¾ in)
Di base 25 cm (9⅞ in)
Manufacturer: One Off, UK

London underground. *The design
scene in London is still largely
dominated by unique products and
limited editions, which is a shame
given the vast creative potential
available, but it is also an
advantage, since, without the
commercial pressure of mass
production, there is still some room
for adventurous designers with a
taste for the bizarre. The Israeli
designer Ron Arad and the Austrian
designer Thomas Eisl play with
light, corrugated iron, aluminium
and concrete to create an
underground design in a twofold
sense of the term: not only is their
work far removed from the public at
large, but its distinctive bunker
aesthetic is a sure indication that it
was never intended to see the light
of day.*

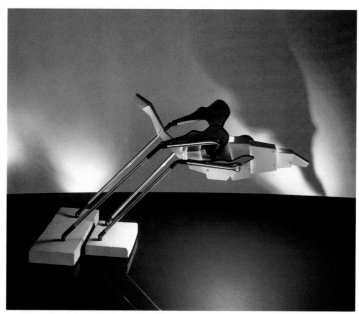

A renaissance of symbols. At the beginning of the twentieth century, electric light still had an aura of wonderment to it. Lamps were held aloft by ecstatic goddesses of light and mythological creatures, their glass decorated with flowers and other ornaments. At a later date, when light became the preserve of technicians and engineers, that sense of magic was lost. By the end of the 1980s, however, there were increasing signs that light was again acquiring its deeper significance as a symbol of life. Designers such as Gehry, Branzi, Lindfors and Viemeister/Krohn have brought light back from the laboratory and returned it to the biosphere. Leaves, birds and fish now herald a new age of lighting design which is once again in harmony with nature and where there is no contradiction between economy and ecology.

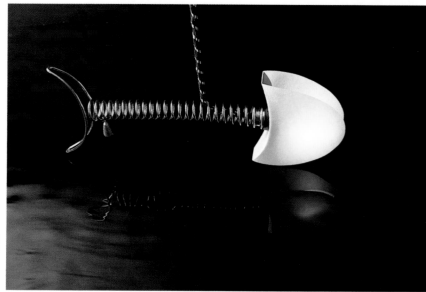

51, 54 FRANK D GEHRY
Fish lamp
sculptures
Designed for the 'Surface and Ornament Competition'. Gehry chipped and tore Colorcore into tiny pieces like fish scales, and built the pieces into a fish. When the light inside is lit, the material becomes semi-translucent. The lamp stand is made of wooden sticks and irregular pieces of Colorcore. (1984/5)

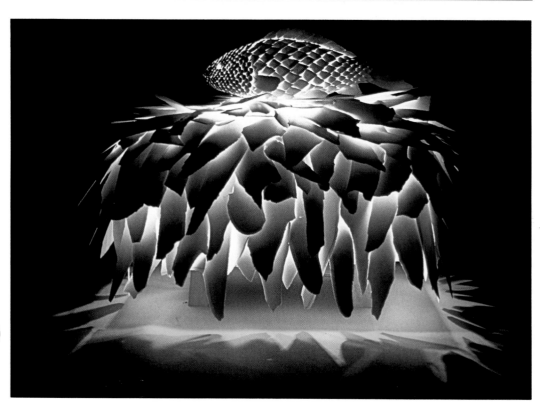

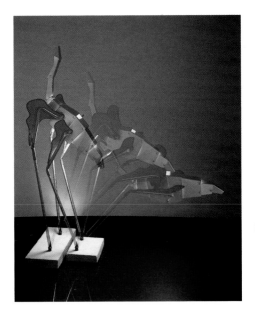

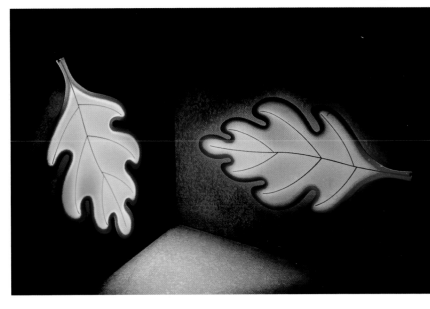

49, 52 STEFAN LINDFORS FOR THE INGO MAURER TEAM
Floor lamp, *Scaragoo*
Aluminium, steel, plastic
Takes one 50W 12V halogen bulb
H53 cm (20⅞ in) to 79 cm (31 in)
W33 cm (13 in) L46 cm (18 in)
Manufacturer: Design M Ingo Maurer,
West Germany (1988/9)

50 TUCKER VIEMEISTER
& LISA KROHN
Ceiling lamp, *Sardine Light*
Metal spring, lead, paper shade
Uses any voltage with a matching bulb;
this one is a standard 110V with a 40W
chandelier bulb. Prototype
H12.5 cm (5 in) W5 cm (2 in)
L46 cm (18 in)
Manufacturer: Gallery 91, USA (1988/9)

53 ANDREA BRANZI
Wall lamp, *Foglia*
Electro-luminescent glass
The electrical current of this low-voltage
lamp is generated through the veins of
the leaf.
W25 cm (9⅞ in) L45 cm (17¾ in)
Manufacturer: Memphis, Italy (1988/9)

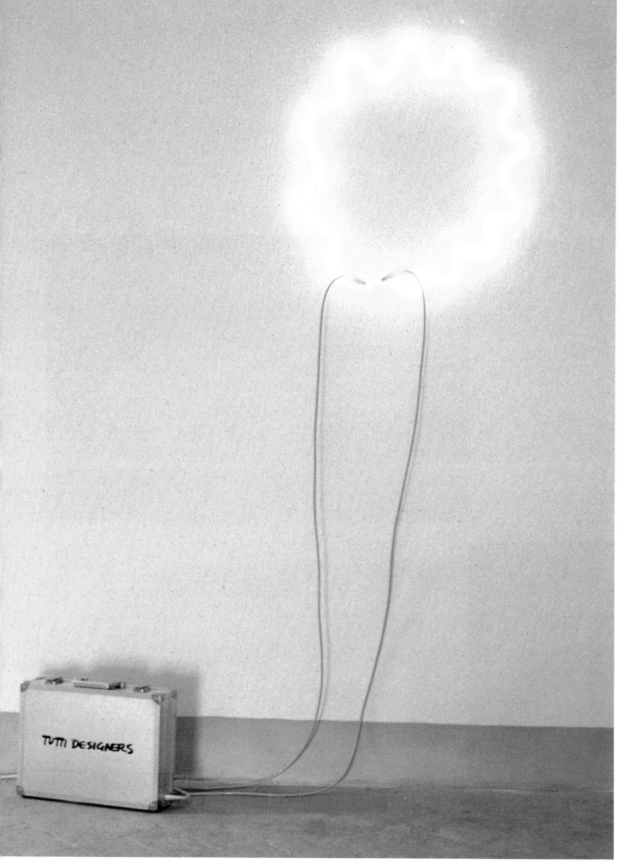

55 MICHELANGELO PISTOLETTO
Neon wall lamp, *Tutti Designers*
Neon lamp with silkscreened aluminium briefcase
H69 cm (27⅛ in) L71 cm (27⅞ in)
D12 cm (4¾ in)
Manufacturer: Metamemphis, Italy (1989)

Artwork. *The imagination bears strange fruit indeed. The lamps that are illustrated on these pages are like so many peals of scornful laughter aimed at industrial design – strange and sinister hybrids of handicraft and art that look like commercial readymades. None of their creators is a designer by profession. The Turin-born artist Michelangelo Pistoletto is the leading representative of* arte povera *and the Austrian-born Franz West is an object artist, while the rococo revival in the centre is the work of the photographer Mark Bayley. This is 'beautiful living' from a distorted version of our world, in which Batman, Dracula and Big Brother read magazines about home furnishings.*

57 FRANZ WEST
Floor lamp, *Privatlampe des Künstlers I*
Welded iron chains
H170 cm (66⅞ in)
Manufacturer: Metamemphis, Italy (1989)

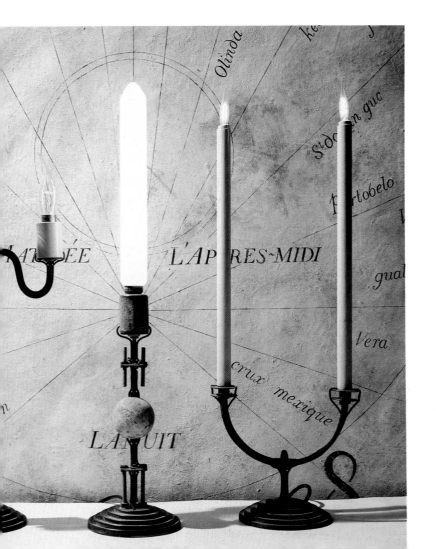

56 MARK BAYLEY
Candelabra, single candlestick, fork candlestick
Fibreglass resin, steel studding
Limited batch production
Candelabra Takes three 15W lamps
H100 cm (39½ in) W25 cm (9⅞ in)
Di base 14 cm (5½ in)
Single candlestick Takes one
60W lamp
H75 cm (29½ in) Di base
14 cm (5½ in)
Fork candlestick Takes two 15W
chandelier lamps
H50 cm (19⅝ in) Di base 14 cm
(5½ in) Di arch 18 cm (7 in)
Manufacturer: Mark Bayley, UK (1987/8)

The brave new world of cyberpunk. *The mid-eighties saw the development of a new and fascinating branch of science fiction called 'cyberpunk', a made-up word deriving from 'cybernetics' and 'punk' and used to describe a run-down future world in which high tech and low life, uncontrolled progress and uncontrollable barbarism are inextricably linked. (Anyone who has seen the film*

Blade Runner will have an idea of what is meant.) The lamps reproduced on these pages look as though they are imports from this future world, linking together the high and the low in a form that is little short of extreme. The table lamp by Toshiyuki Kita and Keith Haring has an electro-luminescent shade (an innovation previously used only in industry) with graffiti crudely scratched on its surface by

way of contrast. Equally provocative is Gaetano Pesce's Airport Lamp, which combines the most modern low-voltage halogen lamps with a melted object of synthetic material looking like some objet trouvé from a world destroyed by nuclear warfare. These are the lights of an age of darkness. May we never live to see it.

58

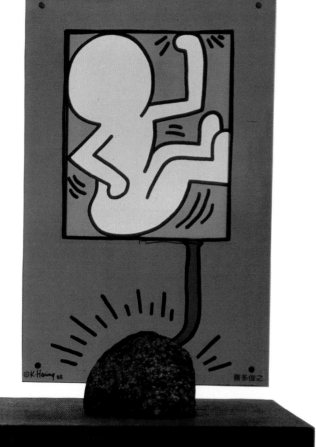

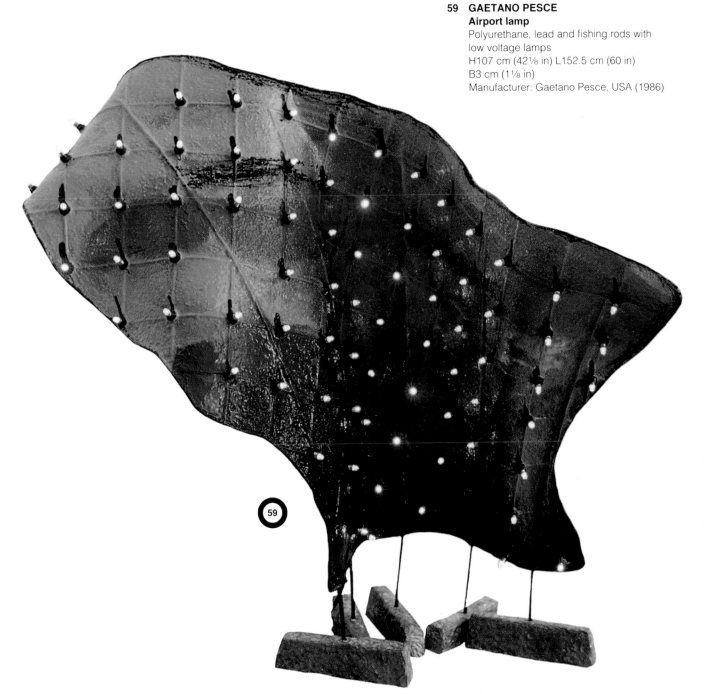

59 GAETANO PESCE
Airport lamp
Polyurethane, lead and fishing rods with
low voltage lamps
H107 cm (42⅛ in) L152.5 cm (60 in)
B3 cm (1⅛ in)
Manufacturer: Gaetano Pesce, USA (1986)

59

58 TOSHIYUKI KITA & KEITH HARING
Table lamp, left: *On Taro*, **right:** *On Giro*
Natural stone, glass
The electro-luminescent fixture can be
plugged into 110V or 220V. The
consumption is minimal, about 4W, and
the lifetime is over 10,000 hours.
H52 cm (20½ in) W29 cm (11⅜ in)
D15 cm (6 in)
Manufacturer: Kreon, Belgium (1988/9)

The world of tableware differs in many respects from what we have seen so far. Italy's design supremacy is not as marked here as in the areas of furniture and lamps. The influence of other regions of the world, most notably Scandinavia, Spain, the USA and, above all, Japan, is more pronounced, while current stylistic trends are, conversely, rather less clearly discernible. The dominant factor in tableware is the

3 TABLEWARE

personality of the designer, with fashions and trends taking second place, even if they figure at all. Moreover, tableware designers seem in their heart of hearts to be more conservative types than their contemporaries, who set their sails to the winds of the *Zeitgeist* on the sea of interior design. Or why do we find so little punk art, so little high-tech and deconstructivism on our dining-room tables?

But even though tableware ignored so many of the stylistic trends of the last decade, it nevertheless paid perfect tribute to the *spirit* of the 1980s, expressing a new delight in decoration in the wake not only of post-modernism but of that conspicuous consumerism with which we flaunt our lifestyles. Both of these are embodied with paradigmatic predictability in what might be termed the 'Alessi phenomenon'. Although little known to date on an international level, this metalware firm from the northern Italian town of Crusinallo scored a major coup in 1979, when it commissioned eleven of the world's leading architects to design a coffee and tea service. The result (1983) turned out to be something of a media event, establishing design as a popular subject in the minds of those responsible for the media; creating demand for new designs in magazines and on TV networks; and providing Alessi with a huge commercial success. This provided a brilliant public relations ploy for the architects concerned (including Meier, Tigerman, Venturi, Portoghesi, Hollein and Jencks), many of whom were encouraged to embark on a second career as furniture and product designers. It was almost as a by-product that it helped to establish the trend towards micro-architecture in design. Even more successful were the kettles by Richard Sapper, Michael Graves and Aldo Rossi, all three of which were among the definitive icons of 1980s' design, developing into considerable commercial hits for Alessi.

1 ALDO ROSSI
Coffee and tea service in six pieces
Part of the Tea and Coffee Piazza series
Coffee-pot: Silver. Truncated cone body
with upper cylindrical band in light blue
stoved enamel. H26 cm (10 in)
Teapot: Silver H22.5 cm (9 in)
Manufacturer: Alessi, Italy (1984/5)

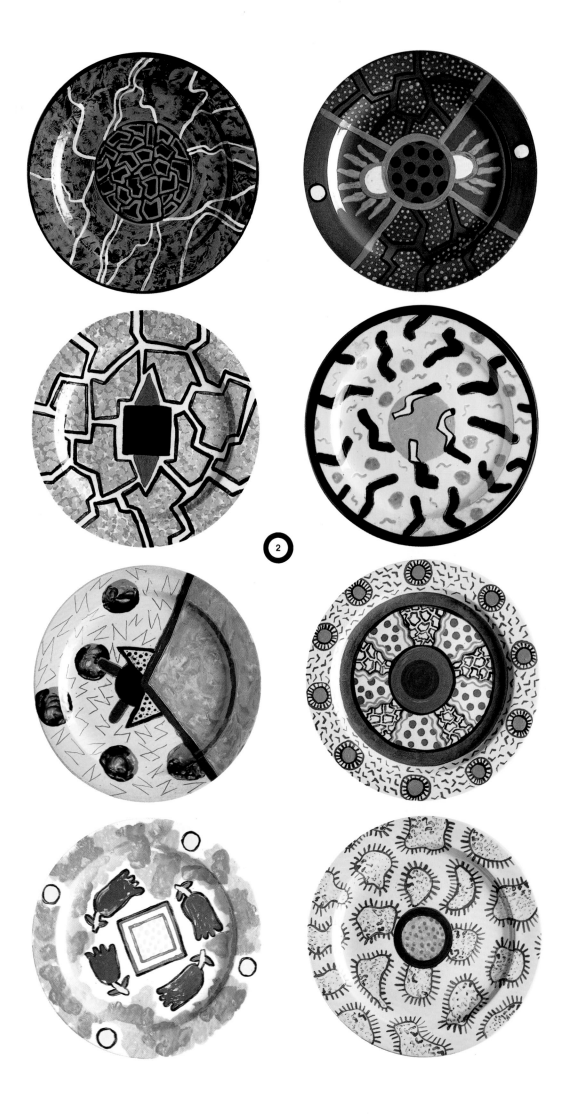

2

Alessi's strategy of ensuring market successes by employing designers with the status of cult figures, together with the company's shrewd manipulation of the media as a public relations machine, soon found other imitators, most notably in the case of the American glass and ceramics firm Swid Powell Design and of the German carpet manufacturers Vorwerk. Unlike Alessi, however, these two firms used their star designers not to design new works but to decorate and give the finishing touches to existing standard products.

In general, the decorative element played a major role throughout the decade under review. Following the rigorous and, ultimately, highly anaemic years of functionalism and Bauhaus-inspired 'good form', post-modernism (however much maligned it may have been) opened the floodgates and allowed the designer's delight in ornamentation, flourishes and, not least, in kitsch that had long been held in check to find renewed expression. The freedom to give uninhibited pleasure was exploited to the full. Tableware was made of wood or even concrete; colours no longer maintained a decent reserve; far from having a uniform look, services were thrown together from a multiplicity of varied parts, each of them differently designed and decorated; and objects appeared on the scene in which decoration and form were no longer in any recognizable harmony. It is no wonder, then, that insecure souls sought refuge in the numerous re-editions that were produced at this time, preferring teapots by Frank Lloyd Wright or Alvar Aalto.

But, in spite of all these escapades and inconsistencies, tableware in the 1980s shared a common feature, namely, the desire to restore an aura of distinction to the processes of serving, eating and drinking. The need for a living liturgy of enjoyment is greater now than it has been for a very long time. People want to escape from excessive rationality, since all too often rational functionalism has reduced the act (and art) of eating to a mere ingestive process. Fast food, TV dinners and standardized cafeterias have secularized the action of sitting together round a table to eat. More and more people are growing aware of the vacuum that has arisen. The widespread feeling of emptiness that besets our modern industrial societies is the result, not least, of too much 'practical' thinking, too much predictable ordinariness and common sense. The formal dinner, afternoon tea or morning coffee with its ritual vessels and actions offers the chance to escape, for however brief a span, into happier times. That is why Japan, where this form of ceremonial has long been part of everyday life, has exerted more and more influence on western table manners. In Japan there is no distinction between art and utilitarian objects, between the sacred and the profane. This holistic philosophy is bound to influence western design during the coming years. Perhaps the 1990s will be the decade not only of the yen but also of Zen?

2 **NATHALIE DU PASQUIER**
Plates
Decorated ceramic
One-off
Maker: Nathalie du Pasquier, Italy (1986/7)

4 MICHAEL GRAVES
Kettle
Stainless-steel kettle with blue polyamide handle and red whistle in the shape of a bird
Capacity 2.27 litres (4 pints)
Manufacturer: Alessi, Italy (1985/6)

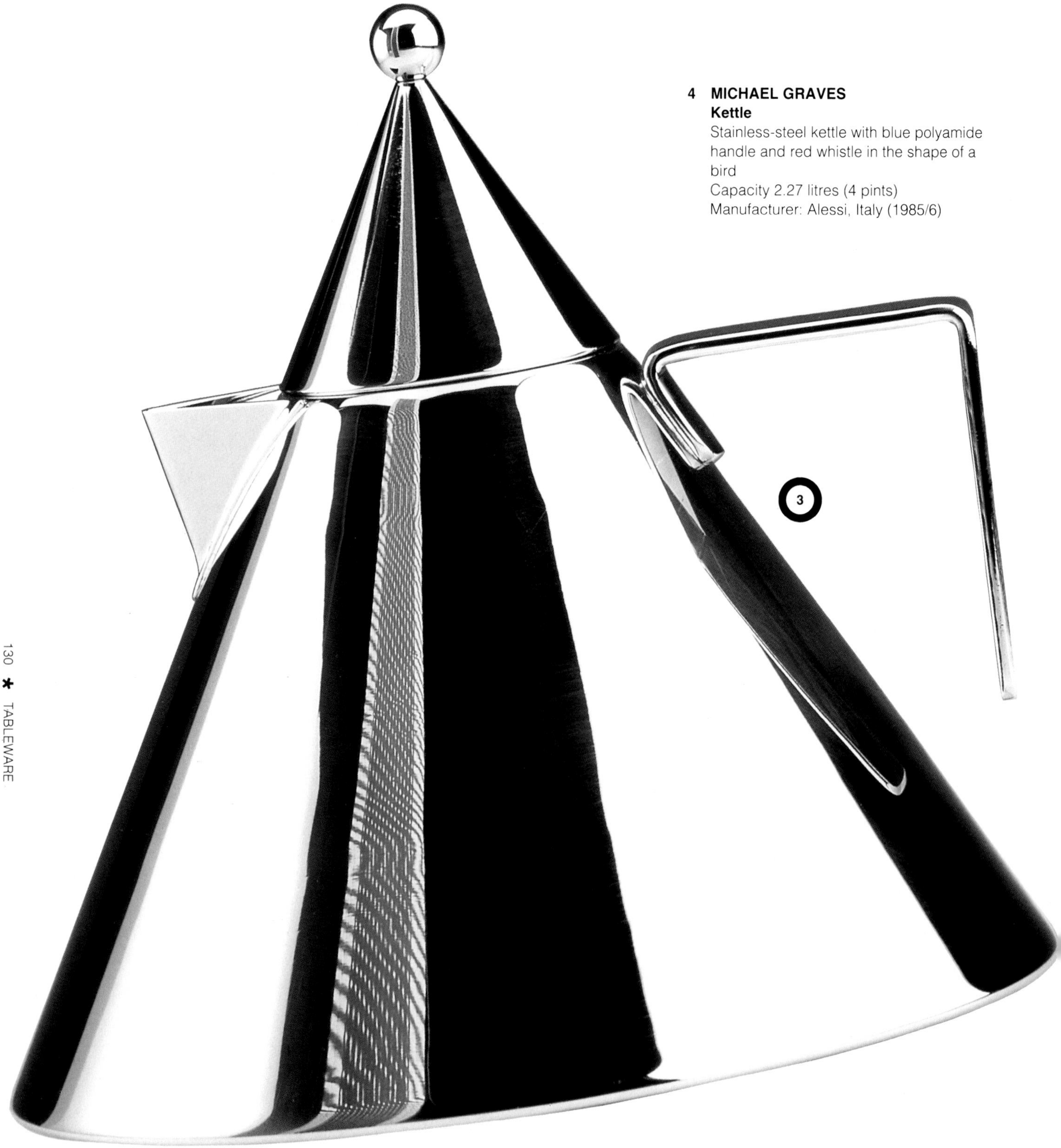

6 RICCARDO DALISI
Caffettiera Napoletana
Stainless steel, wood
A coffee-maker in stainless steel with a 'canaletto' walnut handle
Capacity: 11 oz/6 cups
H23.5 cm (9¼ in)
Manufacturer: Alessi, Italy (1987/8)

3 ALDO ROSSI
Kettle, *Il Conico*
Stainless steel
H20.2 cm (8 in) Di21.9 cm (8⅝ in)
Manufacturer: Alessi, Italy (1986/7)

5 RICHARD SAPPER
Kettle with melodic whistle
Stainless steel with copper heat-diffusing
bottom, brass whistle, pitched notes E and
B, polyamide-covered handle. In two
sizes: 2 litre (70 oz) and 3 litre (106 oz)
Also available in silver-plated stainless
steel. The whistle reproduces the sound of
an American steam locomotive.
Manufacturer: Alessi, Italy (1984/5)

Coffee and tea service of four pieces
Part of the Tea and Coffee Piazza series
Coffee-pot: silver; rectangular section
body; hinged lid; handle and spout
made of double tubular segments;
knob tubular, bent to form the initial C (coffee)
H22.5 cm (9 in)
Teapot: silver; square section body; knob
tubular, bent to form the letter T (tea)
H19.5 cm (7½ in)
Milk jug: silver; rectangular section body,
knob tubular, bent to form the letter S
H15 cm (6 in)
Tray: relief seams on surface determine
the arrangement of the pieces H1.5 cm
(¾ in) L51 cm (22¼ in) D16 cm (6¼ in)
Manufacturer: Alessi, Italy (1984/5)

Fruit bowl, *Murmansk*
Silver
H35 cm (13¾ in) Di 35 cm (13¾ in)
Manufacturer: Memphis, Italy (1982)

7

8

9

8 HANS HOLLEIN
Coffee and tea service with
five pieces
Part of the Tea and Coffee
Piazza series
Coffee-pot: silver with blue
metacrylate handle; square
section body with spout and
handle pivoted at the corners;
lid hinged on the spout side
with concealed hinge H17 cm
(6¾ in)
Teapot: silver with feet and
handle in blue metacrylate; lid
with internal central hinge and
opening next to the spout.
H18 cm (7¼ in)

Milk jug: silver with handle in
blue metacrylate; cylindrical
section body with truncated
conical base H13 cm (5¼ in)
Sugar bowl: silver, three
quarters of a circle section
body; knob in blue metacrylate
H7 cm (2¾ in)
Tray: electro-plated brass;
surface has a satin-finished
transversal band; shaped like
an aircraft-carrier deck, on
which the pieces have a
precise position H4.5 cm (2 in)
L92.4 cm (36 in) D31 cm
(12 in) Manufacturer: Alessi,
Italy (1984/5)

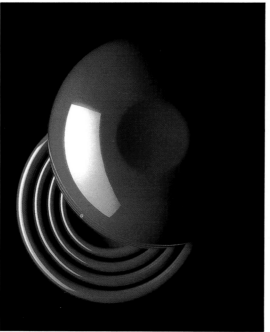

10 **TOSHIYUKI KITA**
Bowl
Wajima lacquer
Bowl for salad, antipasto,
etc from the *Urushi*
range of tableware
H from 3.1 cm-10.1 cm
(1¼ in-4 in) Di from 13 cm-24.5 cm
(5⅛ in-9⅝)
Manufacturer: Koshudo, Japan
(1986/7)

12 **LINO SABATTINI**
Cutlery, *Insect Legs*
Silver, titanium
L21 cm (8¼ in)
Manufacturer: Argenteria Sabattini,
Italy (1986/7)

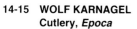

14-15 **WOLF KARNAGEL**
Cutlery, *Epoca*
Sterling silver, heavily
silver-plated
A complete set of tableware
comprising nearly 40 items
Manufacturer: Wilkens Bremer,
West Germany (1986/7)

16 RICHARD SAPPER
Casserole
Black-enamelled cast iron
An item from the *La Cintura di Orione* range
of cooking utensils, produced in
collaboration with six leading international
chefs. Capacity 7l (6 quarts)
H11.5 cm (4½ in) W32 cm (12½ in)
D23 cm (9 in)
Manufacturer: Alessi, Italy (1986/7)

11 MAKOTO KOMATSU
Plate, *Infinity*
Porcelain
Part of the *Infinity Collection* of tableware
Available in three sizes
W31 cm, 24.5 cm or 17.5 cm (12¼ in,
9⅝ in or 6⅞ in) D27 cm, 22 cm or 15 cm
(10⅝ in, 8⅝ in or 6 in)
Manufacturer: Ceramic Japan, Japan (1986/7)

13 LINO SABATTINI
Tableware, *Insect Legs*
Silver-plated metal, anodized black titanium
Tray: L32 cm (12½ in) W25 cm (9⅞ in)
Cutlery: L21.5 cm and 29 cm (8½ in and
11⅜ in)
Bowls: H4.3 cm and 4.8 cm (1⅝ in and
1⅞ in) Di 7 cm and 10.2 cm (2¾ in and 4 in)
Manufacturer: Argenteria Sabattini, Italy (1986/7)

**17 RICHARD
SAPPER**
Cooking utensils
Stainless steel,
copper and
stainless-steel
laminate, black
steel, enamelled
cast iron. A series
of cooking utensils
in the *La Cintura di
Orione* range,
produced in
collaboration with
six leading
international chefs
Manufacturer:
Alessi, Italy
(1986/7)

18 ANDREA BRANZI
Silver and glass
H40 cm (15¾ in)
Manufacturer: Memphis,
Italy (1982)

18

19 LINO SABATTINI
Cutlery, *P-1*
Prototypes of cutlery for Rosenthal in
brass alloy, heavily silver-plated
L22 cm (8⅜ in)
Manufacturer: Argenteria
Sabattini, Italy (1987/8)

20 LINO SABATTINI
Vase, *Colonnato*
A vase in brass alloy, heavily silver-plated
H27 cm (10½ in)
Manufacturer: Argenteria
Sabattini, Italy (1987/8)

21 PHILIPPE STARCK
Cutlery, *Objects Pointus 1*
Stainless steel
Sticks: L24.5 cm (9⅔ in)
Teaspoon: H15.5 cm (6⅛ in)
Dessertspoon: H22 cm (8⅔ in)
Fork: L22.5 cm (8⅞ in)
Knife: L25 cm (9⅞ in)
Manufacturer: Owo, France/
Sasaki, Japan (1988/9)

22 DOROTHY HAFNER
Teaset, *Flash*
Ceramic
A fifteen-piece teaset
Manufacturer: Rosenthal,
West Germany (1987/8)

23 ALI SCHERHAUFER
Tableware, *The Fifties*
Earthenware
Limited batch production
Cup: H10 cm (4 in) W15 cm (6 in)
D9.5 cm (3¾ in)
Saucer: Di16.5 cm (6½ in)
Milk jug: H10 cm (4 in) W10.5 cm (4⅛ in)
D9.5 cm (3¾ in)
Coffee pot: H23 cm (9 in) W19 cm
(7½ in) D15 cm (6 in)
Sugar bowl: H10 cm (4 in) Di9.5 cm (3¾ in)
Plate: Di21 cm (8¼ in)
Manufacturer: Villeroy & Boch, West
Germany (1988/9)

24 AMBROGIO POZZI
Cup and saucer
Porcelain
A cup in the *Collector's Cups* series
Limited batch production
Cup H8 cm (3⅛ in)
Saucer Di15 cm (6 in)
Manufacturer: Rosenthal, West
Germany (1987/8)

25 MARIO BELLINI
Teapot, *Cupola*
Porcelain
Teapot from the *Cupola* teaset
H19.7 cm (7¾ in) Di including spout
and handle 25.6 cm (10 in)
Manufacturer: Rosenthal,
West Germany (1987/8)

26 RENATE HATTINGER
Tableware, *Turkey*
Earthenware
Milk jug: H9.5 cm (3¾ in) W13.5 cm
(5⅖ in) D8.5 cm (3⅜ in)
Egg cup: H10 cm (4 in) Di5 cm (2 in)
Plate: Di21 cm (8¼ in)
Coffee pot: H29.5 cm (11⅝ in)
W19.5 cm (7⅗ in) D15 cm (6 in)
Cup: H7.5 cm (3 in) W12.5 cm (5 in)
D8.5 cm (3⅜ in)
Saucer: Di14.5 cm (5¾ in)
Manufacturer: Villeroy & Boch, West
Germany (1988/9)

27 MARGIT DENZ
Tableware, *Liberty I, II and III*
Earthenware
Limited batch production
Manufacturer: Villeroy & Boch,
West Germany (1988/9)

Comix ceramix. In the Spirit of the
USA was the subject which Matteo
Thun set his students at the Vienna
Academy of Applied Art. The result
was fast food for the eyes – an
agglomeration of visual clichés,
colourful, superficial, unconcerned.
Take it or leave it. What emerged
was something scarcely destined
for the Hall of Fame of purist

designers but rather for the
breakfast table where the day could
begin with a little bit of showbiz.
Everything looks so spontaneous
and ephemeral but, as we know,
Pop Art and clichés can go on for
quite some time.

28 MARIA WIALA
Tableware, *Catch the Line*
Earthenware
Limited batch production
Manufacturer: Villeroy & Boch,
West Germany (1988/9)

29 JOHANNA SCHMEISER
Tableware, *American Football*
Earthenware
Limited batch production
Manufacturer: Villeroy & Boch,
West Germany (1988/9)

30 KLARA OBEREDER
Tableware, *Coca Cola*
Earthenware
Limited batch production
Manufacturer: Villeroy & Boch,
West Germany (1988/9)

31 MICHAELA LANGE
Tableware, *Fly High*
Earthenware
Limited batch production
Manufacturer: Villeroy & Boch,
West Germany (1988/9)

32 INGRID SMOLLE
Tableware, *Blue Magic*
Earthenware
Limited batch production
Manufacturer: Villeroy & Boch,
West Germany (1988/9)

33 MARGIT DENZ
Tableware, *Bronx*
Earthenware
Limited batch production
Manufacturer: Villeroy & Boch,
West Germany (1988/9)

Zen design. *'It shows an absence of good taste to add all manner of unnecessary extras to what one already owns in order to invest it with a strange and more valuable appearance. Household goods should look old, they should not be immediately eyecatching nor excessively expensive, and they should be made of solid material – that is all that is needed.'*
From the Tsurezuregusa by Yoshida Kenkô (1283–1350)

34 MARCELLO MORANDINI
Cup and saucer, *Tazzina da Thè*
Ceramic
A teacup and saucer that fit together so snugly that they look like a single piece
H6 cm (2⅜ in) Di20 cm (7⅞ in)
Manufacturer: Unac Tokyo, Japan (1987/8)

(34)

35 SACHIKO KAWABE
Tableware, *Kan Kan*
Set of raised plates
Lacquered wood
Made using the traditional lacquerware method of Urushi
H8.6 cm (3⅜ in) Di24.5 cm (9⅔ in)
H7.5 cm (3 in) Di18 cm (7 in)
H6.5 cm (2½ in) Di16 cm (6¼ in)
Manufacturer: Yamada-Heiando, Japan (1988/9)

(36)

(35)

36 MINORU SUGAHRA
Tableware, *Indigo and Clear Frost*
Limited batch production
Left to right:
Plates: W12 cm (4¾ in) L12 cm (4¾ in)
W18 cm (7 in) L18 cm (7 in)
W24 cm (9⅜ in)
Vases: H18 cm (7 in) Di4 cm (1½ in)
H20 cm (7⅞ in) Di5 cm (2 in)
Flowers: L25 cm (9⅞ in) to 35 cm (13¾ in)
Manufacturer: Sugahara Glass Corporation, Japan (1988/9)

37 SMART DESIGN
Dinnerware
In Melamine and styrene
plastic, including
plates, bowls and servers
Dinner plate: D25 cm (10 in)
Salad bowl: H13-15 cm (5-6 in)
D25-30 cm (10-12 in)
Salad server: L29-34 cm
(11½-13½ in)
W9-11 cm (3½-4¼ in)
Manufacturer: Copco,
USA (1985/6)

38 LELLA & MASSIMO VIGNELLI
WITH DAVID LAW
Dinnerware, Aneic cutlery, *Bordin*
Stoneware, stainless steel
Modern stoneware with a high-gloss body
and a matt-finished rim. Cutlery of stainless steel
Manufacturer: Sasaio Crystal, USA (1986/7)

A MARTINE BEDIN
Vase, *Cucumber*
Ceramic
H30 cm (12 in)
Manufacturer: Memphis,
Italy (1985/6)

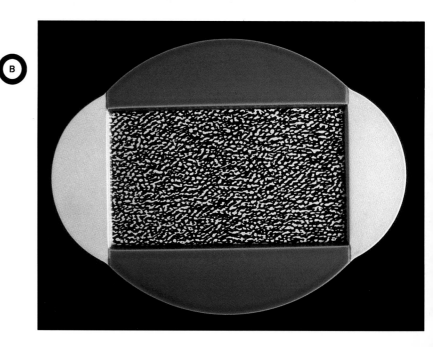

Made for today. *In recent years, many designers have tried to smuggle their products past the world of everyday use and into New York's Museum of Modern Art or some other important gallery. They have sought to create an instant classic right from the very beginning, although this is clearly not possible. Cult films and cult objects cannot be planned as such: they are raised to that status by time and by the public's reaction to them. This was always self-evident to the designers who worked for Memphis: they never worked for eternity, but for the here-and-now. For the present is brief and fleeting, and by tomorrow everything may be completely different. In its unpredictability and spontaneous transformations, the long series of Memphis collections reveals an almost philosophical belief in the here-and-now and in the transitoriness of being within the flux of time. What is important, therefore, about the objects depicted here is not their distant echos of constructivism or De Stijl. No, what matters is that they are used – at least until such time as something new is found to replace them.*

B MICHELE DE LUCCHI
Plate, *Celery*
White ceramic serving plate with decoration
L42 cm (16½ in) W32 cm (12½ in)
Manufacturer: Memphis, Italy (1985/6)

C MARCO ZANINI
Bowl, *Broccoli*
Ceramic fruit bowl, decorated in three
different shapes and colours
Di35 cm (14 in)
Manufacturer: Memphis, Italy (1985/6)

D MARIA SANCHEZ
Ashtray, *Squash*
Ceramic ashtray, in three
different primary colours
15 cm (6 in) square
Manufacturer: Memphis,
Italy (1985/6)

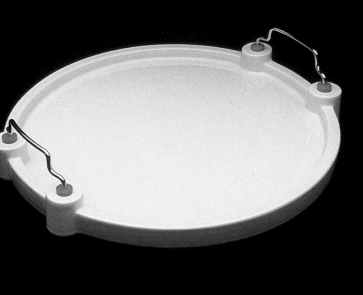

E GEORGE SOWDEN
Tray, *Potato*
Ceramic with metal handles
Di31 cm (12 in)
Manufacturer: Memphis,
Italy (1985/6)

40 DAVID TISDALE
Coasters
Anodized aluminium, acrylic
W7.5 cm (3 in) L7.5 cm (3 in)
Manufacturer: David Tisdale
Design,
USA (1987/8)

39 GEORGE SOWDEN
Plates
Decorated ceramic
One-offs
Manufacturer: George Sowden, Italy (1986/7)

42 DAVID TISDALE
Salad bowl with spoons
Anodized aluminium
Bowl: H25.5 cm (10 in) Di33 cm (13 in)
Spoons: W7 cm (2¾ in) L33 cm (13 in)
Manufacturer: David Tisdale Design,
USA (1987/8)

41 DAVID TISDALE
Picnic flatware
Anodized aluminium
Fork: W2.5 cm (1 in) L18 cm (7 in)
Knife: W2.5 cm (1 in) L20.5 cm (8 in)
Spoon: W3.8 cm (1½ in)
L16.5 cm (6½ in)
Manufacturer: David Tisdale Design,
USA (1987/8)

43 HELEN SHIRK
Bowl, *Bare Tracery*
Copper, brass
A double bowl. The outer bowl is
copper, spray-etched and patinated.
The inner bowl is brass, etched, copper-
plated, patinated and heat coloured.
One-off
H12.5 cm (5 in) Di43.5 cm (17 in)
Manufacturer: Helen Shirk, USA (1987/8)

44 SHARI M. MENDELSON
Bowl No. 1
Copper, patina, gold foil
One-off
H46 cm (18 in) Di46 cm (18 in)
Manufacturer: Shari M. Mendelson,
USA (1987/8)

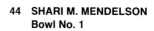

45 FREI OTTO
Pitchers
Ceramic pitchers designed for he
'Golden Eye' exhibition at the Cooper-
Hewitt Museum
Prototypes (1985/6)

Back to the roots. *If centuries-old traditional crafts are currently being revived, it is as a reaction to the sheer anonymity of modern production techniques. Memphis inspires Murano. In ceramics, too, the trend is to go back to long-established techniques. The bowls by Helen Shirk and Shari Mendelson are classic examples of the medieval Japanese ideals of wabi ('patinated and weathered') and sabi ('the melancholy and lonely'). An alternative solution is that proposed by Rajiv Sethi and his 'Golden Eye' project. Sethi uses designs by European and American designers in an attempt to revive oriental craftsmanship, which, having suffered beneath the onslaught of western technology, is threatening to fall into total oblivion. The German architect Frei Otto has found an ideal solution which is modern, independent and suitable for non-industrial production.*

46-47 NATHALIE DU PASQUIER
Vase, *Carrot*
Ceramic
H30 cm (12 in)
Manufacturer: Memphis, Italy (1985/6)

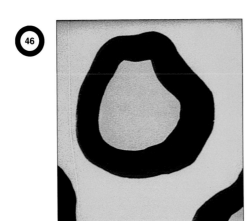

46

47

**48 PERRY A. KING &
SANTIAGO MIRANDA
Bowl,** *Bergamo*
Transparent and coloured glass with
Murino glass supports
Limited batch production
H12 cm (4¾ in) Di35 cm (13¾ in)
Manufacturer: Veart, Italy (1987/8)

(48)

**49 SOICHIRO SASAKURA
Tableware,** *San Marino*
Glass
Left to right:
Black goblet: H16 cm (6¼ in)
Di8.4 cm (3¼ in)

Clear goblet: H16 cm (6¼ in)
Di8.4 cm (3¼ in)
Black decanter: H19 cm (7½ in)
Di11.2 cm (4½ in)

Black jug: H16 cm (6¼ in)
Di11 cm (4⅜ in)
Manufacturer: Sasaki Glass Co,
Japan (1988/9)

(49)

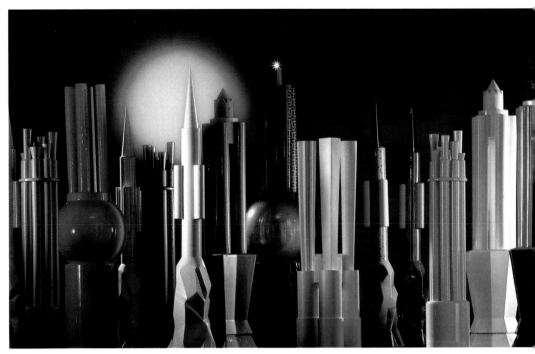

51 MATTEO THUN
Vases, *Urban Signals: Andy*
Ceramic
H71 cm (28 in) Di28 cm (11 in)
Manufacturer: Anthologie Quartett,
West Germany (1988/9)

50 MATTEO THUN
Vases, *Castelli in Fiore*
Ceramic
Five different vases in a range of colours
and finishes
Far left: ***Castel Fondo***
H76 cm (30 in) Di15 cm (6 in)
Second from left: ***Castel Altaguardia***
H106 cm (41¾ in) Di30 cm (11⅞ in)
Third from left: ***Castel Thun***
H94 cm (37 in) Di 20 cm (7⅞ in)
Sixth from left: ***Castel Brughier***
H97 cm (38¼ in) Di26 cm (9 in)
Eighth from left: ***Castel Cagno***
H72 cm (28½ in) Di23 cm (9 in)
Manufacturer: Anthologie Quartett, West
Germany (1988/9)

52 SACHIKO KAWABE
Tableware, *Kan Kan*
Twelve-cornered plates
Lacquered wood
Made using the traditional lacquerware
method of Urushi
Di67 cm (26⅜ in) and 48.5 cm (19 in)
Manufacturer: Yamada-Heiando,
Japan (1988/9)

53 PHILIPPE STARCK
Vase, *3 Etrangetes sous un mur*
Glass
H46 cm (18 in) W40 cm (15¾ in)
L50 cm (19⅝ in)
Manufacturer: Daum, France (1988/9)

Designer glass. *The success of
Alessi and Swid Powell Design has
shaken many traditional European
firms out of their aristocratic
reserve. In the past it was only the
manufacturer's name (if at all) that
influenced people in their choice of
glassware, whereas now the major
glassworks are setting increasing
store on the marketing potential of
the name of a prominent designer.
In Austria, Swarovski has
commissioned works from Sottsass
and Sipek, while the French firm of
Daum Frères has turned, bien sûr,
to Philippe Starck, who has helped
the company flourish with a series
of vases that play a fragile game
with gravity. In the meantime
Monsieur Starck has become such
a master of marketing strategies
that he has even given these vases
the shape of his unofficial
trademark, a horn.*

55 PHILIPPE STARCK
Vase, *Une Etrangete sous un mur*
Glass
H55 cm (21½ in) D2 cm (¾ in)
Vase H50 cm (19⅝ in)
Manufacturer: Daum, France (1988/9)

57 PHILIPPE STARCK
Vase, *L'Etrangete*
Glass
H13.5 cm (5¼ in) L55 cm (21½ in)
Manufacturer: Daum, France (1988/9)

54 PHILIPPE STARCK
Vase, *4 Etrangetes contre un mur*
Glass
H60 cm (23½ in) W46 cm (18 in)
L50 cm (19⅝ in)
Manufacturer: Daum, France (1988/9)

56 PHILIPPE STARCK
Vase, *4 Etrangetes sous un mur*
Glass
H46 cm (18 in) W55 cm (21½ in)
L60 cm (23½ in)
Manufacturer: Daum, France (1988/9)

58 PHILIPPE STARCK
Vase, *Une Etrangete contre un mur*
Glass
H70 cm (27½ in) D2 cm (¾ in)
Vase H38 cm (15 in)
Manufacturer: Daum, France (1988/9)

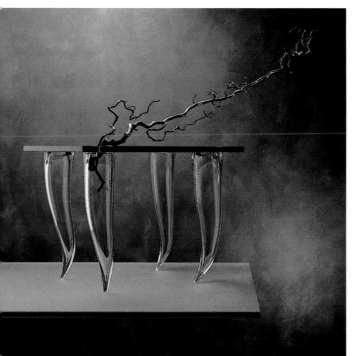

59 ACHILLE CASTIGLIONI
Goblet, *Paro*
Full-lead crystal glass, hand-blown
and ground. The glass
can be reversed according to use.
H20 cm (7¾ in) D8 cm (3 in)
Manufacturer: Alessi, Italy (1984/5)

60

60 **ANGELO MANGIAROTTI**
Glass, *First Glass*
H14.5 cm (5¾ in) Di7 cm (2¾ in)
Manufacturer: Colle, Italy (1988/9)

61

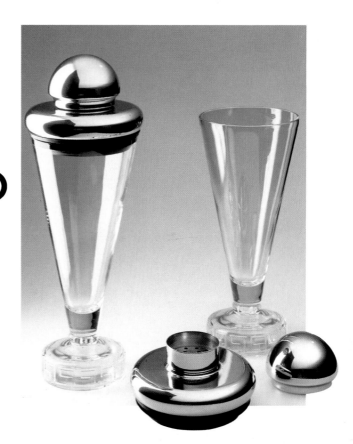

61 **MATTEO THUN**
Cocktail shaker, *Campari*
Stainless steel, glass, silicon rubber
H27.7 cm (10⅞ in) Di10.5 cm (4⅛ in)
Manufacturer: Alessi, Italy (1988/9)

62 ETTORE SOTTSASS
Vase, *Mizar*
Clear blue glass with multicoloured handles
H32 cm (12⅝ in) 30 cm (11⅞ in)
Manufacturer: Memphis, Italy (1982)

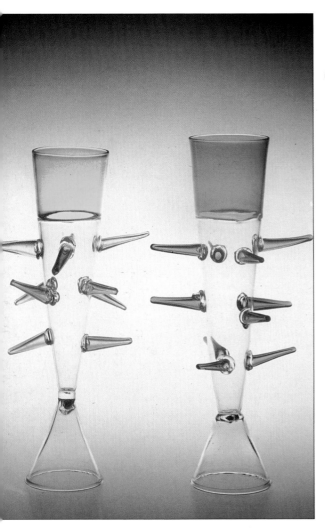

64 BOŘEK ŠIPEK
Glass
A vessel that can be used as a
centrepiece for the table or as a fruit
holder. In two parts that can be used
independently as a vase and a large
plate. Hand-blown by the traditional
Murano glass manufacturing method.
Limited batch production
H28 cm (11 in) Di base 10.5 cm (4⅛ in)
Di top 33.5 cm (13⅛ in)
Manufacturer: Sawaya & Moroni,
Italy (1987/8)

63 BOŘEK ŠIPEK
Neboi Champagne Glass
Glass
A champagne glass, hand-blown by the
traditional Murano glass manufacturing
method. The points are designed to
keep the hand away from the glass and
to minimize spillage when it is set
down. Limited batch production
H29.5 cm (11⅝ in) Di base
7 cm (2¾ in) Di top 7.5 cm (3 in)
Manufacturer: Sawaya & Moroni,
Italy (1987/8)

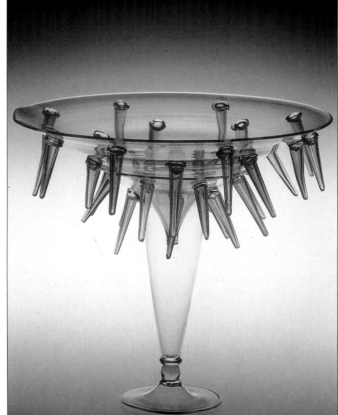

Dusted-down heirlooms. *The sparkling cut of Bohemian glass was once as world-famous as the colourful magic of glassware from Murano. But Europe's leading glass-blowers gradually slipped back down from the Olympian heights of their skill as craftsmen, into the depths of souvenir kitsch. With only a few important exceptions, hard currency and a quick profit were more important than integrity and a sense of genuine identity. Design in the 1980s altered all this. New designs were commissioned from the citadels of art glass. The craftsmen concerned could once more take pride in their work, since the results were spectacular in every respect, whether it be the spikey creatures of the Czech designer Borek Sipek or the charming, brightly coloured creations of Marco Zanini and Ettore Sottsass – both of whom are now engaged in an exciting neck-and-neck race for the most creative and sensitive glass designer of the decade.*

65 BOŘEK ŠIPEK
Glass
A carafe with a cap that can also be used as a drinking glass. Hand-blown by the traditional Murano glass manufacturing method. Limited batch production
H37 cm (14½ in) Di base
10.5 cm (4⅛ in)
Di top 9.5 cm (3¾ in)
Manufacturer: Sawaya & Moroni, Italy (1987/8)

(65)

(66)

66 MARCO ZANINI
Bowl, *Rigel*
Blue, black, green, red and clear glass
H35 cm (13¾ in)
Manufacturer: Memphis, Italy (1982)

Textile design has always been a peaceful 'region' of the design world. In this distant province life goes by more slowly, and trends that do not fit in with the more introspective mode are simply ignored, while innovations, to put it mildly, are rare. Little of all this

4 ★ TEXTILES

changed in the 1980s, except that this underdeveloped area on the edge of the design world suddenly gained in popularity. The textile departments of all the major furniture stores are growing larger and larger, and textiles fill up more and more space in furnishing and design magazines.

There is little doubt that textiles, like tableware, have profited from the return of conspicuous consumption in the 1980s. Memphis and other post-modernist movements have had a variety of effects, from simple pleasure in the decorative interplay of colours and forms to neo-conservative splendour reminiscent of rococo courts, not to mention the obliquely ironical treatment of the garish, tasteless and kitschy. All these approaches require new coverings for furniture, walls and floors. And this in turn means lots and lots of new designs. The ailing textile industry was quick to realize that design could offer it the long-sought opportunity to free itself from thinking in terms of cost per square metre and hence from competitive pressures from cheap suppliers in the Far East. Those buyers who value good design are prepared to pay high prices for it, with the result that design has helped a whole section of industry take on a new lease of life.

As in so many other areas, the most important motivating forces came from Japan. Textile designers such as Junichi Arai, Eiji Miyamoto, Hiroshi Awatsuji and Yoshiki Hishinuma have created textiles in which the traditional predominance of the

1 **SCOT SIMON**
Wallpleats
Vinyl
Wall-covering made of pleated vinyl and
backed with fabric. Available in various
matt and pearlized colours
W76 cm (30 in)
Manufacturer: Innovations, USA (1987/8)

TRACEY J. BULLEN
Frabic, *CH22/CH30*
100 per cent cotton
Hand-printed and painted frabrics
using helizarin dyes. Suitable for
furnishing and available in a
choice of colours. Limited batch
production
W127 cm (50 in) L300cm (118 in)
Manufacturer: Chameleon
Textiles, UK

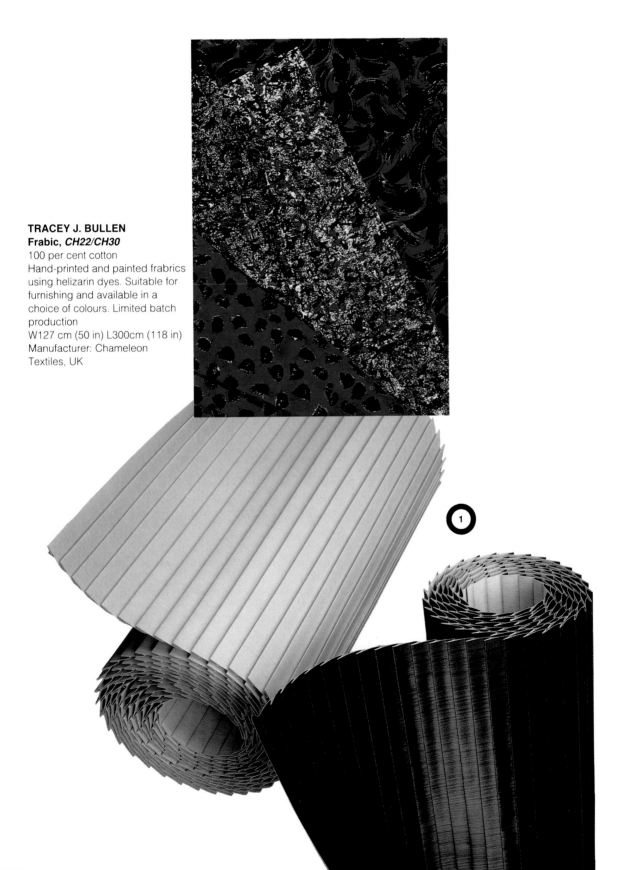

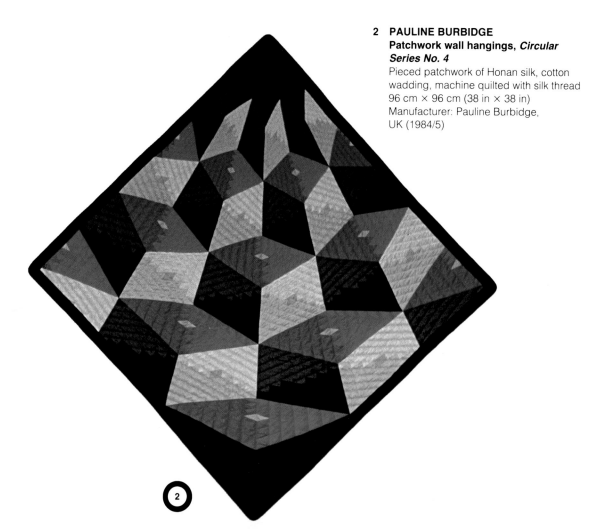

2 PAULINE BURBIDGE
Patchwork wall hangings, *Circular*
Series No. 4
Pieced patchwork of Honan silk, cotton
wadding, machine quilted with silk thread
96 cm × 96 cm (38 in × 38 in)
Manufacturer: Pauline Burbidge,
UK (1984/5)

pattern has been replaced by an emphasis on the *structure* of the fabric. The printed or smoothly woven surface can once again become a tactile adventure, so that the semantic link between 'textile' and 'texture' begins to make sense once more: fabrics can be experienced not only by the eye but also by the hand, drawn across the surface. A part of the attraction of these textiles is that they give the impression of being handmade: in fact they are manufactured on computer-driven looms, with random generators ensuring built-in flaws in the weaving.

Minimalist materials in nondescript colours were also used by fashion houses such as Issey Miyake or 'Comme des Garçons', thereby proving that the distinctions between fashion textiles and homemade textiles are beginning to disappear. The

way to the *haute couture* curtain now lies open before us.

A second important force in terms of modern textile design has been the influence of ethnic cultures from all around the world. Folklorist motifs from Morocco, South Africa, Mexico, Indonesia and Polynesia, sometimes in transmuted form, have become increasingly common. One does not need to be a prophet to see that this trend will increase, since the vitality, *joie de vivre* and natural harmony of this ethnic art is so irresistible that it can continue to inspire us for many years to come. It is interesting to see the way in which this trend is paralleled by an increasing interest in international music or ethno-pop. Both musical and visual influences come from the same parts of the world – from Morocco and Algeria, South Africa and the Homelands, and from Creole and Polynesian roots. It appears that an international culture is beginning to emerge, a culture which, by spanning several regions of the earth, has proved to be mutually stimulating. What a wonderful world it would be if politicians thought in the same way as musicians and designers.

Nonetheless, there is no denying that textile design in the 1980s was also guilty of a tendency towards decorative

superficiality and aesthetic escapism. Laura Ashley and Ralph Lauren were never out of fashion, and the seductive beauty of the designs by English fabric designers such as Susan Collier & Sarah Campbell or Natalie Gibson have even breathed new life into the genre of floral and landscape prints. Alcantara has found its way out of hotels and banking halls and into our homes and living rooms. And, hard to believe, velvet and velour have made a comeback, as though time itself had stood still. The decade that began with the hot suburban jazz of Memphis drew to a close to the sound of the pleasant harmonies of a tuneful casino dance band. In a decade when everything was possible, conservatism acquires the exotic thrill of progressiveness. Anarchy sinks back in its deep armchair and enjoys the feeling of comfort.

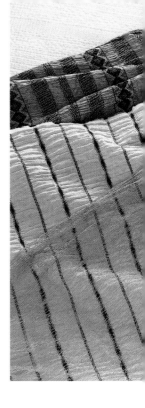

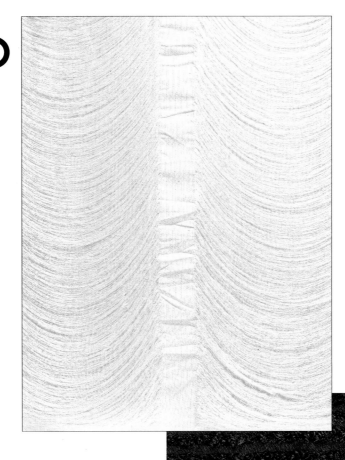

3 EIJI MIYAMOTO
Fabric
Cotton, rayon
One-off
Manufacturer: Miyashin,
Japan (1987/8)

4 EIJI MIYAMOTO
Fabric
100% cotton
One-off
Manufacturer: Miyashin,
Japan (1987/8)

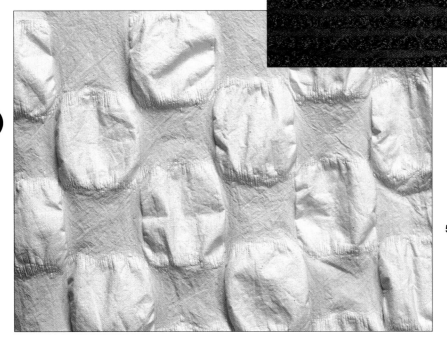

5 EIJI MIYAMOTO
Fabric
100% cotton
One-off
Manufacturer: Miyashin,
Japan (1987/8)

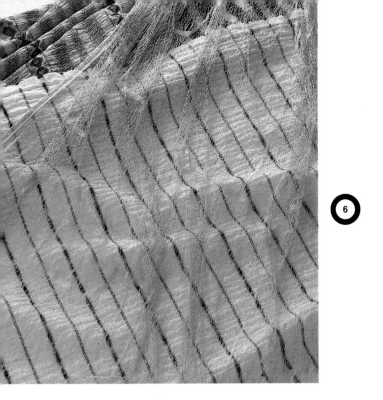

6   JUNICHI ARAI
Fabrics
Top: *Tube*
Polyester
Made using the Jacquard technique with
several different kinds of polyester yarns
W50 cm (19⅝ in) Repeat 12 cm (4¾ in)
Middle: *Striped Pucker*
Polyester
Made using the Jacquard technique with
several different kinds of polyester yarns
W95 cm (37½ in) Repeat 9 cm (3½ in)
Bottom: *Silk Lace*
Silk
Made using the Raschel technique
W100 cm (39½ in) Repeat 135 cm (53¼ in)
Manufacturer: Nuno, Japan (1988/9)

7   FUJIWO ISHIMOTO
Fabric, *Uoma*
100% cotton
Tablecloth, part of the
Sydantalvi collection
W140 cm (55⅛ in)
Manufacturer: Marimekko,
Finland (1987/8)

Woven haikus. The new fabrics by
the leading Japanese textile
designers have the same
impressionistic quality as the
traditional three-line haiku. By
saying enough, but not too much,
they create an idealized picture of
snow, sand, ashes, shingle
beaches and broken ice floes in the
observer's mind. Almost all these
designs reflect the central theme in
Japanese art – nature through the
changing seasons. But what looks
entirely natural is the result not of
traditional handicraft but of untiring
experimentation with fabrics,
processing treatments and the most
modern computer technology. And
yet, for all their intellectuality and
introversion, these fabrics have an
immense emotional power so that
everyone who sees them feels the
silent command to touch them.

8 JUNICHI ARAI Fabrics
Fabrics designed and
manufactured for
fashion designer
Yoshiki Hishinuma. Left:
thin transparent threads
– nylon, crushed
polyester and 'ceramic
yarn' made of titanium.
Right: nylon, cotton and
rayon. Manufacturer:
Anthology, Japan
(1986/7)

*The mathematics of
aesthetics.* Perhaps the
most interesting textile
designer at present is the
Japanese designer Junichi
Arai, one of the few to
bridge the gulf between
art and science and to
return with amazing results
from his forays across the
great divide. For Arai,
designing textiles involves
an act of mathematical
calculation, a form of
applied geometry. He
uses computer programs
to create and vary
patterns, testing the
properties of new fabric
mixtures with scientific
thoroughness in order to
establish how adaptable
they are, when they tear,
when they are liable to
split, and so on. In the
course of these
experiments, Arai has
produced many novel
combinations of materials,
including natural fabrics

9 JUNICHI ARAI Fabric
'Ceramic yarn'
(titanium), wool and
stretch polyurethane
thread.
After weaving, felt
is attached to the back
to create a wrinkled
effect. One-off
Manufacturer:
Anthology, Japan
(1986/7)

164 ✱ TEXTILES

10 JUNICHI ARAI
Fabrics designed and manufactured for Issey Miyake. Left: silk and 'ceramic yarn' (titanium). Centre: a printed version of the same material. Right: cotton and stretch polyester, double-woven Manufacturer: Anthology, Japan (1986/7)

such as cotton and silk, manmade fibres, plastics, and even metal wires made of titanium and aluminium. Among the favourite materials of this Leonardo of textile design are 'ceramic yarn' made of titanium, together with threads which contract or even disappear completely in the course of the production process. Arai's designs also reveal the admiration that he feels for ethnic patterns from Indonesia, Mexico and Polynesia. Junichi Arai is that rare phenomenon, a man who combines the intuition of the artist with the purposeful progressiveness of a research and development scientist.

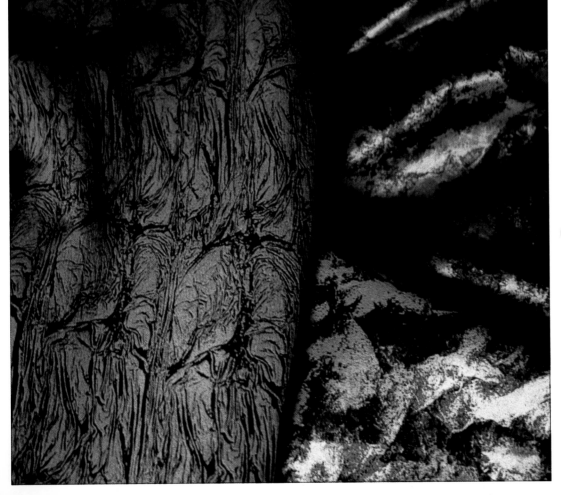

11 JUNCHI ARAI
Fabrics specially manufactured for Toray Industries using a super-fine polyester thread, double-woven Manufacturer: Anthology, Japan (1986/7)

12 JUNICHI ARAI
Fabrics
100% polyester fabrics in a range
of bright colours achieved by
using metal plates
Manufacturer: Junichi Arai,
Japan (1985/6)

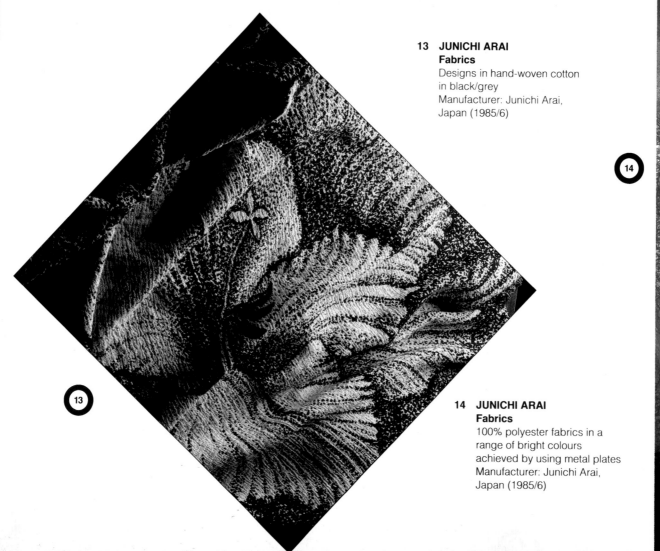

13 JUNICHI ARAI
Fabrics
Designs in hand-woven cotton
in black/grey
Manufacturer: Junichi Arai,
Japan (1985/6)

14 JUNICHI ARAI
Fabrics
100% polyester fabrics in a
range of bright colours
achieved by using metal plates
Manufacturer: Junichi Arai,
Japan (1985/6)

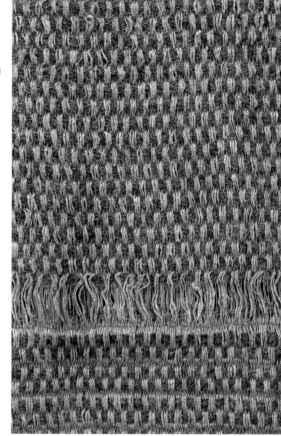

16 EIJI MIYAMOTO
Fabric, *Ancient Look*
Silk, wool
One-off
W110 cm (43½ in)
Repeat 70 cm (27½ in)
Manufacturer: Miyashin,
Japan (1988/9)

15 REIKO SUDO
Fabric, *Film Stripe*
Cotton, polyurethane
Made using the double-weave Jacquard
technique. The double layers of the wide
coloured stripes create a billowing effect
when the white polyurethane yarn in the
narrow stripes shrinks during finishing.
W60 cm (23½ in) Repeat 21 cm (8¼ in)
(1988/9)

17 EIJI MIYAMOTO
Fabric
Polyester, cupra, wool, acrylic
Three-layered quilting, highlighted with
looped wool thread. One-off
W110 cm (43½ in) Repeat 1.5 cm (⅔ in)
Manufacturer: Miyashin, Japan (1988/9)

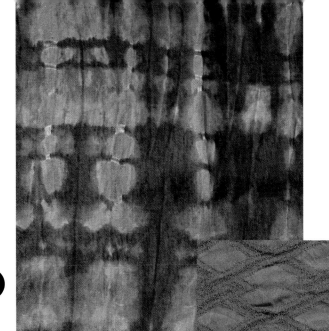

18 EIJI MIYAMOTO
Fabric
Linen
Made using the
tie-dye technique
One-off
W150 cm (59 in)
Manufacturer: Miyashin,
Japan (1988/9)

20 EIJI MIYAMOTO
Fabric
Linen, cotton
Crimped effect created by pulling the
weft thread tightly on the back of the
fabric. One-off
W60 cm (23½ in)
Manufacturer: Miyashin,
Japan (1988/9)

19 EIJI MIYAMOTO
Fabric
Linen, cotton
Made using the crimped Jacquard
technique. One-off
W90 cm (35½ in) Repeat 6 cm (2½ in)
Manufacturer: Miyashin,
Japan (1988/9)

21 EIJI MIYAMOTO
Fabrics
Left to right:
Silk
One-off
W130 cm (51⅛ in)
Repeat 2 cm (¾ in)
Cotton
One-off
W130 cm (51⅛ in)
Wool
W130 cm (51⅛ in)
Manufacturer: Miyashin,
Japan (1988/9)

22 JUNICHI ARAI
Fabrics
Designs in undyed hand-woven cotton
Manufacturer: Junichi Arai, Japan (1985/6)

23 JUNICHI ARAI
Fabrics
100% cotton
Top and middle: patterns inspired by
African designs. Bottom: pattern
inspired by Micronesian designs. In
strong cotton woven to give different
stretch patterns. Limited batch
production
Manufacturer: Arai Creations System,
Japan (1987/8)

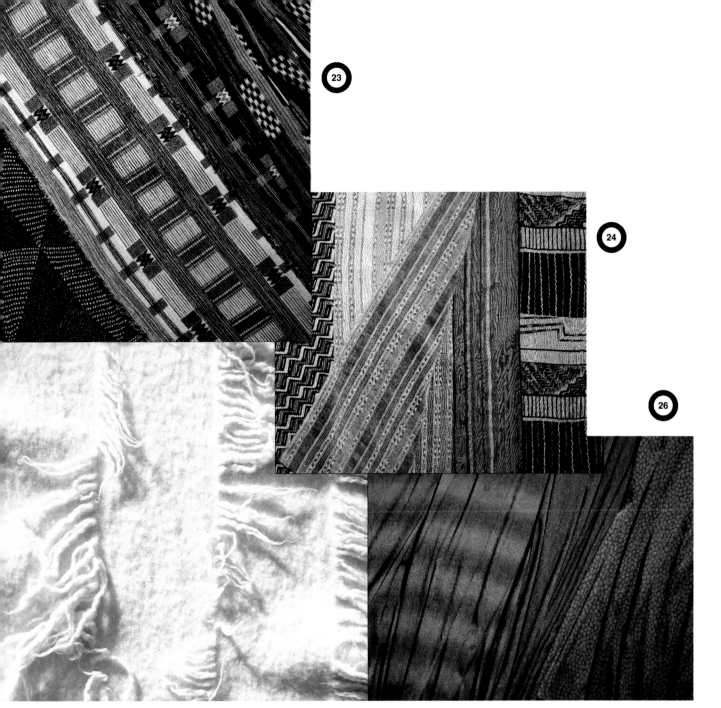

26 JUNICHI ARAI
Fabric
Cotton, polyester
Limited batch production
Manufacturer: Arai Creations System,
Japan (1987/8)

24 JUNICHI ARAI
Fabric
Cotton, hemp
A pattern inspired by Micronesian
designs, in cotton thread coated with
hemp fibres. Limited batch production
Manufacturer: Arai Creations System,
Japan (1987/8)

25 JUNICHI ARAI
Fabric
Wool
Limited batch production
Manufacturer: Arai Creations System,
Japan (1987/8)

27 **VERNER PANTON**
Furnishing fabric, *Diamond Collection*
Plain fabric, *Mira Plaza*;
printed fabric, *Mira-Rubin*
100% cotton chintz
W140 cm (55 in)
Manufacturer: Mira-X,
Switzerland (1984/5)

28 **H-DESIGN**
Furnishing fabric,
Mira-Terrazzo 20,
Mira-Terrazzo 40
Former 59% Polyester, 41%
cotton; latter 100% cotton
W130 cm (51 in)
Manufacturer: Mira-X,
Switzerland (1984/5)

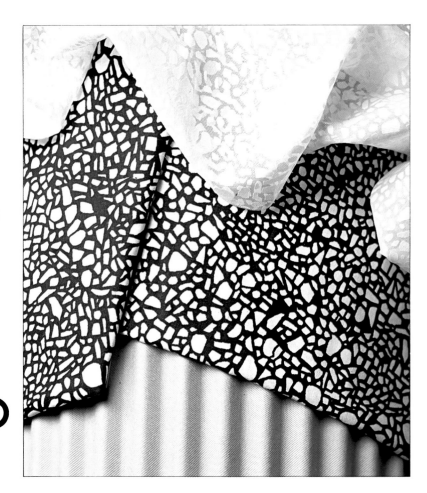

30 TOSO & MASSARI
Furnishing fabric, *Selene*
Part of the *Mosaico Collection*
Manufacturer: L Marcato,
Italy (1984/5)

29

29 H-DESIGN
Furnishing fabric,
Mira-Terrazzo 10,
Mira-Terrazzo 30
Former of 100% cotton; latter 59%
polyester, 41% cotton
W130 cm (51 in)
Manufacturer: Mira-X,
Switzerland (1984/5)

Camouflage. *A striking micro-trend
of the 1980s can be seen in those
fabrics which sought not to look like
fabrics at all. There were piece
goods of counterfeit marble, stucco
and wood. The patterns shown here
are characteristic examples. Most
were produced by the Swiss firm
Mira-X, which includes among its
designers such famous
architectural designers as Verner
Panton and Trix and Robert
Haussmann. Fabrics such as these
conceal themselves behind a false
identity, conveying the impression
of wall or floor mosaics, ice-cream
parlour floors from the 1950s, or
rough plaster stained with water.
When used to cover sofas, they can
have a somewhat disturbing effect.*

Computer folklore. *Of all the members of the Memphis group, Nathalie du Pasquier and George Sowden are probably the two who have been most intensely involved in the decorative aspect of design. Above all, the designs by Nathalie du Pasquier exude an unbridled delight in the variegated world of colours, signs and symbols. Her carpets for the firm of Palmisano in the northern Italian province of Como reveal how receptive she is to cultural influences from around the world, influences which she reworks through a process of association. For Nathalie du Pasquier is not interested in recreating an authentic ethnological design but in producing, on her computer screen, a synthetic global folklore every bit as powerful as the models she adopts. That she has also stored graffiti, comics, children's book illustrations and the images of Art Deco in the visual encyclopaedia of her imagination will be clear from*

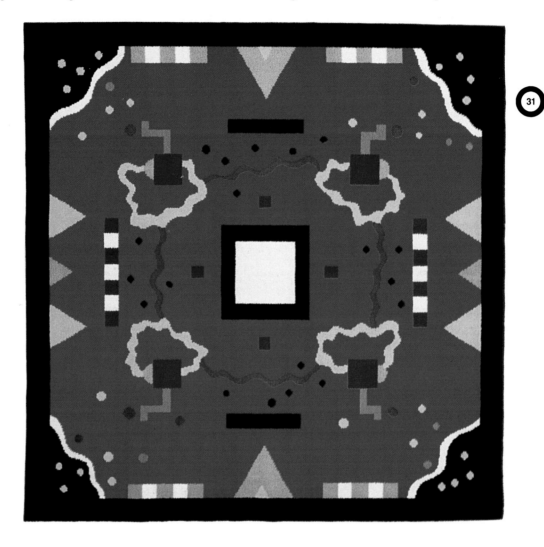

(31)

174

★

TEXTILES

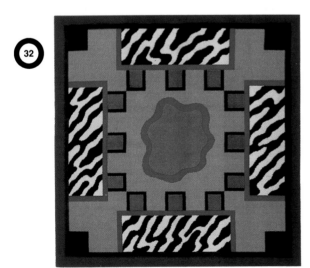

(32)

(33)

32 NATHALIE DU PASQUIER
Carpet, *Equador*
Hand-made carpet with 40,000 Ghiordes pure wool knots per square metre, on a cotton weft and with hemp warp W200 cm (78¾ in) L200 cm (78¾ in)

Manufacturer: Palmisano Edizioni Tessili, Italy (1986/7)

the following pages. Experienced observers will also sense a sweetly psychedelic perfume here, wafting across the years from Haight Ashbury in San Francisco and London's Notting Hill Gate to Memphis's home in Milan.

31 GEORGE SOWDEN
Carpet, _India_
Wool
L200 cm (78¾ in) W200 cm (78¾ in)
Manufacturer: Palmisano Edizioni Tessili,
Italy (1986/7)

33 NATHALIE DU PASQUIER
Carpet, _Messico_
Hand-made carpet with 40,000 Ghiordes knots per square metre, on a cotton weft and with hemp warp. The yarn used for the knots is long-fibre New Zealand wool, combed, spun and dyed in Italy.
W200 cm (78¾ in) L100, 200, 300 or 400 cm (39⅜, 78¾, 118 or 157½ in)
Manufacturer: Palmisano Edizioni Tessili,
Italy (1986/7)

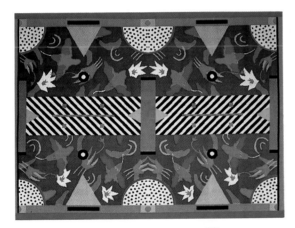

35 GEORGE SOWDEN
Carpet, _Palm Spring_
Wool
L300 cm (118 in) W200 cm (78¾ in)
Manufacturer: Palmisano Edizioni Tessili,
Italy (1986/7)

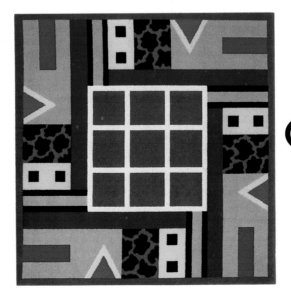

34 NATHALIE DU PASQUIER
Carpet, _Riviera Grande_
Hand-made carpet with 40,000 Ghiordes knots per square metre, on a cotton weft and with hemp warp. The yarn used for the knots is long-fibre New Zealand wool, combed, spun and dyed in Italy.
W250 cm (98½ in) L350 cm (137¾ in)
Manufacturer: Palmisano Edizioni Tessili,
Italy (1986/7)

36 NATHALIE DU PASQUIER
Carpet, _America_
Hand-made carpet with 40,000 Ghiordes knots per square metre, on a cotton weft and with hemp warp. The yarn used for the knots is long-fibre New Zealand wool, combed, spun and dyed in Italy.
W200 cm (78¾ in) L200 cm (78¾ in)
Manufacturer: Palmisano Edizioni Tessili,
Italy (1986/7)

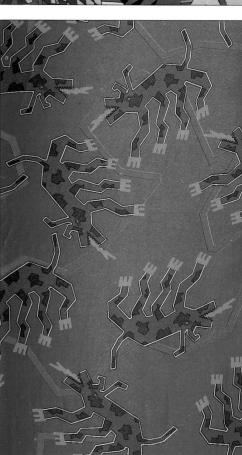

37 **NATHALIE DU PASQUIER**
Fabric
Brightly-patterned cotton – colourful
motifs on a white background
Manufacturer: Esprit, USA (1985/6)

38 **NATHALIE DU PASQUIER**
Fabric
Velvet patterned with flowers
and birds in reds, pink and mauves
Manufacturer: Harriet Selling,
Italy (1985/6)

39 **NATHALIE DU PASQUIER**
Fabric
Brightly-patterned polyester
Manufacturer: Esprit, USA (1985/6)

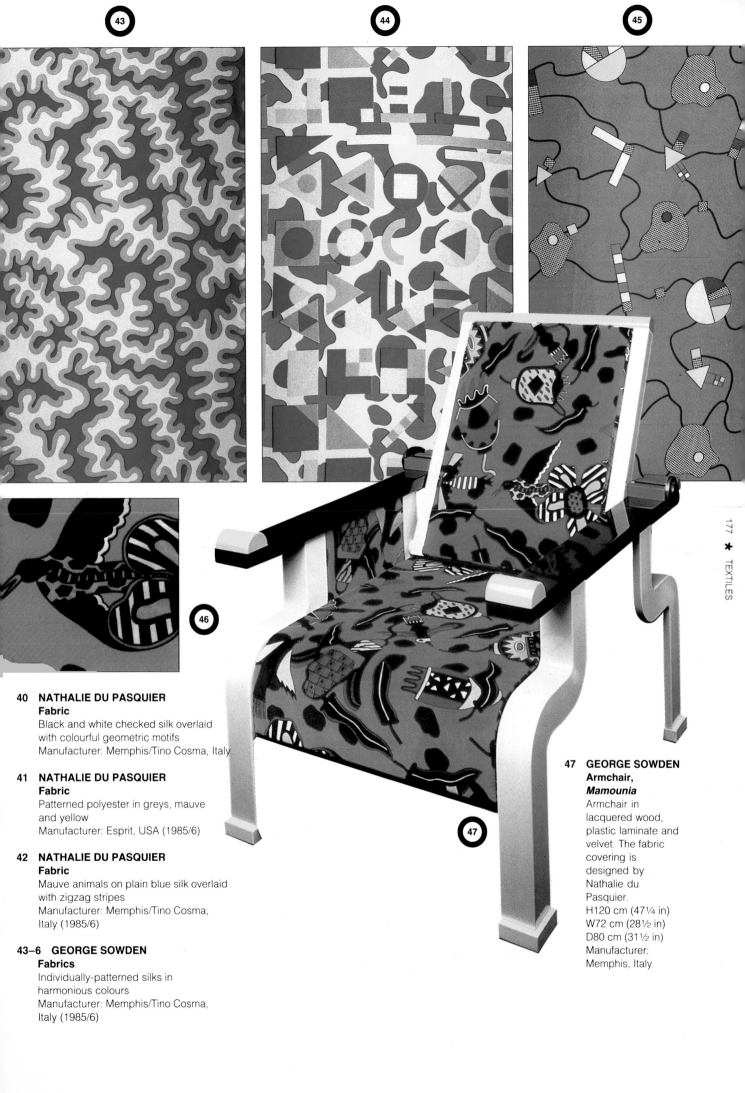

43

44

45

46

47

40 NATHALIE DU PASQUIER
Fabric
Black and white checked silk overlaid
with colourful geometric motifs
Manufacturer: Memphis/Tino Cosma, Italy

41 NATHALIE DU PASQUIER
Fabric
Patterned polyester in greys, mauve
and yellow
Manufacturer: Esprit, USA (1985/6)

42 NATHALIE DU PASQUIER
Fabric
Mauve animals on plain blue silk overlaid
with zigzag stripes
Manufacturer: Memphis/Tino Cosma,
Italy (1985/6)

43–6 GEORGE SOWDEN
Fabrics
Individually-patterned silks in
harmonious colours
Manufacturer: Memphis/Tino Cosma,
Italy (1985/6)

47 GEORGE SOWDEN
Armchair,
Mamounia
Armchair in
lacquered wood,
plastic laminate and
velvet. The fabric
covering is
designed by
Nathalie du
Pasquier.
H120 cm (47¼ in)
W72 cm (28½ in)
D80 cm (31½ in)
Manufacturer:
Memphis, Italy

48 FUJIWO ISHIMOTO
Fabric, *Lainehtiva*
Printed cotton
W145 cm (57 in)
Repeat 109 cm (43 in)
Manufacturer: Marimekko,
Finland (1988/9)

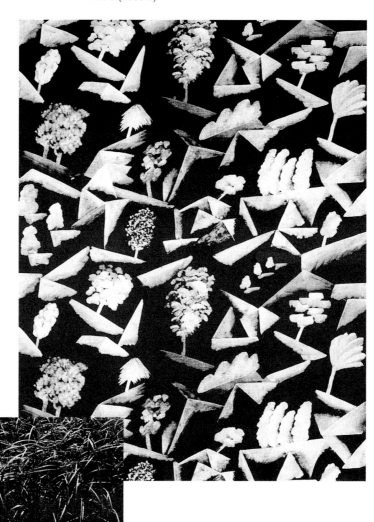

Museum of collective memories.
*Pictures form the only language that
is understood in every corner of the
world. And there are special
pictures to which people always
react in exactly the same way
despite the cultural differences, be
they from Korea, Kenya or Canada.
Foremost among these pictures are
representations of nature – plants,
animals, mountains, water and
clouds – which may be collective
memories of 'Paradise', expressing*

49 FUJIWO ISHIMOTO
Fabric, *Atlas*
52% linen, 48% printed cotton
W145 cm (57 in) Repeat 96 cm (37¾ in)
Manufacturer: Marimekko,
Finland (1988/9)

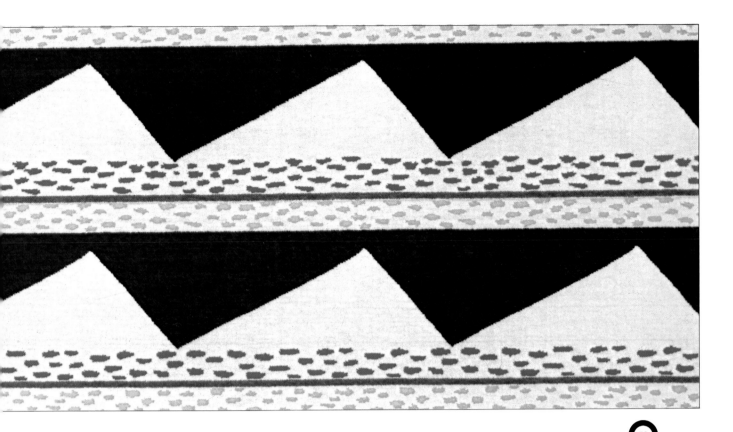

50 **MARC VAN HOE**
Furnishing fabric, *Etnic*
Polyacryl-PC W140 cm (55 in)
Manufacturer: Ter Molst International,
Belgium (1984/5)

51 **FUJIWO ISHIMOTO**
Fabric, *Taival* **(left),** *Karhusaari* **(right)**
100% cotton
W145 cm (58 in)
Manufacturer: Marimekko,
Finland (1984/5)

a longing for a mythical land of
innocence and beauty. Only in this
way can one understand how a
Japanese designer working in
Finland can design materials
inspired by Indonesian culture and
how these same materials can find
a ready market throughout the
whole of Europe; or that motifs from
Soweto can turn up in the Belgian
town of Oostrozebeke. It is a small
but by no means an unimportant
step on the way to global solidarity.

52 **FUJIWO ISHIMOTO**
Fabric, *Taival*
100% cotton
W145 cm (58 in)
Manufacturer: Marimekko,
Finland (1984/5)

Pictures from an exhibition.

Increasingly, printed fabrics are reprints from artistic movements from periods earlier than our own. Pop Art, Op Art, Cubism, Expressionism, art informel, Suprematism – there is scarcely a twentieth-century style that has not found its way out of museums and galleries and into our living rooms, where it has given furniture and curtains the character of connoisseurship. Management experts would describe this as image transfer, while the writers of feature articles would tend to call it cultural sampling. But the principal aspect is altogether more prosaic: textile designs such as these can give the buyer a sense of security. After all, you can't go far wrong with a Vasarély or a Braque . . .?

55 VERNER PANTON
Fabric, *Cubus Collection*
100% cotton
A printed furnishing fabric based on a square grid with a three-dimensional appearance
Manufacturer: Mira-X, Switzerland (1987/8)

56 INDEPENDENT DESIGNERS FEDERATION CRESSIDA BELL
Fabric
Furnishing fabric and two cushions made of cotton sateen
Manufacturer: Cressida Bell, UK (1986/7)

53 INDEPENDENT DESIGNERS FEDERATION JANE SPURWAY
Wall hanging, *Painting on Silk*
Wool delaine
W137.2 cm (54 in) L274.3 cm (108 in)
Manufacturer: Jane Spurway, UK (1986/7)

54 INDEPENDENT DESIGNERS FEDERATION CHRISSIE SGUBBI
Rug, *Ribbons*
100% wool
One-off
Maker: Tai-Ping, UK (1986/7)

53

54

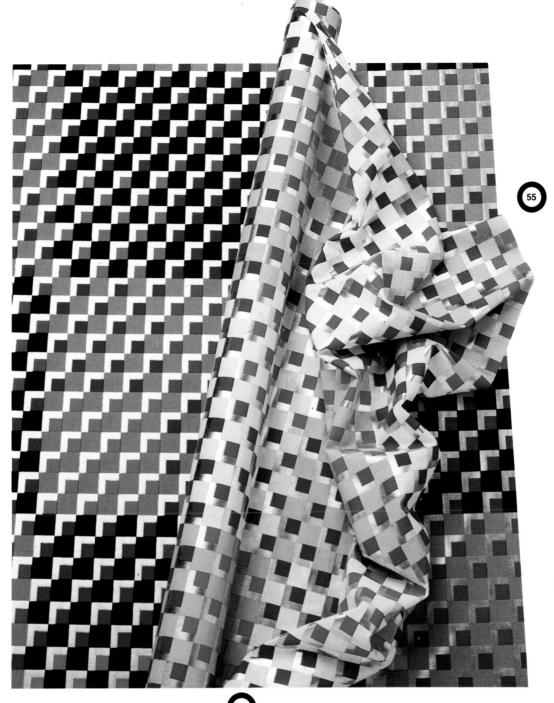

55

56

**57 JASON POLLEN &
LARSEN DESIGN**
Fabric, *Ravenna*
100% cotton
W127 cm (50 in)
Manufacturer: Jack Lenor
Larsen, USA (1986/7)

58 FUJIWO ISHIMOTO
Fabric
Pink and red squared design
based on crayon sketches
Manufacturer: Marimekko,
Finland (1985/6)

59 LEAH NELSON
Rug, *Conception*
Inlaid carpet, paint, nylon, polyester
An area rug or wall-hanging inspired by
Zuni Indian symbols. Limited batch
production.
W109cm (43 in), L223 cm (93 in)
Manufacturer: Leah Nelson, USA

60-61 UGO NESPOLO
Rug, *Ottocentoquaranta*
Wool, cotton, hemp
Hand-knotted carpet made with 40,000
Ghiordes knots per square metre. Cotton
weft and hemp warp. Limited batch
production
W135 cm, 175 cm, 200 cm or 250 cm
(53¼ in, 69⅞ in, 78¾ in or 98 in)
L200 cm, 250 cm, 300 cm or 375 cm
(78¾ in, 98 in, 118 in or 147½ in)
Manufacturer: Palmisano Edizioni
Tessili, Italy (1987/8)

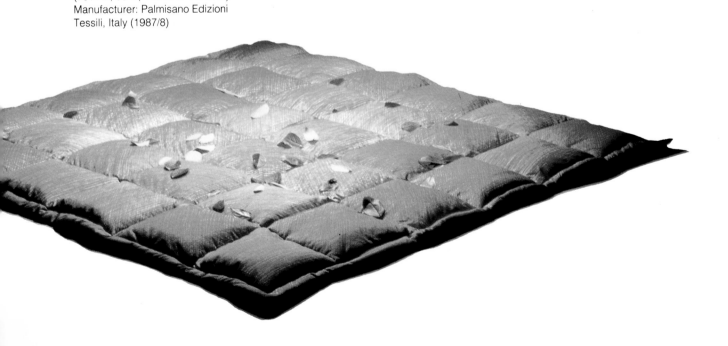

62

63

**64 INDEPENDENT
DESIGNERS FEDERATION
SALLY ANN HEARTSHORNE**
Fabric, *Summer Fruits*
Cotton hand-painted with metallic paints
W137 cm (54 in)
Manufacturer: Sally Anne Heartshorne,
UK (1986/7)

**65 INDEPENDENT
DESIGNERS FEDERATION
LYNNE HUGILL**
Collage
Examples of designs for surfaces – textiles,
ceramics, stationery, household linens, etc
Manufacturer: Lynne Hugill, UK (1986/7)

66 YOSHIKI HISHINUMA
Fabric, *Horse*
95% rayon plus 5% silk
Manufacturer: Hishinuma Institute,
Japan (1986/7)

67 YOSHIKI HISHINUMA
Fabric, *Toros*
80% nylon plus 20% polyurethane
Manufacturer: Hishinuma
Institute, Japan (1986/7)

68 YOSHIKI HISHINUMA
Fabric, *Skeleton*
Polyester
Manufacturer: Hishinuma
Institute, Japan (1986/7)

62 PAUL BURGESS
Fabric, *Man-Flag*
Wool
Monoprint/silk-screened
furnishing fabric using acid
dye on wool delaine
One-off
W137 cm (50 in)
L300 cm (118 in)
Manufacturer: Paul Burgess,
UK (1987/8)

63 YOSHIKI HISHINUMA
Fabric, *Dance*
Polyester
Limited batch production
Manufacturer: Hishinuma Associates,
Japan (1987/8)

69 YOSHIKI HISHINUMA
Fabric, *Sorceress*
95% rayon plus 5% silk
Manufacturer: Hishinuma
Institute, Japan (1986/7)

Diseño d'España. *At the very time that Spain was in the process of joining the European Community, Spanish design was undergoing a meteoric rise in popularity: from catatonia to Catalonia. Virtually everything of any significance in the field of Spanish design comes from Catalonia or, to be more exact, from Barcelona, the Iberian Milan. As in Italy, all the country's important designers (with the one exception of Javier Mariscal) are architects by profession, and yet they are far more deserving than their colleagues in other parts of the world when it comes to their claim to have designed a universal range of things from spoons to entire cities. They are also very active in the field of interior design and have peppered Barcelona with*

spectacular discothèques, boutiques and restaurants. As advocates of comprehensive interior design they also accord an important role to textiles and specifically to carpets. Their delight in experimentation is totally uninhibited and extends from coolly calculated alienation in the case of Oscar Tusquets Blanca to the violent gestural language of neo-Expressionist art in that of José Luis Ramón-Solans, whose carpets are manufactured solely and exclusively by a company in Madrid. All the country's other leading manufacturers, including B. d. Ediciones de diseno and Nani Marquina, are in Barcelona. Were he alive today, Antoni Gaudí would not be lonely.

71 JOSE LUIS RAMÓN-SOLANS
Carpet, *Magic carpet*
Hand-made wool carpet using Spanish knot
L200 cm (78¾ in) W300 cm (118⅛ in)
Manufacturer: Alfombras Ariás Tronco,
Spain (1986/7)

(71)

72 OSCAR TUSQUETS BLANCA
Rug, *Luna*
Wool
Circular carpet, handmade in Turkish
knots, representing the moon. Limited
batch production
Di120 cm (47¼ in)
Manufacturer: B.d. Ediciones de diseño,
Spain (1987/8)

(72)

70 JOSE LUIS RAMÓN-SOLANS
Carpet
Hand-made wool carpet using Spanish knot
L230 cm (90½ in) W230 cm (90½ in)
Manufacturer: Alfombras Ariás Tronco,
Spain (1986/7)

73 MARCELLO MORANDINI
Rug, *Progetto 22*
Wool
L240 cm (94½ in) W240 cm (94½ in)
Manufacturer: Teppichfabrik Melchnau,
Switzerland (1988/9)

Unlimited possibilities in limited editions. *The series of carpets* Progetto *by the Italian designer Marcello Morandini encapsulates a number of important trends in modern carpet design. Controlled as they are by punch cards, the looms at the avant-garde Swiss firm of Melchnau allow an almost limitless number of colours and forms to be used. Morandini takes advantage of this to manufacture carpets which include other shapes and sizes apart from the classic rectangular form. (Triangles, circles and polygons are not in the least unusual.) As so often, the man from Varese plays with the possibilities that are offered by optical illusions to produce* trompe-l'oeil *effects in black and white which, though only two-dimensional, appear to be three-dimensional thanks to the metaphysics of geometry. The new dimensions, however, are immediately restricted, since each motif in this limited edition exists in only thirty-three copies. Many carpet manufacturers have recently begun to use the well-tried mechanism of the limited edition to ensure that exclusivity is a built-in part of their product.*

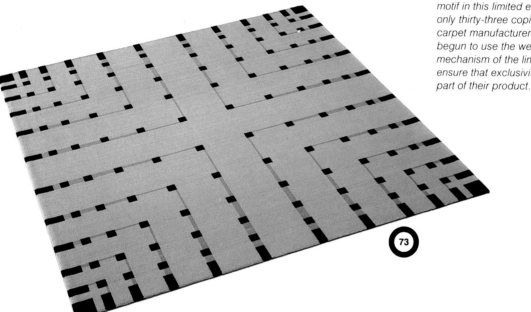

73

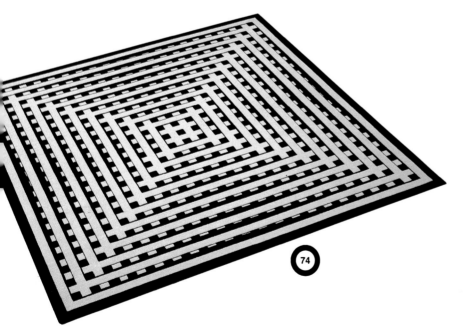

74

74 MARCELLO MORANDINI
Rug, *Progetto 21*
Wool
L240 cm (94½ in) W240 cm (94½ in)
Manufacturer: Teppichfabrik Melchnau,
Switzerland (1988/9)

76

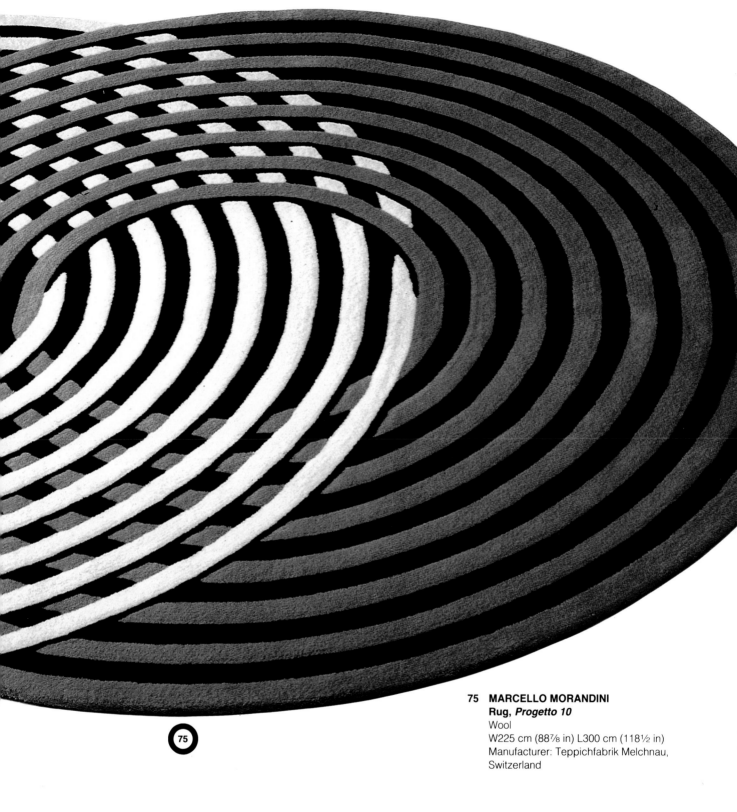

75 **MARCELLO MORANDINI**
Rug, *Progetto 10*
Wool
W225 cm (88⅞ in) L300 cm (118½ in)
Manufacturer: Teppichfabrik Melchnau,
Switzerland

76 **MARCELLO MORANDINI**
Rug, *Progetto 6*
Wool
L300 cm (118½ in) W300 cm (118½ in)
Manufacturer: Teppichfabrik Melchnau,
Switzerland (1988/9)

77 MATTEO THUN
Carpet, from the *Dialog* collection
Polyamide
W400 cm (157½ in) Repeat W20.5 cm
(8 in), L19 cm (7½ in)
Manufacturer: Vorwerk, West
Germany (1988/9)

78 MICHAEL GRAVES
Carpets, from the
***Dialog* collection**
Polyamide
W400 cm (157½ in)
Repeat W50 cm (19⅝ in),
L92.5 cm (36¼ in)
Manufacturer: Vorwerk, West
Germany (1988/9)

Parquet for the masses. *In days gone by, the floor was the basis of any interior design, in the truest sense of the word. Costly parquet or stone floors, laid out in ingenious patterns, gave rooms such a sense of perspective and beauty that they created their effect without the need for any other furnishing. But this was an art which fell into oblivion, being ousted by endless wastes of monochromatic carpets which* come to life only when other furnishings are added. The German firm of Vorwerk, however, decided to invest the humble carpet with a new sense of dignity and to turn uninteresting piece-goods into one of the high points of modern interior design. Alessi had already shown the way. What was important was to win over famous designers who, to quote Vorwerk's managing director Peter Littmann, 'would lend their

authority to the implementation of new and innovative ideas'. The plan succeeded. Vorwerk was able to obtain the services not only of design stars such as Norman Foster, Michael Graves, Arata Isozaki, Matteo Thun and Oswald Mathias Ungers, but also famous artists such as Sam Francis, David Hockney, Roy Lichtenstein and Sol LeWitt. But – and it is this that

deserves the highest praise – Vorwerk did not adopt the elitist approach of bringing out a limited edition: theirs was the democratic course, involving mass production. Everyone can buy these images for his or her own floor, images in which art and industrial design come together in an ideal synthesis. Well done!

79 ARATA ISOZAKI
Carpets, from the *Dialog*
collection
Polyamide
W400 cm (157½ in) Repeat W50 cm
(19⅝ in), L31.5 cm (12⅜ in)
Manufacturer: Vorwerk, West
Germany (1988/9)

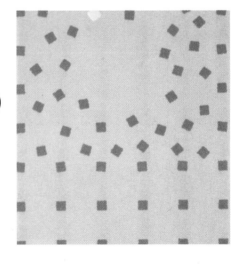

80 HANS-ULLRICH BITSCH
Carpet, from the *Dialog*
collection
Polyamide
W400 cm (157½ in) Repeat W100 cm
(39½ in), L92.5 cm (36¼ in)
Manufacturer: Vorwerk, West
Germany (1988/9)

81 DAVID HOCKNEY
Carpets, from the *Dialog*
collection
Polyamide
W400 cm (157½ in) Repeat W100 cm
(39½ in), L92.5 cm (36¼ in)
Manufacturer: Vorwerk, West
Germany (1988/9)

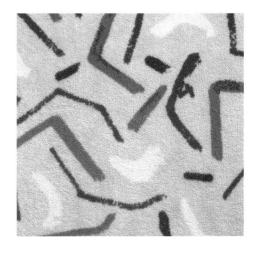

83 ROY LICHTENSTEIN
Carpet, from the *Dialog*
collection
Polyamide
W400 cm (157½ in)
Manufacturer: Vorwerk, West
Germany (1988/9)

82 SAM FRANCIS
Carpet, from the *Dialog*
collection
Polyamide
W400 cm (157½ in) Repeat W200 cm
(78¾ in), L92.5 cm (36¼ in)
Manufacturer: Vorwerk, West
Germany (1988/9)

83

There is a sense in which this is the most important chapter in this book, for products determine our lives in a way that is not the case with furniture or lamps. How much influence does Kita's *Wink* chair, or an Alessi kettle, exert in comparison to that of a Walkman or an Apple MacIntosh? Products have the advantage over all the other objects in this book in that, (a) they are produced in

5 ✱ PRODUCTS

enormous numbers and, being impossible to avoid, they leave their mark on all our everyday lives, and (b) they deal with new products and new technologies and thereby help to shape the way that the future will look. Next to products, furniture design – to quote the somewhat unsubtle expression of a German design magazine – is an 'overploughed field'.

Product design in the 1980s was therefore extraordinarily eventful, yet virtually everything that happened can be summarized in two basic, interlinked and opposing tendencies which, for the sake of simplicity, may be referred to as New Freedoms and New Constraints. The new sense of freedom came from microchips, printed circuits and new materials. The technology which had hitherto been the very heart of the product became so small, so cheap, so self-evidently reliable, and hence so boring, that in the majority of cases it came to play no more than a secondary role. Product design, previously strictly functional in its orientation, has been liberated from material constraints, form is no longer tied to function, and designers have learned to exploit this freedom with a pleasure which, held in check for so long, has sometimes erupted with altogether anarchical force. 'Snoopy' telephones, concrete record-players, paper watches – nothing is impossible. What was three-dimensional now becomes two-dimensional, shrinking to cardboard thinness, macro turns into micro, what was static now becomes mobile. But this play with form, with influences from the world of fashion, with ironical quotations that extend to include the silliest kitsch emanates not only from the designers, but is also a result of consumer expectations. Technology has now become so commonplace it no longer occupies a special place on the pedestal of science: it has lost its magic and authority. It is something we take for granted and are grateful therefore if it does not give itself airs and play the professor but simply proves a staunch companion. This, however, does not entitle us to speak of post-functionalism with contempt as many writers do, since all these curious and brightly coloured products function quite splendidly in their own way. Perhaps the term 'post-rationalism' sums up the phenomenon better.

1 ETTORE SOTTSASS
Telephone, *Enorme*
With 10-number memory,
redial facility
Plastic
H19 cm (7½ in) W4.5 cm (2 in)
D5.5 cm (2¼ in)
Manufacturer: Enorme, Italy (1988)

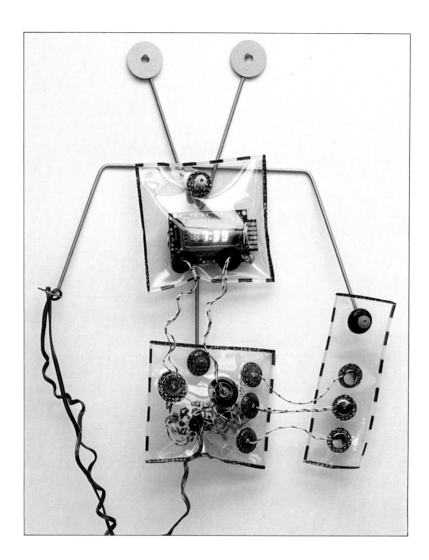

2 DANIEL WEIL
Radio fm/am, *Andante*
Part of the Anthologie Quartett Collection
H30 cm (11 in) L30 cm (11 in) D4 cm (1½ in)
Manufacturer: Quartett, West Germany (1984/5)

As so often, these new freedoms are matched with new constraints, all of which are commercial in nature. Design is no longer the formal exercise that it once was. During the 1980s it established itself as a marketing instrument, and, indeed, as one of the most important. Producers saw it as the ideal means not only of making themselves appear more attractive and more distinctive in markets already saturated with interchangeable products and overrun by cut-price competitors, but of opening up new niches in those markets. From a purely technical point of view, there is no doubt that this is a mere cosmetic exercise, offering, as it were, new brands of make-up in place of old products. Yet, this is too rational an assessment, for a product which used to be grey but is now manufactured in pink is in fact felt by the buyer to be something new. More and more of today's designs are meant to create what Marx would have called a 'surplus value', an emotional value that transcends the product's objective qualities. In a word, the trend has been to move away from product design to what may be termed 'experience design': materiality has given ground to immateriality. As such, the trend is in keeping with the old cosmetics adage: we are not selling lipstick, we are selling beauty.

Design, to quote Malcolm Forbes, has become a 'capitalist tool'. In doing so, it has placed itself under the pressure to be successful. Business is now more important than aesthetics. Famous design studios and design-orientated businesses are bought up by larger concerns that are not always very sensitive and which want to see their profit margins rise. Marketing plans must be realized. Compromises and concessions dilute what used to be good design. The design revolution devours its children or, at the very least, it compromises them. For, if product design becomes no more than a sales instrument, this is bound to mean that the designer not only loses his independence, he even changes sides. Traditionally, the designer, if he took sides at all, tended to side with the buyer and user; his aim was to make the product clear, straightforward and easy to use (in a word, to make it functional). But far less thought is given now to the advantages to the user than to the conditions governing marketing strategies. Instead of the object's utility, it is now its retail success that dominates our thinking. Or, to put it more succinctly: commercial design such as this is no longer primarily the partner of the consumer but the partner of the producer. This is a fundamental reversal of values and one whose importance cannot be underestimated. There are, however, encouraging signs that a change may be on the way. Many design studios have recognized that their integrity and independence are under threat and in consequences are setting up design initiatives in the form of project studies which may allow them to stop merely reacting to what already exists and to abandon the role of the slave and revert to that of the master.

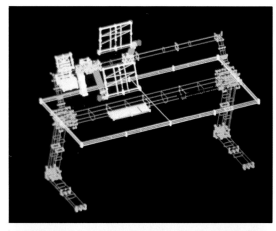

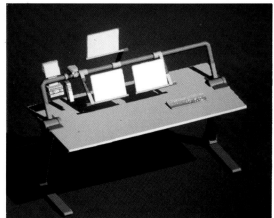

3 FROGDESIGN
Office system based on a furniture
arrangement designed for K&N, with a
folded-steel structure, adjustable
mechanism and optional electronic extra (1986/7)

4

**4 LISA KROHN WITH
TUCKER VIEMEISTER/
SMART DESIGN
Telephone and answering
machine, *Phonebook***
Plastic
A machine that combines the functions
of both a telephone and a telephone
answering machine. The prototype,
produced by Neste, Finland, won first
prize at the international 'Forma
Finlandia' plastic design competition
H5 cm (2 in) W20 cm (7⅞ in)
L30 cm (11⅞ in)
Manufacturer: Smart Design,
USA (1987/8)

The shape of things to come.
*Some of the world's most important
buildings have never been built, yet
this has not prevented the utopian
designs of Boullée, Ledoux,
Sant'Elia, Tatlin, El Lissitzky,
Tchernikov, Soleri, Fuller, Cook,
Herron and Hadid from leaving a
lasting mark on architectural history.
The same phenomenon can now be
seen in the area of design, where
the pragmatism that was practised
for decades is being replaced by
attempts to develop more visionary
concepts. Or, to put it another way,
the conviction that form follows
function has now been superseded
by the belief that function follows
form. This is a welcome*

*development. Design needs visions
and there were far too few of these
in the past. Yet it is, of course, a
commercial investment as well. The
first person to meet the challenges
of the future and design the
appropriate products may not
inherit tomorrow's world, but he will
at least control tomorrow's markets.
As a result, large concerns
throughout Japan and Europe have
set up project studies which,
although the projects are never
realized, make a decisive
contribution to the shape of things
to come. And if no clients present
themselves, there are enough
design firms such as Frogdesign in
Germany, Moggridge Associates in
Great Britain, and Design Logic and
Smart Design in the USA to take the
future into their own hands.*

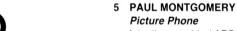

5 PAUL MONTGOMERY
Picture Phone
Injection-moulded ABS, rubber
Prototype of a telephone that
transmits a digital image using fibre-
optic technology and functions as a
conventional telephone when the lens
cover is down. Calls can be made using
the touch-screen key pad or the
electronic directory
H30.5 cm (12 in) W15 cm (6 in)
D15 cm (6 in)
Manufacturer: Paul Montgomery,
USA (1987/8)

**6-10 DESIGN LOGIC/D M
GRESHAM, MARTIN THALER,
JAMES N LUDWIG**
Telephone answering machines
Semantic studies of digital
answering machines produced for
Sandor F Weisz of Dictaphone,
USA. The design in 6 is based
on the conventional flat model; that
in 7-8 is a Constructivist view of
the human face; and that in 9-10 is
based on the design of the US
mailbox (1987/8)

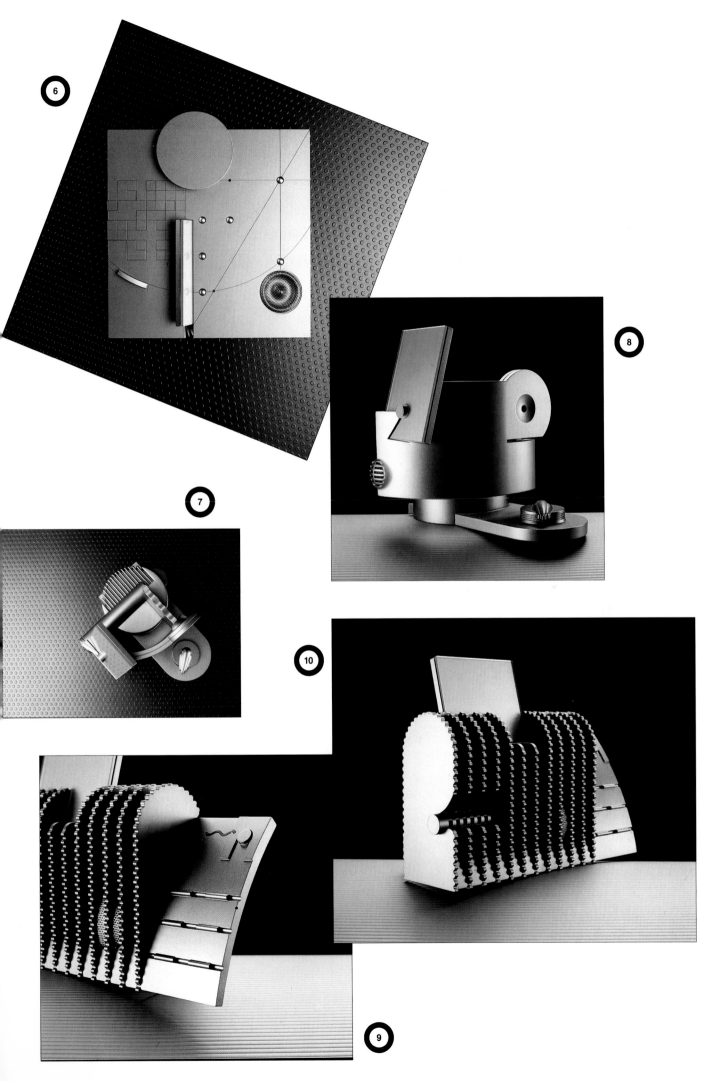

12 **HEINZ JUNGER**
TV, *Loewe Art 1*
Large flat-screen red TV in wooden case
H95.5 cm (37½ in) D46.5 cm (18 in)
W64.5 cm (25 in)
Manufacturer: Loewe Opta, West
Germany (1985/6)

11 **I·DE·A INSTITUTE DESIGN TEAM**
Television
Plastic
700-line horizontal resolution with a
12-hour on/off timer and a remote
control unit. The piece is designed to
house two video recorders and
to store video tapes
H107.9 cm (42¹⁄₁₆ in) W68.8 cm
(27¹⁄₁₆ in) D51 cm (20 in)
Manufacturer: Toshiba, Japan (1988/9)

12

11

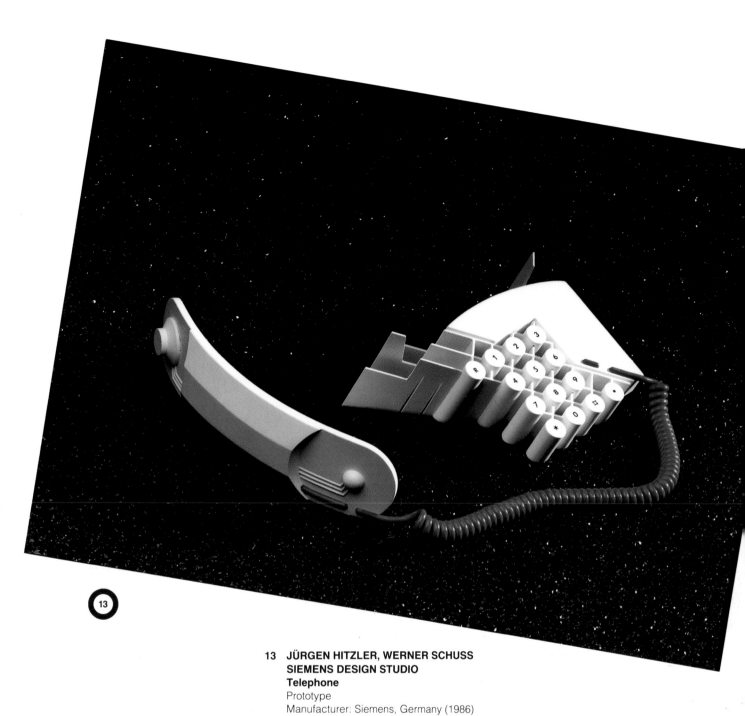

13

**13 JÜRGEN HITZLER, WERNER SCHUSS
SIEMENS DESIGN STUDIO
Telephone**
Prototype
Manufacturer: Siemens, Germany (1986)

The colour of pride. *For a
particular sort of person (especially
male), only one colour can be
considered as far as technological
products are concerned, and that is
black. On the one hand, black is
intimidatingly aggressive, while, on
the other, it suggests the victor's
noble reserve: it seems technocratic
and at the same time elegant, but
most of all it is sexy. For a Porsche,
no other colour can ever be really*
*seriously considered, and the same
is true of pocket calculators,
bosses' armchairs, cameras, hi-fi
equipment and television sets. Even
Toshiba and Loewe-Opta follow the
unwritten rules that govern this
black art. With their powerful
presence and coolly prestigious
aura of innovative technology, these
television sets are precisely what
the brilliant English design critic
Deyan Sudjic once described as an
'indoor BMW'. (This certainly makes
sense in the case of Loewe-Opta,*
*which is after all a subsidiary of
BMW.) In contrast to these, the
design for a telephone by Jürgen
Hitzler and Werner Schuß is bound
to strike the purist as rather too laid
back – which may explain the
reason why this, like so many other
brilliant ideas produced in the
Siemens Design Studio, will never in
fact be realized. It looks like a
space station circling the earth –
and that is too far away from Ulm.*

From utopia to Armageddon.
Product design is one of the last remaining refuges in which to indulge a positive vision of the future. Here the future is still exactly how we always imagined it would be in the past, clean, efficient, progressive and altogether rational. Beocenter 9000 still recalls this promised land of Utopia with its coolly erotic technology and feeling of omnipotence. But we have learned in the meantime to see the future as a sombre place of environmental destruction and possible nuclear threat. Ron Arad's hi-fi system reminds us just how thin is the ice on which we are currently skating. It is so successful because it is so disturbing. Does it not look like some archaeological find that survived the nuclear winter? But maybe I'm being too profound, maybe it's just a visual gag on which to play Da Doo Ron Ron.

14 RON ARAD
Hi-fi system
Hi-fi system in an outer covering of concrete. Includes speakers, amplifier and deck
Record player: H7.5 cm (3 in) W46 cm (18 in) D38 cm (15 in)
Speakers: H89 cm (35 in) W20 cm (8 in) D20 cm (8 in)
Pre-amp with power amp: H20 cm (8 in) W30.5 cm (12 in) D25 cm (10 in)
Manufacturer: One-Off, UK (1985/6)

14

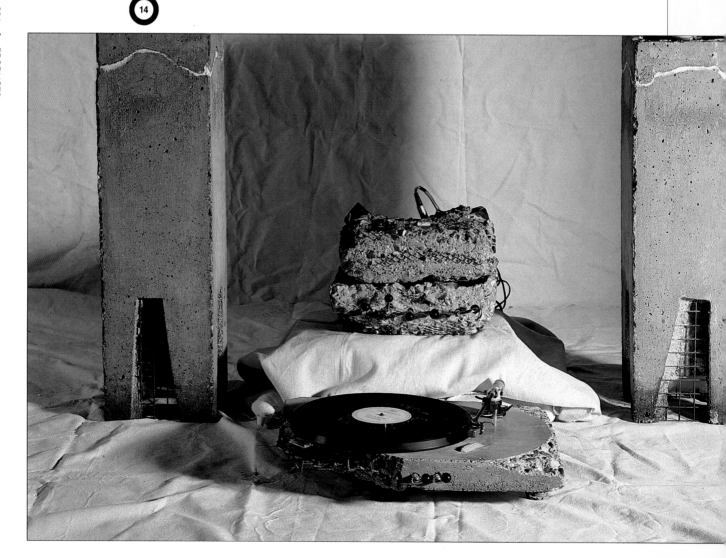

15

15 JACOB JENSEN/B & O DESIGN TEAM
Beocenter 9000
Glass, metal, plastic
A music system comprising FM/AM
radio, cassette tape recorder and
compact disc player
H11 cm (4⅜ in) W76 cm (30 in)
D34 cm (13⅜ in)
Manufacturer: Bang & Olufsen,
Denmark (1987/8)

Love Hertz. *We live in the age of total communication. Hertz and Watt, and bits and bytes determine our professional lives as much as they do our leisure time. Progress is rampant in this field. New and revolutionary products are constantly being evolved and marketed commercially, demanding a type of design that ensures that their novelty value is given due expression. This becomes increasingly hard to achieve, since every solution has already been attempted, from the ultra-high-tech look to the amplifier box of rusty steel. But let us stick here to three stylistic trends that typify the rest: first, the professional look of Sony monitors, which give the impression of having come straight from the studio; second, the jokey look as embodied by Joachim Stanitzek's tower, which looks as though caught in an aerobic pose; and third, a kind of New Age design that strives to play a mediatory role between man and technology without any love of ostentation and with no intimidatory mechanisms. This can all change very quickly. The Media Laboratory at MIT sets out from the premise that in twenty years' time a television set will have the capacity of a Cray computer. The consequences are scarcely imaginable. But perhaps we shall then prefer a neo-Baroque CD-player. Or a tiny portable box that will interface a Sensorama film directly into our brains. Will the electronic hermits of the future still have a taste for design or will these data-addicted junkies care in the least if design exists or not? Think about it.*

17   JOACHIM STANITZEK
Media component holder, *BG 1*
Lacquered steel and wood
The built-in loudspeakers are height-adjustable. Prototype
H110 cm (43¼ in) W49 cm (19¼ in)
L220 cm (86⅝ in)
Manufacturer: Designwerkstatt, West Germany (1988/9)

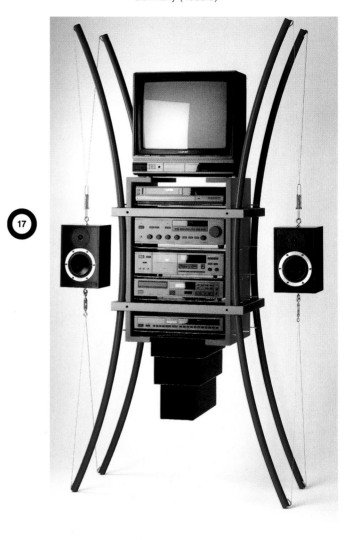

16   DESIGN CENTRAL
Personal electronic terminal
Plastic, glass
Prototype of an electronic terminal for
use in word-processing, data and office communication
H28 cm (11 in)
W42 cm (16½ in)
Manufacturer: Design Central, USA (1987/8)

18 SONY DESIGN TEAM
Colour monitor, *Profeel Pro*
Colour monitor available in two sizes
H50.8 cm or 40.9 cm (20 in or 16 in)
W65.3 cm or 51.6 cm (25¾ in or 20⅜ in)
D48.9 cm or 47.9 cm (19¼ in or 18⅞ in)
Manufacturer: Sony, Japan (1986/7)

**20 TIM BROWN FOR MOGGRIDGE
ASSOCIATES**
Facsimile machine, *Concept*
Acrylic, glass
The printer, containing the paper roll,
plugs in at the back of the processing
unit. To operate, the glass screen top
has touch-sensitive icon keys. Messages
can be drawn or written directly on the
screen for transmitting. Prototype
H12 cm (4¾ in) W40 cm (15¾ in)
L50 cm (19⅝ in)
Manufacturer: IDM, UK (1988/9)

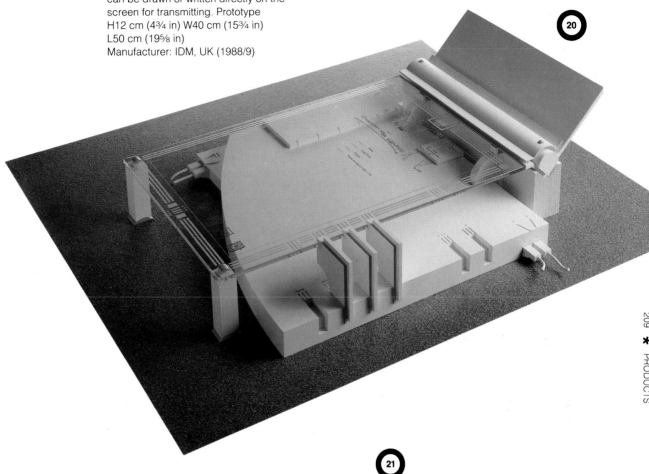

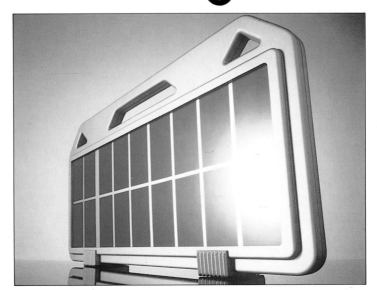

**19, 21 MOGGRIDGE
ASSOCIATES
HEDDA BEESE**
Solar lantern, *SL 48*
Moulded
polycarbonate, sheet
metal chassis
Portable solar lantern
which can be hung
up or placed on a
surface. It is robust
and requires almost
no maintenance as
well as being
environmentally
sealed and capable
of operating under
extremes of
temperature
H56 cm (22 in)
W33.7 cm (13¼ in)
D9 cm (3½ in)
Manufacturer: BP
Solar International,
UK (1986/7)

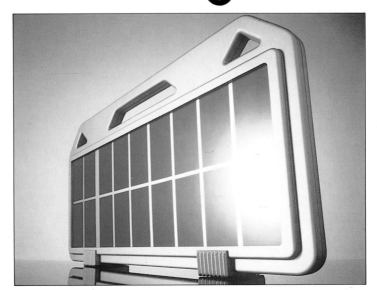

22

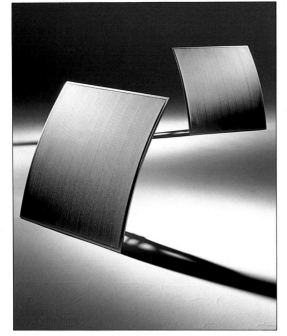

23

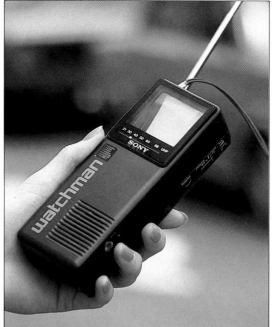

24

25

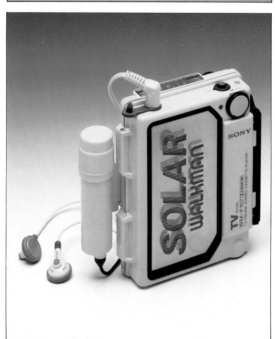

22 MASAYUKI KUROKAWA
Flat-wave speaker
GRP, metal
Speaker designed for use on the wall or
floor or with a stand. Maximum input 60W;
frequency characteristic 50 Hz-20 kHz/85 dB Wm
H60 cm (23⅝ in) W60 cm (23⅝ in)
D5 cm (2 in)
Manufacturer: Seidenko, Japan (1986/7)

23 SONY DESIGN TEAM
Portable TV, *Watchman*
Plastic
Hand-held TV with a 5 cm (2 in) screen,
magnifying viewfinder and external aerial socket
H64 cm (25⅛ in) L157 cm (61⅞ in)
D42 cm (16½ in)
Manufacturer: Sony, Japan (1986/7)

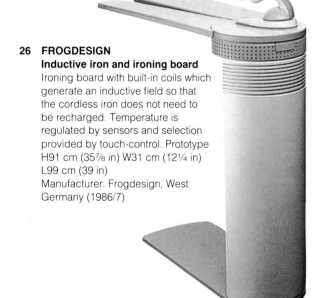

26

26 FROGDESIGN
Inductive iron and ironing board
Ironing board with built-in coils which
generate an inductive field so that
the cordless iron does not need to
be recharged. Temperature is
regulated by sensors and selection
provided by touch-control. Prototype
H91 cm (35⅞ in) W31 cm (12¼ in)
L99 cm (39 in)
Manufacturer: Frogdesign, West
Germany (1986/7)

24 MOGGRIDGE ASSOCIATES
NICHOLAS DORMON
Fuel-computer exhibition display
Acrylic
Free-standing exhibition display designed
for the Ford Motor Company to
demonstrate their car fuel computer. With
a sound system and interchangeable
graphics panel. One-off
H30.6 cm (12 in) W19 cm (7½ in)
L45 cm (17¾ in)
Manufacturer: IDM, UK (1986/7)

25 SONY DESIGN TEAM
Solar Walkman, *F107*
Walkman with built-in solar-power cell/
rechargeable battery, lightweight folding
sports headphones. Dolby B noise
reduction and belt clip
H11.4 cm (4½ in) W9.2 cm (3⅝ in)
D3.4 cm (1⅜ in)
Manufacturer: Sony, Japan (1986/7)

The bonus system. *If, in spite of all attempts to distinguish them on the part of their designers, products remain too much alike, extras must be added in order to point up their differences. Products then become ultra-flat, ultra-small, ultra-light, ultra-comfortable, cordless, plugless, fitted with solar batteries, and so on. The design process begins at a very early stage here and is closely bound up with the way the product develops. Ideas such as these often emanate from the design department in the form of project studies rather than from the development section. The design department is thus a kind of think tank for the enterprise. Who would have thought this possible twenty or thirty years ago?*

27 FROGDESIGN
Rotating TV set
The main feature of this TV set is a rotating screen which enables the viewer to watch comfortably from any sitting or lying position. Prototype designed for an exhibition of the Helen Hamlyn Foundation aimed at identifying the needs of the elderly in product design
H (base) 42 cm (16½ in)
W (base) 38 cm (15 in)
Di52 cm (20½ in)
Manufakturer: Frogdesign, West Germany (1986/7)

27

For kids of all ages. *Technical appliances which Daddy used to be able to use only after reading a 30-page manual, concentration writ large on his furrowed brow, are now used as a matter of course by the children of today. Children and adolescents are the group that marketing managers and designers consciously target, creating*

products in brightly coloured Kiddy Design, with the ulterior motive of making a conquest: the user will then be wedded to that particular make for life – 'my first Sony'! For those who are somewhat older there is then the Sports Walkman *in sunshine yellow, a model which is even shower-proof, so that the wearer does not need to break off 'Swinging in the rain'. The* QT *by contrast is a real beauty, a*

candy-coloured Miami Art Deco streamlined baby that goes round looking like the Beverly Hills version of a ghetto blaster. It looks cool, above all when you hold it in the crook of your arm and ride round with it on your Vespa scooter. Young people like it for its chic appeal, their parents buy it because it evokes nostalgic memories. Do you still remember, Susie, the summer of '65? As we have said elsewhere, this is not really product design, but experience design.

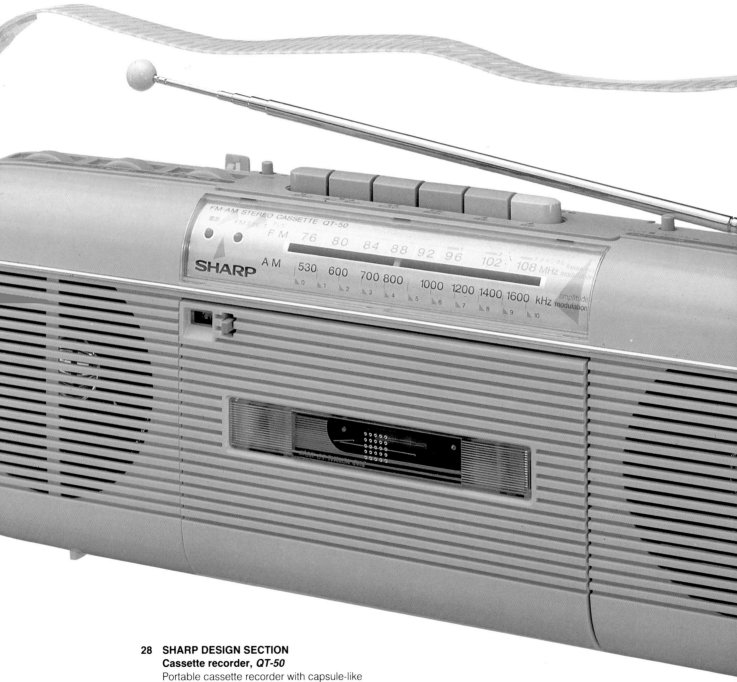

28   **SHARP DESIGN SECTION**
Cassette recorder, *QT-50*
Portable cassette recorder with capsule-like
design comes in a range of
ice-cream colours and has
stereo sound for both
radio and cassettes
H40.2 cm (15¾ in) W13.7 cm (5⅜ in)
D8.1 cm (3⅛ in)
Weight: 2 kg (4 lb 6½ oz) including batteries
Manufacturer: Sharp, Japan (1985/6)

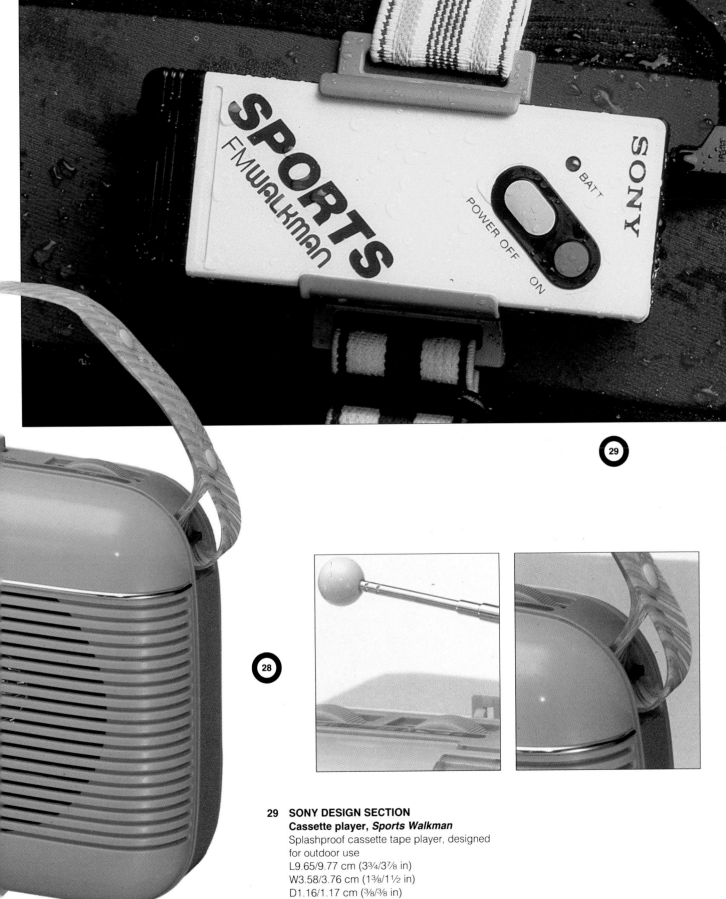

29 **SONY DESIGN SECTION**
Cassette player, *Sports Walkman*
Splashproof cassette tape player, designed
for outdoor use
L9.65/9.77 cm (3¾/3⅞ in)
W3.58/3.76 cm (1⅜/1½ in)
D1.16/1.17 cm (⅜/⅜ in)
Weight 290/320 g
(10¼/11¼ oz) including batteries
Manufacturer: Sony, Japan (1985/6)

A GIORGIO ARMANI
Telephone, *Notturno*
ABS
An electronic telephone with a 'visual
alert system', a luminous line that
produces a green beam to signal each
incoming call. Limited batch production
H4.9 cm (1⅞ in) W6.5 cm (2½ in)
L21.9 cm (8⅝ in)
Manufacturer: Italtel Telematica,
Italy (1987/8)

E SONY DESIGN TEAM
Personal radio
Plastic
One credit-card sized plastic card is
slotted into the clip for each radio station
Card: W5.4 cm (2¹/₁₆ L8.85 cm (3⁵/₁₀ in)
Manufacturer: Sony, Japan (1988/9)

 E

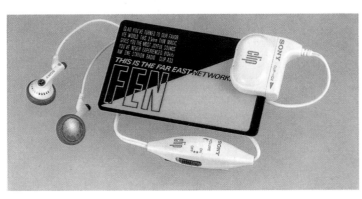

Form follows fun. *Where technology is taken for granted and therefore treated as irrelevant, design becomes the decisive factor in whether or not we buy the product. It must look great and be good fun. But in far too many cases it achieves these aims only by submitting to the dictates of some passing fashion. And when technological design is treated as something à la mode, why not commission a fashion designer to dress up a telephone in some new disguise? Giorgio Armani found it funny to give a 'phone the very form that had become so unpopular in product design, that of the black box. And he managed to silence it in the process: here is a phone that does not ring, it merely flashes. Toshiba, too, sets store by fashion. They have realized that since their* Walky *is worn in public, it must, like any other accessory, match the current fashions by Esprit, Benetton, Boss and Marc O'Polo. Even Sony's* Personal Radio *makes sense when seen in this light. At first sight, of course, it seems unnecessarily complicated to mess around with plastic cards, and yet it looks tremendously important,* quite apart from the fact that the choice of cheque card reveals that the listener is really with it.

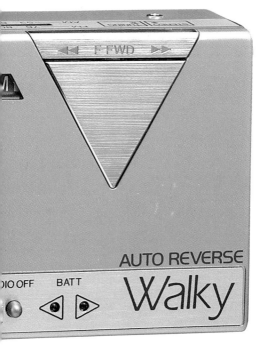

 D

B-D TOSHIBA DESIGN DEPT
Walky Headphone Stereo Cassette Player
Slim-line cassette and radio player
available in a variety of finishes
L11.85/11.85/11.6/11.6/10.35/12.4 cm
(4⅝/4⅝/4½/4½/4⅛/4⅞ in)
W7.8/8.35/8.35/8.5/8.7/8.8 cm
(3⅛ /3¼/3¼/3⅜/3⅜/3½in)
D3.55/3.55/2.95/3.05/3.2/4.1 cm
(1⅜/1⅜/1⅛/1⅛/1¼/1⅝ in)
Manufacturer: Toshiba, Japan (1985/6)

**30 CORPORATE INDUSTRIAL
DESIGN (CID)**
Refrigerator, *Mix & Match*
Refrigerator with a selection of different
handles and accessories available in
different colours
H160 cm (72 in) W55 cm (21⅝ in)
L55 cm (21⅝ in)
Manufacturer: IRE, Italy (1986/7)

31 ROBERTO PEZZETTA
Fridge/freezer, *The Wizard's Collection*
A new concept for a free-standing fridge/
freezer. There are four models available:
black, metal, marbled and stone
H162 cm (63⅞ in) W55 cm (21⅝ in)
D60 cm (23⅝ in)
Manufacturer: Zanussi, Italy (1986/7)

Nouvelle cuisine. *Eating habits
have changed a great deal in
recent years, while kitchens, by
contrast, have largely remained
conventional. A handful of kitchen
appliance manufacturers, however,
are now attempting to produce
designs of a kind prescribed by the
nouvelle cuisine – light and
decorative, and with a soupçon of
élitism. Roberto Pezzetta, the head
of design at Zanussi, has designed
a refrigerator for his firm which is as
different from other fridges as the
maître de cuisine is from the man
who washes the dishes. Perhaps
the Wizard's authority derives not
least from the fact that, like the head
cook, it has a hat, a pyramid-
shaped Rossi roof with a little
pennant attached. By contrast, the
tops of the Mix & Match fridges by
IRE look like posters for a
supermarket competition. Pezzetta
reused his successful design in the
Wizard electric cooker, the hotplate
of which he transformed into a
user-friendly surface of the choicest
graphic design. Alessandro
Mendini's high-grade steel pans for
Alessi are similarly indebted to this
decorative revival. The Rossi
pennant, however, took on worrying
transmutations: lid handles that
could be purchased separately and
stuck to existing pans were thought
up by four different designers –
Michael Graves, Arata Isozaki, Yuri
Soloviev and Philippe Starck. A
question of scraping the bottom of
the barrel?*

32 ALESSANDRO MENDINI
Cookware
Stainless steel, plastic
Part of a range of 25 items
Prototypes
Big stockpot: H30 cm (11⅞ in)
Di34 cm (13⅜ in)
Small stockpot: H19 cm (7½ in)
Di24 cm (9⅜ in)
Saucepan: H15 cm (6 in) Di30 cm (11⅞ in)
Small casserole: H13 cm (5⅛ in)
Di24 cm (9⅜ in)
Manufacturer: Alessi, Italy

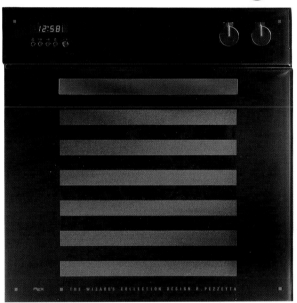

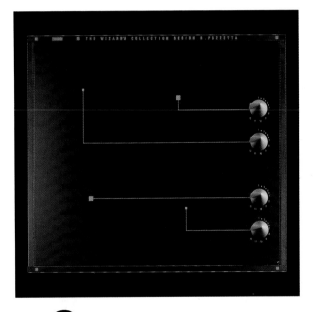

33-35 ROBERTO PEZZETTA
Electric oven, *Wizard Multiblack*
Glass, melamine resin, enamelled
steel, aluminium
A multi-function oven with an electronic
timer and programmer, using 2.5 kW
H59.5 cm (23⅜ in) W59.5 cm (23⅜ in)
D56 cm (22 in)
Manufacturer: Zanussi, Italy (1988/9)

36 ALCHIMIA
BRUNO GREGORI
Il Mondo in Cucina, *Neo-spatial*
Workstation for a new model kitchen with
electronic equipment and a computer
designed by Philips. Experimental concept
Manufacturer: Alchimia/Salvarani, Italy (1986/7)

37 SMART DESIGN
Iron, *Steam Ship Travel Iron*
The iron has a polycarbonate shell and
handle and a non-stick coated metal sole plate
H11 cm (4½ in) L19.5 cm (7¾ in)
W5 cm (2 in)
Manufacturer: Sanyei America,
USA (1985/6)

Brave new household. Founded in 1976, the design group Alchimia can always be relied upon to provide us with some healthy provocation. Their Kitchen World project was devised in the mid-1980s as an answer to the increasing uniformity of fitted kitchens. Bruno Gregori, a founder member of the group, designed a robot-like kitchen monument in which you can burn your roast with the help of a microcomputer. It is the only known example of an early deconstructivist chef. Microchips with everything. And since designers are clearly fond of science-fiction films, the steam iron from Smart Design looks rather like a reconnaissance vessel sent out by Sirius IV. 'Well, officer, it suddenly swooped down out of the sky and started to iron my trousers.' In the world of modern product design, Starship Enterprise is always just around the corner.

(37)

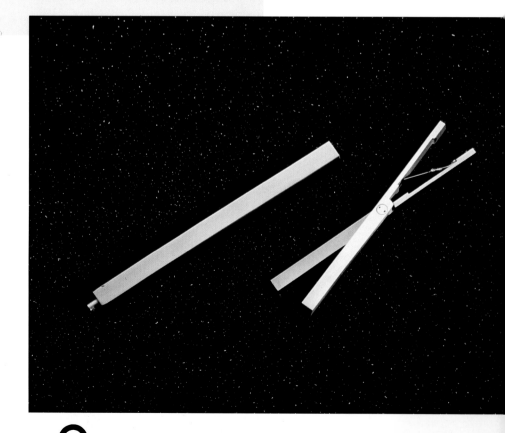

Bonsai design. *Small objects are paid only scant regard in western civilizations, while everyday objects receive even less attention, and virtually no one pays any heed to products that are both ordinary and small. This is hardly a field in which a designer can make a name for himself. Things are different in Japan. What counts here is not so much what one does as the fact that one does it well. And miniature art is traditionally held in high regard here, an art which inspires the country's craftsmen to patient and loving work. What would presumably be unthinkable for Michael Graves or Ron Arad is taken for granted in Japan: a prominent designer like Masayuki Kurokawa devotes himself to designing drawing pins. If we in the west were to pay more attention to so-called 'low-interest' products such as these, our everyday lives would be more attractive. There is much that we can still learn.*

38 **MASAYUKI KUROKAWA**
Pencils, *Archi Version K*
Aluminium alloy
Mechanical pencils
W1.3 cm (½ in) L14.7 cm (5¾ in)
D1.6 cm (½ in)
Manufacturer: Sakura Color Products,
Japan (1987/8)

39 **KAZUO KAWASAKI**
Scissors, *X & I*
Stainless steel
Forged in the traditional method with fire, the scissors open and shut by means of a flat spring. A plate spring at the fulcrum joint increases accuracy. With safety carrying case
H0.8 cm (⅜ in) L14 cm (5½ in)
D0.8 cm (⅜ in)
Manufacturer: Takefu Knife Village,
Japan (1987/8)

40 MASAYUKI KUROKAWA
Pushpin, *Metal Wave*
Stainless steel
Type *A-J*: H0.5 to 2.8 cm (¼ in to 1¼ in)
D1 cm to 2 cm (¼ in to ¾ in) Three long
pins *J1–3*: W0.8 cm (¼ in) L3.8 cm to
8.3 cm (1½ in to 3¼ in)
Manufacturer: Daichi Co, Japan (1984/5)

41 MASAYUKI KUROKAWA
Range of ashtrays, coasters and lighters,
Gom Collection
Rubber, stainless steel, plastic. These
objects are included in the permanent
collection of the Museum of Modern Art in
New York
Clockwise from top left:
Square ashtrays: H4 cm to 4.5 cm (1½ in
to 1¾ in) W7 cm to 10 cm (2½ in to
3½ in) L7 cm to 10 cm (2½ in to 3½ in)
Round ashtray: H4 cm (1½ in) D7 cm (2½ in)
Coaster: H0.5 cm (¼ in) D8 cm (3¼ in)
Square lighter: H4.2 cm (1½ in) W7 cm
(2½ in) L7 cm (2½ in)
Round lighter: H4.2 cm (1½ in) D7 cm (2½ in)
Centre left: ashtray H4 cm (1½ in)
D17.4 cm (7 in)
Centre right: ashtray H3.2 cm (1¼ in)
D13 cm (5½ in)
Manufacturer: Fuso Gomund Co,
Japan (1984/5)

The image is the message.

Images are hard to construct, but once they have become established, they can provide a considerable yield. The image of many brand names is so charismatic that in the age of marketing it is tempting to adopt the strategy of gilding the lily (or is it, rather, Venus's flytrap?) and using the name for financial gain in other areas of product design. A lively two-way traffic is thereby created under the name of 'image transfer'. Davidoff becomes a make of perfume, Harley-Davidson a cigarette, and Ferrari is sported round the wrist in the form of a gentleman's watch. Alessi comes out of the kitchen and takes up a place on the mantelpiece and even Louis Vuitton shares in this 'image-imperialism'. Both men work, so to speak, with a safety net, their image enjoying the additional safeguard provided by famous architects also being used as designers. If we then add the highest price we can think of, the mechanism for producing cult objects will swing into action.

42 MICHAEL GRAVES
Mantel clock
Ebonized wood, maple-veneered ABS
H24 cm (9⅜ in) W9 cm (3½ in) L16 cm (6¼ in)
Manufacturer: Alessi, Italy (1988/9)

43 GAE AULENTI
Wrist-watch, *Louis Vuitton I*
18 carat gold case
Anti-magnetic with a quartz mechanism.
As well as local time, this watch displays
the date, the current phase of the moon,
and the time in each of the cities named
D1.45 cm (³⁄₅ in) Di4 cm (1²⁄₅ in)
Manufacturer: Louis Vuitton, France (1988/9)

44 GAE AULENTI
Wrist-watch, *Louis Vuitton II*
Zirconium oxide ceramic, sapphire glass
Watch with an alarm function. The newly
discovered ceramic is waterproof, and
does not scratch or tarnish
D1.27 cm (⁵⁄₈ in) Di3.7 cm (1¹⁄₅ in)
Manufacturer: Louis Vuitton, France (1988/9)

45 RICHARD SAPPER
Wrist-watch, *Uri-Uri*
Stainless steel, black chromium-plated
brass, titanium, gold, sapphire glass
Quartz watch, water-resistant to 30 metres
D0.5 cm (¼ in) Di3.5 cm (1³⁄₈ in)
Manufacturer: Alessi, Italy (1988/9)

Switch to Swatch. Nowhere are the links more obvious between product design and the spirit of the age than in Swatch's success story. It was in the mid-1980s that the Swiss watch-making industry hit back at its rivals in the Far East, but the strategy it adopted was not to retreat into the increasing esotericism of increasingly expensive and luxurious chronometers, but to launch a counteroffensive on the enemy's very own territory, the market for

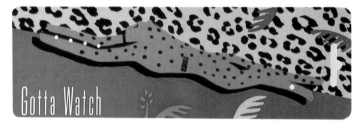

cheap watches. It was a brilliant idea to leave the casing as it was but to use the face of the watch as an invitation to playful decoration. With countless brightly coloured, topically styled motifs to which new ones were added every six months, Swatch threw the market into turmoil, so that watches once again became a trendy product for fashion-conscious buyers. Even status-conscious managers discovered how much more dynamic they appeared with the spirit of the times around their wrist. They put away their Rolexes and bought a Swatch instead. The product was so cheap that those who wore it could flirt with it with impunity, and since it was clear to everyone that they could of course afford a much more expensive watch, Swatch was seen to signal their lifestyle rather than giving a clue to the size of their owners' bank accounts. The idea was copied by other producers, even by those with no experience in the field, but it was the watches by the Italian textile firm of Benetton which came closest in spirit to the original. Recently, Sony went a stage further and began to market the ultimate disposable watch collection, made of paper and colourfully packaged in the trivial myths of our adolescent culture. Watch out for Crocodile Sony!

46 SONY DESIGN TEAM
Disposable digital wrist-watch, *Gotta Watch*
Paper, stainless steel, quartz mechanism
L22 cm (8⅔ in)
Manufacturer: Sony, Japan (1988/9)

47-48 SWATCH
Watches
Quartz watches with plastic faces and
straps. The internal working parts remain
the same but the designs of the faces
(either large or small) change every six
months with the latest fashions
Manufacturer: Swatch, Switzerland (1985/6)

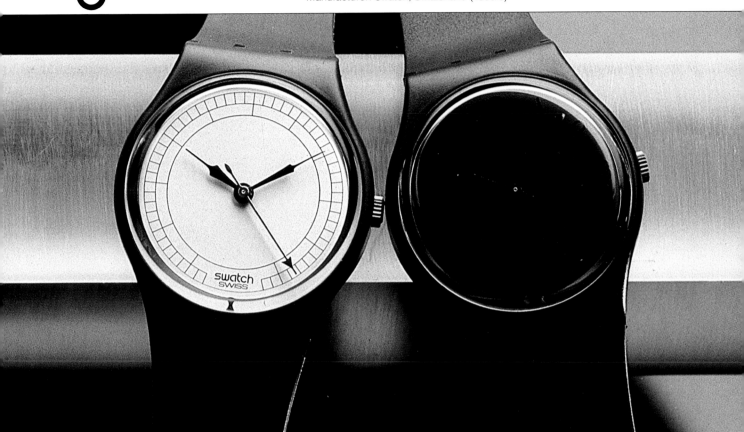

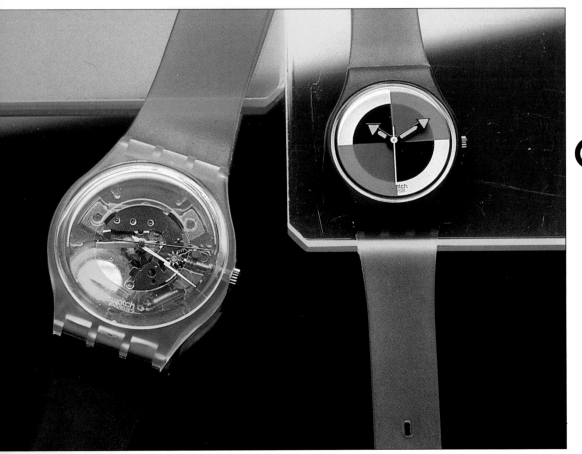

Giancarlo Piretti he designed the *Vertebra* seating system (winner of the Compasso d'Oro) and the *Logotec* track spotlight range (winner of the American National Industrial Design Award in 1980).

Christopher Alviar was born in Manila, Philippines, in 1961 and moved to the United States in 1977. A graduate in Industrial Design from the University of Washington in 1986, he was a freelance designer for various firms in the Seattle area including O'Brien International and Walter Dorwin Teague Associates before joining Ziba in 1987. He was a recipient of IDSA's Merit Award (1985, 1986) and recently IDSA's Merit Award (1985, 1986) and recently IDSA's NW Design Invitational and Design Excellence Awards 1988, both for his work on an electronic transparency system.

Ron Arad was born in 1951 in Tel Aviv, Israel. He studied at the Jerusalem Academy of Art and at the Architectural Association, London, graduating in 1979. After working for a firm of London architects, he founded the design company One-Off Ltd in 1981. He has exhibited widely and designs furniture, products and interiors. He has contributed to furniture collections for Vitra and Aram Design Ltd.

Junichi Arai, born in 1932 in Gunma Prefecture, Japan, is a textile designer and manufacturer specializing in sculptural, heavily

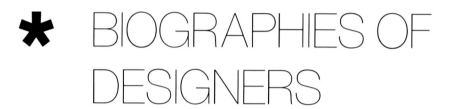

✱ BIOGRAPHIES OF DESIGNERS

Emilio Ambasz earned a Master's degree in Architecture at Princeton University, where he was subsequently a professor. While still in his twenties he helped to found New York's Institute for Architecture and Urban Studies, and served as Curator of Design at the Museum of Modern Art. He has since won international recognition for his work as architect, interior and industrial designer, as well as for his lectures and writings on design. Among his buildings, several of which have won awards, the Museum of American Folk Art and Houston Center Plaza are especially well known. With

textured fabrics. He has supplied Issey Miyake and Comme des Garçons, among other leading Japanese designers. In 1987 he was made an Honorary Member of the Faculty of Royal Designers for Industry.

Giorgio Armani was born in Piacenza, Italy, in 1934. From 1964 to 1970 he worked with Hitman (Cerruti men's fashion company), at the end of which time he began to work freelance for several companies. In 1975 he founded Giorgio Armani SPA which has expanded to include lines for children's fashion, underwear for men and women, accessories for men and women, jeans and perfume. He has received numerous awards, most recently the Gran Cavalière from the Italian government and a Lifetime Achievement Award from the

Council of Fashion Designers of America, both 1987, and in 1988 the Cristobal Balenciaga Award, Madrid, for the best international designer.

Atelier Vorsprung, see Beat Frank and Andreas Lehmann.

Gae Aulenti graduated in architecture from the Milan Polytechnic in 1954. As well as her architectural projects, she has designed stage sets and costumes for opera and drama, lectured extensively on architecture, had exhibitions throughout the world and received many awards. She was responsible for the Musée National d'Art Moderne at the Centre Georges Pompidou and for the interior architecture of the Musée d'Orsay, both in Paris. In September 1987 President Mitterand conferred on her the title of Chevalier de la Légion d'Honneur.

Hiroshi Awatsuji, a textile designer, was born in Kyoto in 1929 and graduated from the Kyoto Municipal College of Fine Arts, establishing his own design studio in 1958. Since 1964 he has collaborated with the Fujie textile company. His principal commissions in Japan include textiles for the government pavilion at Expo 70, and tapestries for the Keio Plaza and Ginza Tokyu hotels. He exhibited at the Victoria and Albert Museum's 'Japan Style' exhibition in 1980, and at the 'Design Since 1945' exhibition in Philadelphia.

Enrico Baleri, born in Bergamo in 1942, is an Italian designer and entrepreneur. He studied in Milan without graduating; since then he has been involved with a number of companies including Pluri and Alias, where he held the position of art director until 1983. He then set up Baleri Italia, a firm which has commissioned work from, among others, Philippe Starck, Hans Hollein and Alessandro Mendini.

Heiko Bartels, born 1947, active as a designer in kitchen technology, cars, camping and motorbikes. Since 1977 lighting systems, lighting design and interior design. Together with the designers Fischer, Hullmann and Hüskes, Bartels founded the Kunstflug group in 1982.

Mark Bayley is a British photographer and interior designer. He studied graphic design at the London College of Printing and photography at the Royal College of Art, London, graduating in 1984. He began work as a freelance photographer, specializing in portraits and fashion photography. His work in lights and interior design was stimulated by creating props for his photographic assignments. He now also undertakes private commissions for interiors and lamps.

Martine Bedin was born in Bordeaux, France in 1957. She studied architecture in Paris, and in 1978 was awarded an Italian scholarship and worked at the Superstudio in Florence. She has worked with Ettore Sottsass, designing lamps and furniture for Memphis. Since 1982 she has been a freelance industrial designer as well as a teacher of design at the Ecole Camondo, Paris.

Hedda Beese was born in 1944 in Germany and educated in Berlin and at the Central School, London. Previously the joint managing director for the London office of Moggridge Associates, she is now establishing the company's German office, Design Drei.

Cressida Bell studied fashion design at St Martin's School of Art, London and textile design at the Royal College of Art, London. After graduating in 1984, she set up her own business designing and hand-printing textiles. In addition to her dress and furnishing fabrics she has designed interiors and decorated furniture. She is a member of the Independent Designers Federation, London.

Carlo Bellini was born in Perugia in 1960 and now lives and works in Milan. He studied architecture at the University of Milan and engineering at the University of Perugia. He was the winner in 1984 of the competition 'Concorso di design regione Toscana'. Two of his works were selected for exhibition at the architecture Biennale of 1985.

Mario Bellini was born in Milan in 1935 and graduated in architecture from the Milan Polytechnic in 1959. He works in architecture and industrial design for firms such as Artemide, B & B Italia, Cassina, Erco, Ideal Standard, Poltrona Frau and Rosenthal. Since 1965 he has been a consultant with Olivetti on electronic machines, and is now editor of *Domus*. He has won several awards, including the Compasso d'Oro in 1986.

Franco Alberto Berg was born in 1948 and studied at the University of Art (HBK) in Brunswick, West Germany, receiving his Master's degree from HBK in 1978. In 1979 he founded the Berg Design Studio for product development in Brunswick, which has since moved to Hanover. Berg has worked on a wide range of consumer and capital goods.

Norbert Berghof, West German architect and designer, was born in 1949 and graduated from the School of Architecture, Technische Hochschule, Darmstadt. In 1981 he established an architectural partnership wtih Michael Landes and Wolfgang Bang. Their architectural projects include master plans for housing projects in Frankfurt, interior-renovation projects, posters and a furniture collection for Draenert.

Hans-Ullrich Bitsch was born in Essen in 1946 and studied architecture and design in Saarbrücken and Chicago. He lives and works in Düsseldorf. His clients in the field of corporate identity include WDR, a radio and television corporation. In the best Bauhaus tradition, he cultivates the unity of architecture, interior design and industrial design.

Leo Blackman, an architect and industrial designer, was born in New York City in 1956. He graduated in architecture from Columbia University, New York, in 1981. He designs furniture and light fixtures. His work has appeared in galleries and exhibitions and has been purchased by the Brooklyn Museum for its permanent collection. Some of his work is undertaken in collaboration with Lance Chantry.

Oscar Tusquets Blanca was born in Barcelona in 1941. He attended the Escuela Técnica Superior de Arquitectura, Barcelona, and in 1964 established Studio PER with Lluis Clotet, with whom he collaborated on nearly all his projects until 1984. He has been a guest professor and lecturer at universities in Germany, France and the USA, and his work has been exhibited in many parts of Europe and the USA. He has received many awards for his work, both as an architect and as a designer.

Mario Botta was born in 1943 in Mendrisio, Switzerland. He attended the Academy of Fine Arts in Milan, then graduated in architecture from the University of Venice. He gained practical experience in Le Corbusier's studio, and established his own architectural practice in Lugano in 1969. He has completed a number of private houses and commrcial buildings in Switzerland generally categorized as 'rationalist'.Since 1982 he has also designed furniture for Alias. Two of his chairs are in the study collection of the Museum of Modern Art in New York.

Andreas Brandolini was born in Germany in 1951. He studied architecture in Berlin and has been a lecturer in Industrial Design at the Hochschule der Künste, Berlin, visiting lecturer at the Architectural Association in London and visiting professor at the Hochschule für Gestaltung, Offenbach. He has been part of a design workshop with Joachim Stanitzek and exhibited in Brazil, France, Germany and Italy.

Andrea Branzi, born and educated in Florence, is educational director of the Domus Academy. He has consistently been a representative of the radical tendency in Italian design. His work was awarded the Compasso d'Oro in 1987. Until 1974 he was with Archizoom Associati, the first avant-garde Italian group. He was involved in the establishment of Studio Alchimia, the Milan-based group which has created pieces closer to artworks than to conventional pieces of design, and with Memphis, collaborating with Ettore Sottsass.

Peter Bremers, born in Maastricht, The Netherlands in 1957, is an artist and designer. He graduated from the art academy in Maastricht in 1980. He began working as a sculptor, since when he has produced furniture as well as wrist watches for the Swiss company Lincoln. He has exhibited at the Neotu Gallery in Paris, at the Biennale in Kortrijk, in Marseilles, Berlin and Arnhem.

Tim Brown was born in Britain in 1962. He studied at Newcastle upon Tyne Polytechnic and the Royal College of Art, London, and won a Royal Society of Arts Bursary Award for business office equipment. He joined Moggridge Associates in 1987 where he has worked on business and office equipment and computer systems. His designs for fax machines for Dancall in Sweden were on show at the 'Leading Edge' exhibition at the Axis Gallery, Tokyo, in December 1988.

Pauline Burbidge was born in Dorset, England in 1950. She studied at Yeovil Technical College, the London College of Fashion, and St Martin's School of Art, London. In 1972 she began designing clothes for a small London company, working in partnership from 1973 to 1976, at which time she started making patchwork quilts. She now teaches and works to commission. Her work has been exhibited and awarded, and she has also published.

Paul Burgess was born in Swindon, UK, in 1961. He studied printed textiles at the Camberwell School of Art and at the Royal College of Art, both in London. His commissions include collections for Extravert Ltd and Extetique/Amescote Ltd and print designs and window displays for Next plc. In 1986 he won the Drapers Record Award at Texprint 86, London.

Santiago Calatrava was born in 1951 in Valencia, Spain. He studied art in Valencia and Paris, took an architecture course in Valencia and studied engineering at the Zurich Federal Institute of Technology. After teaching there for three years, he opened his own architecture and engineering office. Since then he has worked on industrial buildings, engineering structures and, since 1986, on furniture.

Pier Paolo Calzolari, born 1944, Italian conceptual artist close to the *arte povera* movement. Exhibitions at the Sperone and Persano Galleries in Turin, the Galerie Sonnabend in Paris, and the Gladstone Gallery in New York. Has designed furniture for Meta Memphis, Milan.

Anna Castelli Ferrieri graduated in architecture at the University of Milan and worked as a lecturer in industrial design there, as well as an assistant editor of the magazine *Casabella*. Since then she has worked as an architect, planner and industrial designer. Since 1976 she has worked as art director for Kartell, specializing in the design of injection-moulded plastic furniture, for which she was awarded the Compasso d'Oro in 1979. Her designs are on show at the Museum of Modern Art, New York.

Achille Castiglioni was born in Milan in 1918. He began his work as a designer in partnership with his brothers, Livio and Pier Giacomo Castiglioni, specializing in interiors, furniture and lights. He is particularly well known for the latter, notably the *Toio* uplighter. Castiglioni is one of the foremost talents in Italian design, and has been honoured no less than seven times by the Compasso d'Oro, as well as having six of his pieces selected for exhibition at the Musum of Modern Art, New York.

Lance Chantry was born in Chicago in 1954. He now works for major electronics firms, using robotics and advanced electronics in product design and lighting. He collaborated with Leo Blackman on the *Quahog* lamp.

Jaime Tresserra Clapés was born in Barcelona in 1943. He began studying law but switched to the arts, where he pursued an interest in jewellery making. For 15 years he worked in interior design and architecture and then moved into furniture design. He won the 1986 Casa Viva award for best design at the Mogar Fair in Madrid and then established his own company. At the International Furniture Fair in Valencia in 1987 he received Best Design Award. He has recently designed packaging for the Olympic Games to be held in Barcelona in 1992 and is currently working on designs for furniture, lamps and carpets.

Lluís Clotet was born in Barcelona in 1941 where he graduated in architecture. In 1964 he founded Studio PER together with the architects Pep Bonet, Cristian Cirici and Oscar Tusquets Blanca. With the last named, he collaborated on numerous projects until 1983. He is a founder-member of BD Ediciones de diseño, for which he has designed furniture and products. As an architect he received the FAD award for the best interior in Barcelona in 1965 and 1972, and for the best building in 1978 and 1979. He was awarded the Delta de Oro for the best industrial design in 1974, 1979 and 1980, and in 1985 for his last 25 years' work.

Nigel Coates was born in 1949 and graduated from the Architectural Association with the year prize in 1974. He formed an architectural practice with Doug Branson in 1985, which has undertaken commercial and domestic commissions in the UK and Japan, including shops for Jasper Conran, Katharine Hamnett and Jigsaw, and restaurants in Japan and London. He has taught at the AA since 1976 and was a founder-member of the expressionistic and influential NATO (Narrative Architecture Today) group. Despite his increasing international reputation, his furniture has until recently been sold commercially only in Japan.

Pepe Cortées was born in Barcelona in 1945. He has collaborated on numerous projects, including lights, furniture and interiors, with Javier Mariscal.

Coop Himmelblau. See Wolf D. Prix and Helmut Swiczinsky.

Tony Cragg, born 1949, English artist notable for his use of recycled materials and transformations. Numerous one-man shows in many well-known galleries. Represented England at the 1988 Venice Biennale. Lives and works in Wuppertal (West Germany).

Riccardo Dalisi was born in Potenza, Italy, in 1931. Since 1962 he has been conducting experiments on architectural forms using light and geometry, and taking part in various competitions connected with building construction at an academic level. He has written a number of books and teaches at the University of Naples. In recent years he has been developing the theme of the Neapolitan coffee pot for which he won the Compasso d'Oro in 1981. He is credited with revitalizing research into design in southern Italy and has been described by Alessandro Mendini as 'the brains behind design in the South'.

Paolo Deganello was born in Este, Italy, in 1949. He studied in Florence and from 1963 to 1974 worked as a town planner for the Florence municipality. In 1966 he founded, with Andrea Branzi, Gilberio Corretti and Massimo Morozzi, the then avant-garde group Studio Archizoom. In 1975, with Corretti, Franco Gatti and Roberto Querci, he founded the Collettivo Tecnici Progettisti. He has taught widely, including at Florence University and the Architectural Association, London, and has published several books and articles. He has designed products for Marcatrè, Vitra, Driade and Cassina and has taken part in many international exhibitions and competitions.

Michele De Lucchi was born in Ferrara, Italy, in 1951. He studied first in Padua and then at Florence University, where he founded the Gruppo Cavat, which produced avant-garde and radical architecture projects, films, texts and happenings. He graduated from Florence University in 1975 and subsequently taught there. In 1978 he left teaching and began a close collaboration with Ettore Sottsass. He worked and designed for Alchimia until the establishment of Memphis in 1981, for whom he designed and carried out some of their best-known products. In 1979 he became a consultant for Olivetti Synthesis in Massa and in 1984 for Olivetti SpA in Ivrea; under the supervision of Sottsass he designed their *Icarus* office furniture. With Sottsass Associati he designed more than fifty Fiorucci shops in Italy and abroad. Currently he is designing for a wide range of important furniture manufacturers: among others, Acerbis, Artemide, Vistosi, RB Rossana and Fontana Arte.

Margit Denz is a student at the Academy of Applied Arts in Vienna.

Bernhard Dessecker was born in Munich in 1961. He studied interior design and then worked in New York at Studio Morsa from 1983 to 1984. Since 1984 he has been a freelance designer and a collaborator in the design team of Ingo Maurer.

Sergi Devesa is a Spanish designer born in 1961. Following his studies in applied art he has worked with Metalarte on lighting and has now turned his attention to furniture design.

Tom Dixon is a British sculptor and designer, born in 1959. He produces one-off furniture pieces and fixtures such as chandeliers, generally in response to specific commissions.

Nicholas Dormon was born in 1961 and educated at the Polytechnic of the South Bank, London. He is a designer with Moggridge Associates.

Marie-Christine Dorner was born in Strasbourg, France, in 1960. She graduated in 1984 in Paris, and has worked for Patrick and Daniel Rubin and for Jean-Michel Wilmotte. In 1985 her table won a prize from Galeries Lafayette; in 1986 a collection of her work was produced by Idée and shown at the Axis Gallery, Tokyo.

André Dubreuil was born in France in 1951. He studied architecture in Switzerland and design at the Inchbald School of Design in London. He worked as an interior designer and muralist before developing his wrought-iron furniture. He currently lives in London.

Nathalie Du Pasquier was born in Bordeaux, France in 1957. She has lived and worked in Milan since 1979; it was there that she came into contact with the Memphis group. She began working with textiles and later moved on to furniture and graphics as well, undertaking projects for clients such as Fiorucci, Esprit and Lorenz. She often collaborates with George Sowden.

Thomas Eisl was born in Austria in 1947 and has lived in England since 1969. He was educated at the Central School of Art, London, graduating in Fine Arts in 1977. Since 1981 he has been designing lights, mainly one-offs.

Hildegard Erhard German artist, born 1950, lives and works in Berlin.

James Evanson is an American, born in 1946. He trained as an architect at the Pratt Institute, New York, and the Art Center College of Design, New York.

Marco Ferreri, an Italian, was born in 1958. He graduated in architecture from Milan Polytechnic and worked as an architect for Manfiaroti, Zanuso and Munari until 1984, when he established his own office. He has worked since then for Milan City Council, Olivetti, IBM, McCann Erikson and others.

Uwe Fischer German designer, born 1958. With Klaus Achim Heine founded the Ginbande design studio in Frankfurt in 1985. Has designed mechanically convertible furniture for Vitra Edition, also seating for Sawaya & Moroni.

Fulvio Forbicini was born in Ravenna in 1952 and graduated in industrial design in Florence in 1974/75. Following an association with Roche Bobois, he opened a studio with Fabrizio Ballardini where they continue to explore the needs of industry in an aesthetically satisfying way.

Norman Foster, the British architect, was born in Manchester in 1935 and studied architecture at the universities of Manchester and Yale. He started in practice as an architect with Richard Rogers in 1965. Since 1969 he has worked independently as Foster Associates. His major buildings include the Sainsbury Centre, Ipswich, and the Hong Kong and Shanghai Bank, Hong Kong. In 1985 Foster began work on a furniture system for Tecno, known as *Nomos,* Foster is a winner of the Royal Gold Medal for Architecture, and many other awards for his buildings. His work has been exhibited at the Museum of Modern Art, New York, and the Royal Academy, London.

Sam Francis, Abstract Expressionist painter, was born in San Mateo, California, in 1923. He studied medicine 1941–1943 and painting and the history of art, under Mark Rothko, 1948–1950. His work is considered subtler and more European than that of his American colleagues: he is known in America as a 'homo transatlanticus'. Important exhibitions include those at Los Angeles County Museum of Art; Whitney Museum of American Art, New York; Louisiana Museum, Copenhagen/Humblebaek; Musée National d'Art Moderne, Centre Georges Pompidou, Paris.

Beat Frank, Swiss designer, born 1949. In 1986 he and Andreas Lehmann founded the Atelier Vorsprung design studio in Berne.

Albert Fraser was born in Glasgow, Scotland in 1945. He studied architecture at the Rhode Island School of Design, graduating in 1982, and is now resident in Milan. His work includes both furniture and industrial design, as well as lighting. His clients have included Arflex, Mont Blanc, Bausch and Lomb, Stilnovo, Artemide and B&B Italia.

Derek Frost set up his own design consultancy in London in 1984, having previously trained and worked with Mary Fox Linton. His interior design projects, both commercial and residential, are wide-ranging. He also has an interest in one-off furniture design

and works with some of Britain's best cabinetmakers and craftworkers.

Bruno Gecchelin is an Italian architect, born in Milan in 1939. He studied architecture at the Milan Polytechnic and began his career in 1962, working with many major companies.

Frank O Gehry, a principal of Frank Gehry and Associates, Los Angeles, was born in Toronto, Canada, in 1929. He has won many awards and is a Fellow of the American Institute of Architects. His designs have been widely published and exhibited, in particular at the Museum of Modern Art, New York, and at the Louvre, Paris.

Massimo Iosa Ghini is an Italian designer working in furniture, textiles, fashion and advertising. Born in 1959 in Borgo Tossignano, he studied in Florence and graduated in architecture in Milan. In 1981 he joined the group Zak-Ark, and from 1984 has collaborated with the firm AGO. Since 1982 he has worked on a number of discotheques, video projects and magazines. In 1986 he took part in the Memphis group's 12 New Collection.

Ginbande. See Uwe Fischer and Klaus Achim Heine.

Sue Golden is a British artist. After an art-school training in London, she began to produce small, one-off sculptural work, drawing on tribal art: mirrors, vases and, in 1987, the *Shield Chair.*

Piers Gough is a British architect, born in Brighton, England, in 1946. He practised with Wilkinson Calvert and Gough, 1968–72, as Piers Gough, 1972–5, and now with Campbell Zogolovitch Wilkinson and Gough. His *Chaise Longue* was commissioned by Aram Design Ltd.

Michael Graves, the Princeton architect famed for his Post-Modern classicism, was born in 1934. His work, which has received numerous awards, includes the Newark Museum, the Whitney Museum, a library in San Juan Capistrano, the Humana Headquarters in Louisville and a winery in California's Napa Valley. His painting and murals are in several major museums and he has designed furniture for Memphis and Sawaya & Moroni, and products for Alessi and Swid Powell.

Zaha Hadid was born in Baghdad, Iraq, in 1950. She graduated from the Architectural Association, London, in 1977 and in the same year joined the Office of Metropolitan Architecture. In 1982 she was awarded a gold medal in the *Architectural Digest* British Architecture Awards for an apartment conversion in London and in 1983 she won first prize in the Peak International Competition, Hong Kong. Her work is published worldwide and is frequently exhibited. She lives in London.

Dorothy Hafner was born in 1952 in Woodbridge, Connecticut, and studied art at Skidmore Collge, New York. Her hand-painted porcelain is in numerous collections, including the Smithsonian Institute, Washington DC, and the Victoria and Albert Museum in London. Her dinnerware has featured in many exhibitions and she has held solo shows throughout the USA and Europe. In 1982 she began her first porcelain collection for the Rosenthal Studio Line in West Germany, the first American woman to do so.

Renate Hattinger is a student at the Academy of Applied Arts in Vienna.

Sally Ann Heartshorne is a British-born textile designer. She graduated from Leicester Polytechnic, and established the Waterside Studio in London in 1984. She designs and hand-prints cloth, largely hand-painting to individual commission for furnishing and fashion lengths. Her work was selected by the Design Council of Great Britain for exhibition in 1986, and by the Whitworth Gallery at the University of Manchester. She is a member of the Independent Designers Federation, London.

Klaus Achim Heine, German designer, born 1955. In 1985,

together with Uwe Fischer, founded the Ginbande design studio in Frankfurt. Has designed furniture for Vitra Edition and Sawaya & Moroni.

Matthew Hilton, born in the UK in 1957, studied furniture design at Kingston Polytechnic and then worked with the product design consultancy CAPA for five years on a variety of high-technology products. He became an independent furniture and interior designer in 1984, producing lights as well as furniture. In 1986 he designed a range of furniture for Sheridan Coakley which was shown in Milan, and in 1987 held an exhibition in Tokyo with Jasper Morrison.

Yoshiki Hishinuma, a textile designer, was born in Sendai Prefecture, Japan, in 1958. He worked for the Miyake Design Studio in 1978, and is now a freelance fashion, textile and bag designer. In 1984 he established the Hishinuma Design Institute and introduced his first collections.

David Hockney, painter, was born in Bradford, England, in 1937 and now lives in California. He studied at Bradford College 1953–1957, at the Royal College of Art in London 1959–1962, and has held various teaching posts in the USA. He is an exponent of the English variation of Pop Art, his work being divided into three parts: painting, stage design and photography. In 1988, a large retrospective exhibition of his work was held in the Los Angeles County Museum of Art, the Metropolitan Museum of Art, New York, and the Tate Gallery, London.

Jochen Hoffmann was born in Germany in 1940. He studied industrial design at the Hochschüle für Bildende Kunste in Braunschweig. Since 1970 he has worked as a freelance designer in Bielefeld, Germany, and has won several awards.

Hans Hollein was born in Vienna, Austria, in 1934. He received his diploma from the Academy of Figurative Arts in Vienna, attended the Illinois Institute of Technology in Chicago and obtained a Master's degree in architecture at Berkeley University. He has received numerous awards and is a member of various committees and juries. He has undertaken design projects for ocmpanies such as Herman Miller, Cleto Munari, Alessi, Memphis, Poltronova, Knoll International, Baleri and Swid

Powell. Since 1978 he has been the Austrian Commissar for the Venice Biennale.

Bohuslav Horák, Czech sculptor and designer, born 1954. Member of *Atika*, a Prague-based group of designers founded in 1988. Exhibitions of his biomorphic designs, together with other designs by *Atika*, in leading European design galleries and museums.

Lynne Hugill is a British-born print designer who trained in fashion and textiles at Leicester Polytechnic. She has worked on a freelance basis for various companies, including Marks and Spencer and Habitat Mothercare. She is a member of the Independent Designers Federation, London.

Harald Hullmann, German designer, born 1946. Active in the field of medical technology, vehicle assembly and synthetic material design. Together with Bartels, Fischer and Hüskes, founded the Kunstflug group in 1982.

John Hutton is an American designer who joined Donghia Furniture in 1978. His interest lies in producing furniture 'stripped to its very essence to avoid being typecast by trends and periods'.

Fujiwo Ishimoto was born in Ehime, Japan, in 1941 and studied design and graphics in Tokyo. From 1964 to 1970 he was a commercial artist, from 1970 to 1974 a designer at Decembre and from 1974 a printed textile designer for Marimekko, Finland. In 1983 he was awarded both the Roscoe Prize and an honourable mention at the Finland Design Exhibition.

Arata Isozaki was born in Kyushu in 1931 and obtained his diploma at the University of Tokyo. He founded his own studio in 1963 and continued to collaborate with other architects and studios as well. Among his most famous projects are the Gunma Prefectural Museum of Moden Art at Takasaki (1971–2), the Kitakyshu City Museum of Art (1972–4), the Shukosha Building at Fukoka (1975), the Fujimi Country

Clubhouse at Oita (1972–4), the new City Hall in Tokyo and the Museum of Contemporary Art in Los Angeles (both 1986).

Wolf Karnagel was born in 1940 in Leipzig, West Germany. He studied in Braunschwig under Bodo Kampman, and now designs for KPM Berlin, Rosenthal, Amboss, Hutschenreuther and Lufthansa. He teaches at HdK, Berlin.

Sachiko Kawabe was born in Tokyo in 1958. Following her graduation from the Women's Art University, Tokyo, she worked as a fashion stylist for several years and then set up her own design office. Although interested in modern production methods, she is concerned to maintain traditional Japanese craft techniques. She retains an interest in fashion styling and in her work as a make-up artist.

Kazuo Kawasaki was born in Fukui City, Japan, in 1949. He graduated in industrial arts from the Kanazawa University of Arts in 1972. Until 1979 he was creative director for product planning at Toshiba. In 1979–80 he practised as a freelance designer and since 1980 he has been president of Ex-Design Co. He lectures in architectural design at Fukui University and is a part-time instructor at the Kanazawa University of Arts, as well as the Technical Advisor for the Fukui Prefecture.

Perry A King was born in London in 1938 and studied at the School of Industrial Design, Birmingham. He moved to Italy to work as a consultant to Olivetti, designing among other things the *Valentine* typewriter in collaboration with Ettore Sottsass. For the last 13 years he has worked with Santiago Miranda from their office, King–Miranda Associati, in Milan, where they are active in industrial design, furniture, interiors, lighting and graphics. Their work has received several awards and has been exhibited and published in Italy and abroad.

Toshiyuki Kita was born in 1942 in Osaka, Japan, and graduated in

industrial design in 1964. Since 1969 he has divided his time between Osaka and Milan where he has worked on furniture and accessories for many of the major manufacturers. He has received the Japan Interior Design Award, the Kitaro Kunii Industrial Design Award and the Mainichi Design Award. The *Wink* armchair and *Kick* table which he designed for Cassina are in the permanent collection of the Museum of Modern Art, New York. In 1987 he took part in the celebrations for the tenth anniversary of the Centre Georges Pompidou in Paris.

Setsuo Kitaoka was born in Kouchi Shikoku, Japan, in 1946. In 1974 he graduated from the Department of Living Design at the Kuwazawa Design Institute and joined Yamaguchi Co. Ltd. In 1977 he established the Kitaoka Design Office in Tokyo.

Kunstflug. See Harald Hullmann and Heiko Bartels.

Masayuki Kurokawa was born in Nagoya, Japan, in 1937. He graduated from the Department of Architecture at the Nagoya Institute of Technology in 1961 and completed his training in the Graduate School of Architecture at Waseda University in 1967. That same year he established Masayuki Kurokawa Architect and Associates. He has been accorded numerous prizes for his work. In 1970 he won first prize in the International Design Competition for a mass-production house; in 1973 he won first prize in the Competition for Interior Vertical Element of House, and in 1976 he won the annual prize of the Japan Interior Designers' Association for a series of interior elements. He has won six IF prizes for his designs of tables and lighting fixtures.

Michael Landes was born in Frankfurt in 1948. He graduated in architecture from the School of Architecture. Technische Hochschule, Darmstadt, returning to lecture there between 1980 and 1986. He established an architectural partnership with Norbert Berghof and Wilhelm Rang in 1981.

Danny Lane was born in 1955 in the USA. He moved to Britain in 1975 to work with the stained-glass artist Patrick Reyntiens, and then studied painting at the Central School of Art, London, until 1980. The following year he set up his first studio in London's East End. In

1983 he established Glassworks, using glass in unfamiliar and challenging ways in one-off pieces, furniture and interiors. In 1986 his studio was equipped to handle large-scale architectural installations.

Michaela Lange is a student at the Academy of Applied Arts in Vienna.

David Law was born in Pittsburgh, Pennsylvania in 1937, and studied at the Art Center College of Design, Los Angeles. In 1967 he joined Unimark International as an executive designer for the Detroit and Chicago offices. He became a co-founder of Design Planning Group, Chicago in 1972, then manager of packaging design at JC Penney, New York in 1975. He joined Vignelli Associates in 1978. He has designed graphics, packaging, exhibitions, products and furniture, as well as undertaking environmental and interior design. His work is represented in the permanent collection of the Cooper Hewitt Museum.

Andreas Lehmann, Swiss designer, born 1948. Together with Beat Frank founded the Atelier Vorsprung design studio in Berne in 1986.

Stefan Lindfors was born in Mariehamn, Finland, in 1962 and studied interior and furniture design at the University of Industrial Arts, Helsinki, 1982–88. His work has received many awards in Finland and Europe, including the silver medal at the 1986 Milan Triennale; he had his own exhibition of sculpture at the Gallery Titanik in Turku in 1988. His design interests also extend to the stage. He designed the studio and furniture for the Finnish Broadcasting Company's television evening news programme in 1988 and the interior and furniture for the café of the Museum of Industrial Arts in Helsinki in 1989.

Josep Lluscà was born in Barcelona in 1948. He studied design at the Escola Eina, Barcelona, and the Ecole des Arts et Métiers, Montreal. He was vice-president of the Adi-Fad (Industrial Designers' Association) 1985–7. He was also a member of the Design Council of the Catalonian government. He is now a professor at the Escola Eina. He has won several awards and has taken part in international conferences and exhibitions.

Vico Magistretti was born in Milan in 1920. He took a degree in architecture in 1945 and subsequently joined his father's studio. Until 1960 he was mainly concerned with architecture, town planning and the interior layout of buildings. He began designing furniture and household articles for his buildings in the Sixties and collaborates closely with the companies that produce his designs, including Alias, Artemide, Cassina, Conran Habitat, De Padova, Knoll International and OLuce. He has participated in nearly all the Triennales since 1948 and has won numerous awards. Fifteen of his pieces are in the permanent collection of the Museum of Modern Art in New York.

Angelo Mangiarotti was born in 1921 in Milan and educated there, graduating from the Polytechnic in 1948. He has worked as a designer in America and in Italy, as well as teaching at the Illinois Institute of Technology's design school. He has specialized in small sculptural objects, often intended for the table top, including a stainless-steel clock for Portescap and other pieces for Knoll and Munari.

Shari M Mendelson studied jewellery and metalsmithing at Arizona State University and Suny, New Paltz, New York. Her one-off bowls and vessels have been exhibited throughout the USA and she was awarded a Prize for Excellence in 1986 at the Designer Craft Council Show at the Schenectady Museum, New York. She is an instructor in metals and holds workshops and seminars.

Alessandro Mendini was born in Milan in 1931. He was a partner of Nizzoli Associates until 1970, and a founder-member of Global Tools.

He then edited *Casabella* and *Modo* and, until 1985, *Domus*. He has collaborated with a number of companies, has written widely and received the Compasso d'Oro in 1979.

Santiago Miranda is a Spanish designer, born in Seville in 1947. He trained at the Escuela de Artes Aplicadas in Seville before moving to Italy where he has worked ever since with Perry A. King.

Eiji Miyamoto was born in 1948 near Tokyo and graduated from Hosei University in 1970. Miyamoto began developing and designing fabrics in 1975 and now supplies leading Japanese fashion designers, including Issey Miyake.

Paul Montgomery studied at North Carolina State University, the University of Georgia in Cortona, Italy, and Cranbrook Academy of Art, Michigan, where he received his Master's degree in Fine Arts in 1987. He has designed products such as computer systems, televisions, medical products, luggage, typewriters and office furniture and has worked for Texas Instruments in Austin, Texas, PA Technology in Princeton, NJ, and Frogdesign in California. His most recent rewards (1987) were for his digital still camera, from the Industrial Designers' Society of America, 'Designers' Choice' from *ID* Magazine and Frogdesign's *frogjunior* award.

Marcello Morandini was born in Mantua in 1940 and has lived in Varese since 1947. He was educated at the Brera Academy in Milan. In 1963 he opened his own studio and exhibited his first three-dimensional structures in Genoa in 1965. He has subsequently had many exhibitions in Italy and throughout the rest of the world. In 1979 he was invited to Sydney, Australia, and lived and worked for a short time in Singapore. He has been designing ceramics for Rosenthal for several years and was commissioned by them to design the façade of their new offices in Selb, West Germany.

Massimo Morozzi was born in Florence, Italy, in 1941. Trained as an architect, until 1972 he was a member of Archizoom Associati, the leading avant-garde architectural group of the day in Italy. During this period Morozzi collaborated on the design of the *Aeo* chair for Cassina. For five years he ran Montedison's textile design research centre. After

1977 he worked with the CDM group on a corporate identity programme for Rome airport. In 1982 he opened his own studio specializing in consumer goods.

Pascal Mourgue began working as an interior designer at the end of the 1960s. Since 1982 he has been concentrating on furniture designs although he also designs carpets, tableware and even trimarans. He was named French Designer of the Year in 1984, and in 1986 won the Grand Prix de la Critique du Meuble Contemporain. He lives in Paris.

Adolfo Natalini was born in Pistoia, Italy, in 1941. He studied architecture in Florence and in 1966 established an avant-garde group called Superstudio. His work is in town planning and architecture, since 1981 he has been a professor of architecture at the University of Florence. For Volumina he worked with Guglielmo Renzi.

Ugo Nespolo was born in Mosso S. Maria, Italy, in 1941 and lives in Turin. He is a painter, sculptor, avant-garde film-maker and designer. He has exhibited in Turin, Cologne, New York, London, Tokyo, Helsinki, Paris, Venice and Milan. In 1987 he completed seven handmade carpets for Elio Palmisano.

Susanne Neubohn is a Swedish designer born in 1960 who studied industrial design in Berlin and works with John Hirschberg and Inge Sommer as Berlinetta Industrial Design. Their work has been shown at many exhibitions, including '1988 Avant Garde Furniture, Berlin' at the Centre Georges Pompidou, Paris. They also work in urban development and the protection of the environment.

Jean Nouvel, one of France's best-known contemporary architects, was born in 1945. In 1987 he was awarded the Equerre d'Argent for the most outstanding French building of the year (the Institut du Monde Arabe in Paris, for which he also designed the interior of the museum and the furniture for the reception rooms). In 1987 also, the Salon International du Meuble nominated him 'Designer of the Year' for his furniture. He is now working on low-cost housing for Nîmes and has a life-long interest in theatre and set design.

Klara Obereder is a student at the Academy of Applied Arts in Vienna.

Paolo Pallucco is an Italian furniture designer, architect and manufacturer born in 1950 in Rome. He established Pallucco in 1980, producing new designs and re-editions of modern classics and putting his own creations into production. In 1984 he started Pallucco Design to work on designs independently of his other company. He works in conjunction with Mireille Rivier.

Verner Panton was born on the Danish island of Funen in 1926. After completing his studies at the Copenhagen Royal Academy of Fine Arts in 1955, he worked as a freelance architect and designer in several European countries. Since 1969 he has been working for Mira-X in Suhr, Switzerland, developing floor coverings, furnishing fabrics and upholstery weaves. He also designs exhibitions, furniture and lights and has won many prizes for his work.

Maurizio Peregalli, an Italian designer, was born in 1951 in Varese. He studied in Milan and, after graduating, started work on

designing shops for Giorgio Armani. In 1984, along with five other designers, he established Zeus in Milan, a gallery showing avant-garde furniture, textiles, ceramics and glass. He is also a member of Noto, an interior design and manufacturing company.

Gaetano Pesce, artist and designer, is constantly researching into new materials made possible by technological advances. His projects have been exhibited worldwide and many are in permanent museum collections. Born in 1939 he trained as an architect at Venice University. His works include the doughnut-like polyurethane foam *Up 1* armchair in 1969, and a cave-like commune for twelve people shown in 1972. He has lectured worldwide and in 1987 was a visiting professor at the School of Architecture in São Paolo, Brazil.

Roberto Pezzetta was born in Treviso, Italy, in 1946. He has spent most of his career working for household appliance companies. From 1969 to 1974 he worked in the industrial design department of Zoppas, and since then for Zanussi, apart from a brief spell at Nordica. Since 1982 he has been in charge of Zanussi's industrial design department. He was awarded the Compasso d'Oro in 1981 and specially mentioned at the Compasso d'Oro in 1987. He has won gold medals for design in Holland and Ljubljana.

Giancarlo Piretti was born in Bologna, Italy in 1940. He studied and later taught design for several years at the State Institute of Art, Bologna, while working for Anonima Castelli. He holds a number of industrial and mechanical patents, and his works appear in permanent collections in the USA, Austria, Czechoslovakia and Yugoslavia. Several of his prizes have been shared with Emilio Ambasz, with whom he collaborates.

Michelangelo Pistoletto, Italian sculptor, born 1933. Co-founder of the Italian *arte povera* movement in Berlin. Mirror paintings, sculptures

and installations. Furniture designs for Meta Memphis in 1989.

Ferdinand Alexander Porsche was born in West Germany in 1935. He studied at the Ulm Design School, then worked in an engineering company before joining the family car-making business. He was responsible for two sports models including the classic *911*. In 1972 he established his own product-design consultancy, Porsche Design, in Zell-am-Zee in Austria, working on wrist watches and sunglasses, marketed under the Porsche Design label, as well as furniture, lighting and electrical equipment for other firms.

Ambrogio Pozzi was born in Varese, Italy, in 1931. While studying he began work for his family's firm, Ceramica F. Pozzi of Gallarate. As Ambrogio Pozzi Design he has worked for Riedel, Pierre Cardin, Alitalia, Rosenthal, iGuzzini and Rossi. He is a member of the Italian Association for Industrial Design and has won awards worldwide.

Wolf D. Prix, Austrian architect, born 1942. Together with Helmut Swiczinsky founded the architectural studio Coop Himmelblau in Vienna in 1968. In 1988 his work was seen at the *Deconstructive Architecture* exhibition at New York's Museum of Modern Art. Furniture design for Vitra Edition in 1989.

Wolfgang Rang was born in Essen, West Germany in 1949. He graduated in architecture from the Technische Hochschule, Darmstadt and undertook postgraduate work at UCLA, Los Angeles. He established an architectural practice with Norbert Berghof and Michael Landes in 1981. He was a lecturer at the Hochschule, Darmstadt between 1979 and 1985.

Mireille Rivier was born in 1959 in Lyon, France. She graduated in architecture at the Polytechnic of Lausanne before moving to Rome where she works with Paolo Pallucco.

Christopher Robertson is a British furniture designer who graduated from the Royal College of Art, London in 1986.

Aldo Rossi was born in Milan in 1931. In 1956 he began his career working with Ignazio Gardella and later with Marco Zanuso. From 1955 to 1964 he was editor-in-chief of *Casabella-Continuita*. Since 1975 he has held the chair of Architectural Composition at Venice University. He has taught at the Federal Polytechnic of Zurich, and has collaborated with the principal American universities since 1976. In 1983 he was named director of the architecture sector of the Venice Biennale. He has designed many award-winning buildings.

Lino Sabattini is an Italian silversmith, born in 1925. His metalwork first attracted international attention in 1956 when it was exhibited in Paris at a show organized by the architect Giò Ponti. Since then he has continued to be closely associated with a simple, sculptural, essentially modern approach to the design of metal and glassware, working for companies such as Rosenthal and Zani. He exhibits at the Milan Triennale and other major exhibitions. In 1979 he was awarded the Compasso d'Oro. His work is in the collections of the Museum of Modern Art, New York, the Cooper-Hewitt Museum of Decorative Arts and Design, and the British Museum, London.

Richard Sapper was born in Munich in 1932. After studying at the University of Munich, he joined Daimler-Benz's styling department in 1956. Two years later he moved to Italy, working initially with Giò Ponti and then in the design department of La Rinascente before joining Marco Zanuso. With Zanuso he worked on several of the best-known pieces of Italian industrial design from the Sixties, in particular portable radio and television sets for Brionvega. After establishing his own studio, Sapper designed the classic modern adjustable light, the *Tizio*, and the *Tantalo* clock, both produced by Artemide. In addition to furniture for Castelli, Molteni and Knoll, Sapper has designed tableware for Alessi. He participated in 'Italy: The New Domestic Landscape' at the Museum of Modern Art, New York, in 1972, and has worked in the past with Gae Aulenti on transport-planning studies. His numerous awards and distinctions include the Compasso d'Oro and the German Die gute Industrieform prize.

Soichiro Sasakura is a Japanese designer born in 1949. Since his graduation from the Kanazawa College of Art, he has been employed by the Sasaki Glass Company.

Tobia and Afra Scarpa are an Italian husband-and-wife team who have worked together for more than 25 years. Tobia, born in 1935 in Venice, spent a brief time working in the glass industry before their collaboration. Afra, born in Montebelluna in 1937, graduated from the Architectural Institute, Venice. In 1958 they began working in glass with Venini at Murano. They created the *Bastiano* divan and *Vanessa* metal bed for Gavina, and for Cassina the *Sonana* armchair which won the Compasso d'Oro award in 1970 and the *925* armchair which is on permanent display at the Museum of Modern Art, New York. The *Torcello* system, designed for Stildomus, and the *Morna* bed are among their other famous creations. They are responsible for the image of the Benetton shops in Europe and America. They occasionally work as architects as well as designers. Their pieces can be seen in major museums all over the world and many have been chosen for international exhibitions.

Chrissie Sgubbi was born in Caerphilly, Wales in 1957 and studied wallpaper design at Bournemouth College, England. She is a member of the Chartered Society of Designers and the Independent Designers Federation, London. A designer and maker of hand-tufted rugs, she has been commissioned by the British Airports Authority and various British companies.

Helen Shirk was born in Buffalo, New York, in 1942, and received a

Master's degree from Indiana University in 1969. Her bowls and vessels are in the collections of, among others, the National Museum of Modern Art, Kyoto, the Minnesota Museum of Art, St Paul, and the University of Texas in El Paso. Her work is frequently exhibited in galleries and museums. She is currently Professor of Art at San Diego State University, California.

Piotr Sierakowski was born in Warsaw in 1957. He studied industrial design at the Brussels La Cambra National School of Architecture and the Visual Art.

Borek Sipek was born in Prague in 1949. He studied furniture design in Prague, architecture in Hamburg and philosophy at Stuttgart University. His works are included in the collections of the Museum of Modern Art, New York; the Museum of Decorative Arts, New York; the Museum of Decorative Arts,Prague; the Kunstmuseum, Dusseldorf, and PTT in Den Haag. He now lives in Amsterdam and designs for Sawaya & Moroni, Driade, Vitra and Cleto Munari.

Susana Solano, Spanish sculptress, born 1946. Represented Spain at the 1988 Venice Biennale. One-woman shows at numerous European museums. In 1989 designed furniture for Meta Memphis, Milan.

Ettore Sottsass was born in Innsbruck, Austria, in 1917. He graduated as an architect from Turin Polytechnic in 1939, and opened an office in Milan in 1946. Since 1958 he has been a design consultant for Olivetti but is also active in fields as various as ceramics, jewellery, decorations, lithographs and drawings. He has taught and exhibited widely. In 1980 he established Sottsass Associati with other architects, and has designed many pieces of furniture that are part of the Memphis collection.

Philippe Starck was born in Paris in 1949 and works as a product, furniture and interior designer. In

Paris he was commissioned by President Miterand to give a new look to part of the Elysée Palace and designed the Café Costes, together with a number of fashion shops. In New York he remodelled the interior of the Royalton Hotel, and in Tokyo he has designed two restaurants and is currently working on a number of other buildings. His furniture design incldues projects for Disform, Driade, Rateri and Idée. Among his industrial design projects are cutlery for Sasaki, clocks for Spirale and mineral water bottles for Villel.

Axel Stumpf, German designer, born 1957. Representative of avant-garde design in Berlin. Has taken part in exhibition projects *Department Store of the East* and *Feeling Collages* and contributed to the Berlin Design Workshop.

Reiko Sudo was born in Ibaraki Prefecture, Japan, in 1953 and studied at Musashino Art University where she later worked in the textile department. She became a freelance textile designer in 1978, and in 1984 helped to found the Nuno Corporation.

Minoru Sugahara was born in Tokyo in 1940 and graduated from Wasada University. He joined the Sugahara Glass company in 1963 and since 1973 has headed the design team. One of his most successful designs, *BK & WH,* received a Japanese design award in 1986.

Helmut Swiczinsky, Austrian architect, born 1944. Together with Wolf D. Prix, founded the architectural studio Coop Himmelblau in Vienna in 1968. In 1988 his work was seen at the *Deconstructive Architecture* exhibition at New York's Museum of Modern Art. In 1989 designed furniture for Vitra Edition.

Christian Theill was born in Remscheid, West Germany in 1954. He moved to Italy in 1975 and studied in Florence at the Italian State Design University, graduating in 1980. He worked with various design consultancies, including Antonio Citterio. In 1981 he established an independent industrial and interior design consultancy, producing furniture

for, among others, Poltronova, and lights for Eleusi.

Burkhard Vogtherr was born in 1942 and works in Karden-Holzen in West Germany. He graduated in industrial design at the Technical Institute of Kassel and Wuppertal, and was apprenticed for three years. In 1970 he began to work as a freelance designer, having received in 1969 a government award for 'gute Form'.

Daniel Weil was born in Buenos Aires in 1953. He studied architecture at Buenos Aires University and did an MA in industrial design at the Royal College of Art, London. He lives in London, but the reputation he has earned for his work in product design is international. He has exhibited in London, Milan, Venice, Hanover, San Francisco, Philadelphia and Dallas. His works is in the permanent collection of the Museum of Modern Art, New York.

Herbert Weinand was born in Wittlich, Eifel, West Germany, in 1953. After an apprenticeship as a cabinet-maker he studied interior, furniture and product design in Germany and Italy. Since 1984 he has designed many interiors for restaurants and shops in Berlin, Mainz and Luxembourg and has opened his own gallery. His work has been exhibited in Germany, Austria and Italy and has featured at the German avant-garde shows.

Franz West, Austrian object artist, born 1947. One-man shows in Krefeld, Frankfurt, New York and Milan. Nominated for the 1990 Venice Biennale. Lives and works in Vienna. Designed lights and furniture for Meta Memphis in 1989.

Maria Wiala is a student at the Academy of Applied Arts in Vienna.

Stefan Zwicky, Swiss interior designer, born 1952, works for interior design studios of PD Beroulli in Zurich, Trix and Robert Haussmann, Zurich, and Studio Olivetti, Milan. Since 1983 has had his own studio in Zurich.